CONTENTS

PREFACE

The discovery by Alexander Calder and his wife, Louisa, of an abandoned eighteenth-century farmhouse in Roxbury, Connecticut, sparked a moment of inspiration that finds a parallel at Durslade in Somerset.

In 2005, our family moved to the UK from Switzerland and, by chance, when exploring the countryside, discovered the Saxon town of Bruton. Little did we know that this unassuming place would become our new home. (No wonder the American writer John Steinbeck spent six months in this magical place.) By the time we went for a walk in the nearby Cogley Woods, we were sold.

Over time we too, like Calder, came to find inspiration in a collection of derelict eighteenth-century farm buildings in the surrounding fields and farmlands which would become Hauser & Wirth Somerset.

The work of Alexander Calder—like his contemporaries Giacometti, Moore, and David Smith—was a key part of my art education in sculpture. I have distinct memories of visiting the 1975 Kunsthaus Zürich show as a boy and seeing Calder's incredible work, an early source of inspiration.

Many years later, seeing the artist's grandson, Alexander S. C. "Sandy" Rower, interact with the work was a revelation; iconic and valuable works came back to life. Our conversations about art, artists, and food led Sandy and Elan to visit our Somerset home and, of course, the gallery at Durslade farm. There, Sandy enthusiastically responded to our invitation to stage a major Calder show, a presentation that would explore his grandfather's relationship to the countryside.

We are immensely grateful to Sandy Rower, the Calder family, and the Calder Foundation for making this important exhibition a reality.

Manuela & Iwan Wirth

Simplicity of equipment and an adventurous spirit in attacking the unfamiliar or unknown are more apt to result in a primitive, rather than decadent, art. And somehow the primitive is usually much stronger than that in which technique and flourish abound.

Alexander Calder[1]

FOREWORD

Visiting Hauser & Wirth Somerset last year, I was struck by the handsome farm which has been gently converted for exhibiting art, with five human-scaled gallery spaces that encourage visitors to commune directly with the work on display. Not only did the vibrancy of the art spaces affect me but also the surrounding countryside; there is a visceral sense of several centuries of cultivation. The perennial meadows, planned by the extraordinary Piet Oudolf, are at once enchantingly wild and rigorously considered. Central to the experience of the rooms and gardens that Iwan and Manuela have created is a harmonious union of preservation and sustainability. The resulting enterprise is an innovative place where visitors can simultaneously experience art and nature (and great food).

The overall effect in Somerset reminded me of Roxbury, Connecticut, with its similar rolling fields, where my grandparents moved in 1933. Calder commandeered the 1760 farmhouse into a home and studio with the directness and integrity he brought to all of his efforts there; just as we would expect of a great visionary. Louisa planted oriental poppies, peonies, a quince tree, and ever more exotic species in her gardens, and also decorated the house with her own geometries. "To be in a Calder house," wrote satirist and artist Robert Osborn, "is to bask in an unanalyzable beauty which seems more like a living form than an arranged set of contrived objects and walls."[2]

In the process of organizing any exhibition, fresh scholarship often yields unexpected revelations, and this show was no exception. During conservation, I discovered the remnant of a Tiffany & Co. proof mark on a teething rattle made by Calder around 1935 for his first daughter, my aunt Sandra (p. 74). In an act of extreme recycling, Calder destroyed a perfectly fine Tiffany vessel to harvest the antibacterial sterling silver, making what was probably a wedding gift into something actually useful. Throughout his life, my grandfather continued to reimagine the purpose of items otherwise relegated to obscurity. He converted undistinguished porcelain teacups—inherited from his parents—into espresso cups by adding brass wire ornamental holders (known as zarfs) to insulate fingertips from the searing porcelain. Eventually, he reimagined the entire ceremony of freshly brewed coffee, making or improving everything that was required (p. 83).

In addition to the coffee suite, this show includes a refined aluminum table, two wonderfully low chairs, a sculptural chess set, an ingenious standing lamp, and a rug designed by Calder and hooked by Louisa (pp. 68, 69). All of these pieces attest to my grandparents' simple nobility. The Calders' way of life invites us to bypass conventions and see fresh social possibilities.

It's been a truly rewarding experience to see *Alexander Calder: From the Stony River to the Sky* come to fruition, an exhibition that gives visitors an opportunity to connect with my grandfather's creations in a sublime setting. The addition of an intimate gallery of Calder-devised domestic objects provides a unique insight into the immediacy and grace with which my grandparents eschewed decadence and entertained their friends in Roxbury.

Alexander S. C. Rower

1 Calder, "À Propos of Measuring a Mobile," manuscript, Calder Foundation archives, 1943.

2 Robert Osborn, "Foreword," *Calder: An Autobiography with Pictures*, ed. Jean Davidson (New York: Pantheon Books, 1966).

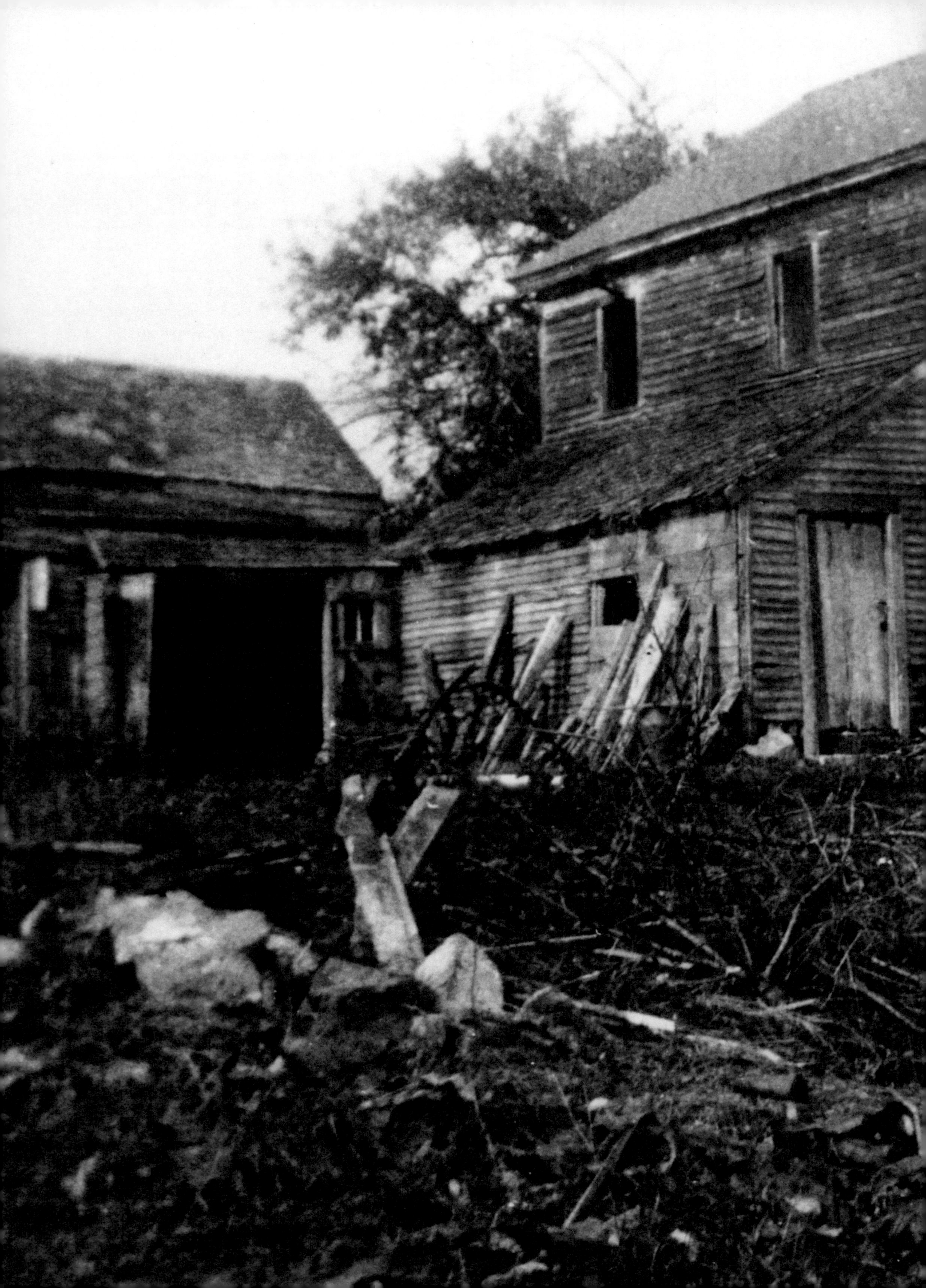

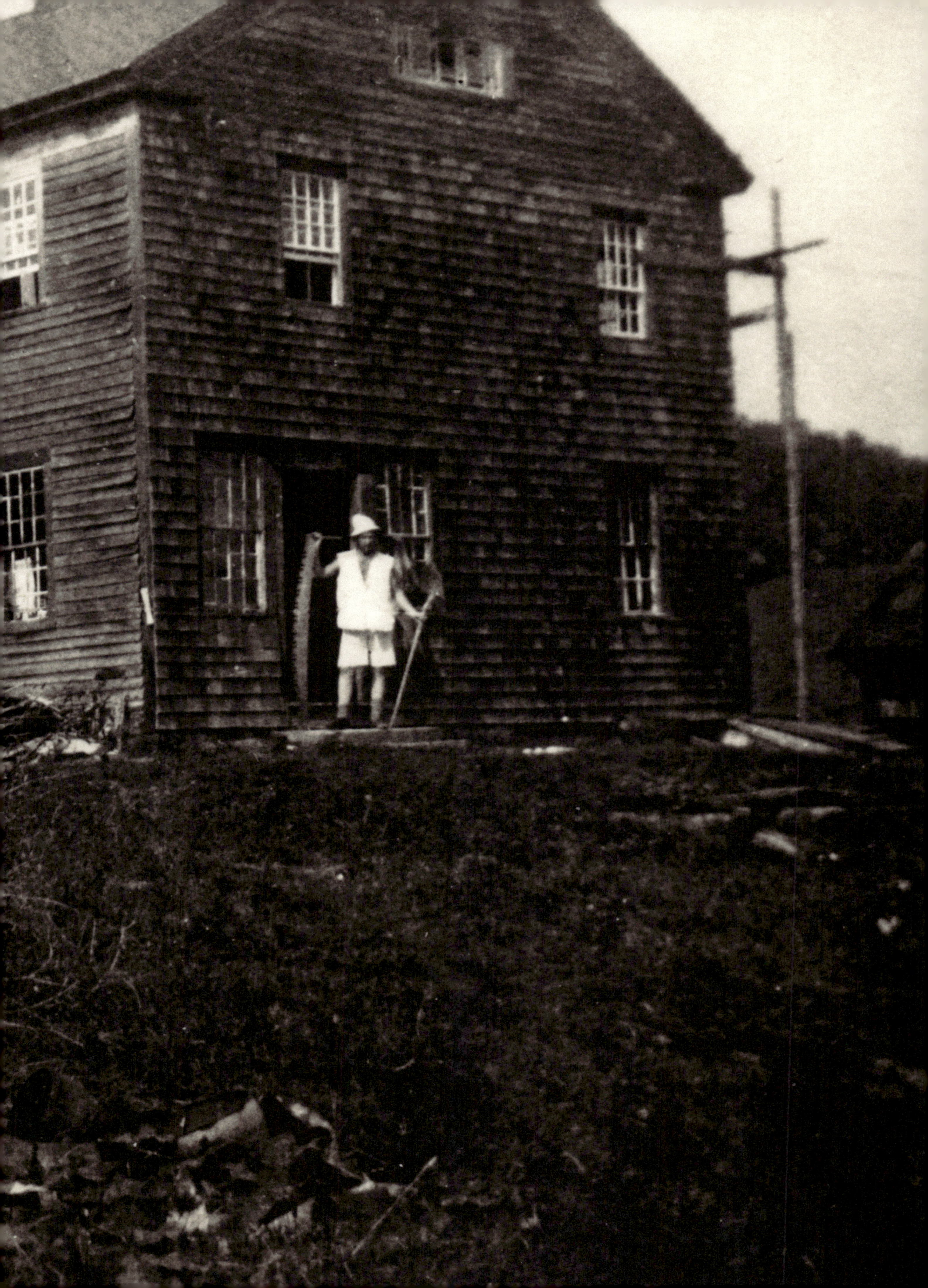

FOR THE OPEN AIR

SUSAN BRAEUER DAM

The art of Calder is the sublimation
of a tree in the wind.

Marcel Duchamp[1]

The landscape has a unifying power for poets, painters, and sculptors alike. For William Wordsworth and Samuel Taylor Coleridge, it was the undulating hills of Somerset, where they composed *Lyrical Ballads* in the 1790s, unearthing the dignity in the everyday. For Thomas Cole, it was the expanse of the Hudson Valley in mid-nineteenth century New York, where he stridently captured the minutia and grandeur of the Catskills. For Alexander Calder, it was the unfolding vistas of Roxbury, Connecticut, in the 1930s, where he unleashed his mobiles into the open air, engaging the caprices of nature. As philosopher Edmund Burke declared in 1757, "Greatness of dimension is a powerful cause of the sublime."[2] In Roxbury, the dimensions of Calder's sculpture responded to the scale of his new environment both in size and sensibility, resulting in objects unruly, untameable, and downright revolutionary.

In July 1933, Calder and his wife, Louisa, returned to the United States from Paris—the city in which they had lived since they were married two years earlier—with the desire to start a family. They set out to find a house in the country close to New York City, where they planned to winter. After searching in Massachusetts, along the Hudson Valley, and on Long Island, the Calders turned to Connecticut, first visiting Westport—where their friend Robert Josephy, an influential book designer, lived—then Sandy Hook. The next day they made their way further inland to Danbury, where they met with an agent's assistant who took them to Roxbury, a rural town in Litchfield County. Here, as they crested the brow of a hill on Painter Hill Road, they caught sight of a derelict eighteenth-century farmhouse (fig. 1). At once they exclaimed, "That's it!" (in his autobiography, Calder maintained that it was he who said it first). "We walked out in the pasture and saw a great rocky mound on top of a gentle hill," he described. "That sealed it."[3] The Calders purchased the property in September 1933, it later becoming the artist's headquarters after his career exploded internationally following World War II.

Previous:

Fig. 1 Calder renovating his Roxbury home, September 1933.

Before the move to Roxbury, Calder had already achieved a "greatness of dimension" that transformed the entire landscape of modern art. In 1931, after having worked on his *Cirque Calder* (1926–31) and wire objects for five years, Calder introduced the fourth dimension of time into sculpture, using motors to diversify the spatial and temporal relationships of abstract elements.[4] It was Marcel Duchamp who coined the term "mobile" (a pun which, in French, refers to both "motive" and "motion") for these works during a visit to Calder's Montparnasse studio that autumn. Among

1 Marcel Duchamp, "Alexander Calder," *Collection of the Société Anonyme: Museum of Modern Art 1920* (New Haven: Yale, 1950), 52.

2 Edmund Burke, *A Philosophical Enquiry into the Origin of Our Ideas of the Sublime and the Beautiful* (1757), in *The Portable Edmund Burke*, ed. Isaac Kramnick (New York: Penguin, 1999).

3 Alexander Calder, *Calder: An Autobiography with Pictures,* ed. Jean Davidson (New York: Pantheon Books, 1966), 144.

the first of these mobiles was *Two Spheres* (1931, fig. 2), a work severely abstract in its constitution, comprising of two spheres painted white, a repurposed black wooden panel, and a motor that moves the spheres in deliberate yet counterintuitive motions. When a reporter writing for the *New York World-Telegram* likened this work to a shooting-gallery target, Calder rejoined:

> The balls in a shooting gallery move for a utilitarian purpose. This has no utility and no meaning. It is simply beautiful. It has a great emotional effect if you understand it. Of course, if it meant anything, it would be easier to understand, but it would not be worthwhile.[5]

What Calder was asking the perplexed reporter to do in 1932 was as challenging then as it is now: to not only leave aside preconceptions and engage in an unalloyed experience in present time but to also recognize how something that has "no meaning" can be intensely emotional. As Calder biographer Jed Perl points out, Calder's statement is on par with what English critic Clive Bell wrote when characterizing a "significant form"—an object that produces "an emotion more profound and far more sublime than any that can be given by the description of facts and ideas."[6] Though intimate in size and minimalist in spirit, *Two Spheres* was grand in its imaginative force.

Calder was no stranger to the profound and the sublime. These themes formed the basis of one of his most fabled aesthetic experiences, dating to 9 June 1922, which resonated throughout his career. "When there is some particularly dramatic effect of nature I am always willing to stay up for that," Calder wrote, "and I remember a very beautiful hot red sunrise off Guatemala with a pale tin moon on the opposite side, a deep blue sky, and the sea all about us."[7] While serving as a fireman on the *H.F. Alexander*, sailing from New York to San Francisco via the Panama Canal, Calder experienced the onset of Civil Twilight, the only time during the lunar cycle when a full moon is situated directly opposite the sun, creating an optical illusion in which the moon appears much larger to the eye. "It left me with a lasting sensation of the solar system," Calder concluded.[8] The term "sensation" is operative here, suggesting a visceral communion with nature's magnitudes—something akin to what his mobiles would later generate in their beholders.

During that sublime moment off the coast of Guatemala, Calder transcended multiple thresholds, conspiring with nature's rapid transformations. He was struck not merely by the dialectical ballet between the sun and the moon, the free-flowing sea and the rotating earth, and the eye and the horizon, but by the circumference of the unseen—a binding force—that circulated infinitely outward, without beginning or ending. As Calder wrote, "The idea of detached bodies floating in space, of different sizes and densities, perhaps of different colors and temperatures, and surrounded and interlarded with wisps of gaseous condition, and some at rest,

4 Notably, Calder's figurative wire objects, though intimate in size, were immense in perceptual complexity, with massless volumes, vibrations, and actual articulations; many of them hung from the ceiling, and their projected shadows on the wall would engage three dimensions within a two-dimensional plane, all within the fourth dimension of time. As the artist wrote in winter 1929, "Although their present size is diminutive, I feel that there is no limitation to the scale to which they can be enlarged." Calder, statement on wire sculpture, manuscript, Calder Foundation archives, 1929.

5 Calder, quoted in "Objects to Art Being Static, So He Keeps It in Motion," *New York World-Telegram,* 11 June 1932.

6 Clive Bell, "The Aesthetic Hypothesis," in *Art in Theory, 1900–2000: An Anthology of Changing Ideas,* eds. Charles Harrison and Paul Wood (Oxford: Blackwell, 2003), 110. See also Jed Perl, *Calder: The Conquest of Time: The Early Years: 1898–1940* (New York: Knopf, 2017), 429.

7 Calder, manuscript, Calder Foundation archives, 1956. Thanks to Ricky Patterson, Senior Scientist, Department of Astronomy, University of Virginia, who dated Calder's experience to 9 June 1922. See author's correspondence with Patterson, 26 April 2010, Calder Foundation archives.

8 Calder, *Autobiography,* 55.

9 Calder, "What Abstract Art Means to Me," *Museum of Modern Art Bulletin* 18, no. 3 (Spring 1951), 8.

10 Writing to James Johnson Sweeney on 27 July 1934, Calder remarked, "I have made [one] wind-mobile so far—but hope to get organized soon." Calder Foundation archives.

11 Calder, "Mobiles," *The Painter's Object,* ed. Myfanwy Evans (London: Gerald Howe, 1937), 67.

12 Calder's other private commission for an outdoor sculpture was *Untitled* (1935), a nine-foot-tall standing mobile created for the Fletcher Steele-designed garden of collector Charlotte Whitney Allen in Rochester, New York.

13 Calder, "Comment réaliser l'art?" *Abstraction-Création, Art Non Figuratif,* no. 1 (1932), 6. Translation courtesy Calder Foundation, New York.

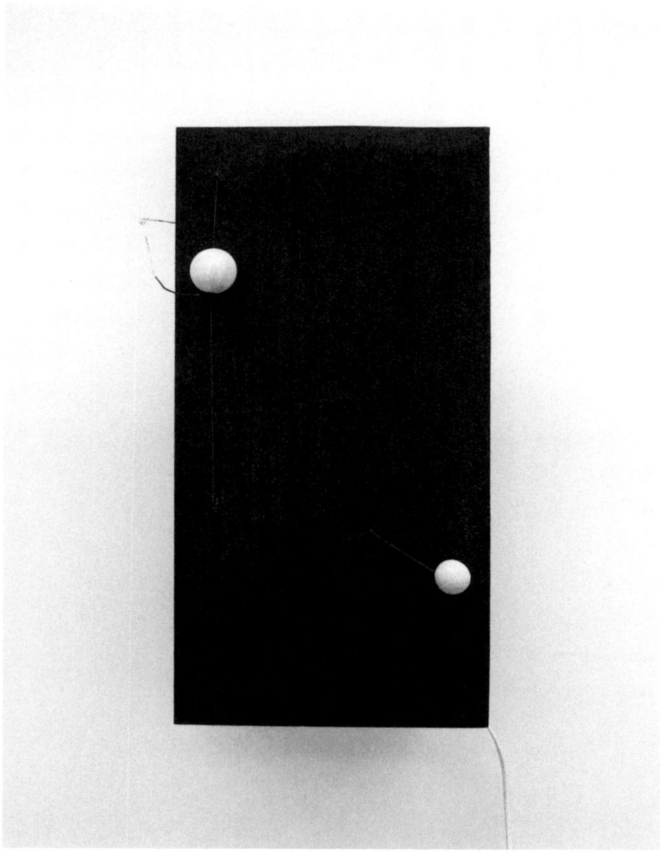

Fig. 2 *Two Spheres* (1931). Wood, wire, and paint, with motor, 21½ × 11 in. (54.6 × 27.9 cm). Calder Foundation, New York. Promised Gift of Holton Rower.

while others move in peculiar manners, seems to me the ideal source of form."[9] With no fixed, identifiable content, Calder's mobiles were not about imitation, but immediacy; they were not about nature, but the nature of all things.

With the departure from his Paris studio and the move to the verdant countryside of Roxbury, Calder's motorized mobiles developed into immense, wind-propelled volumes in space. In the summer of 1934 (less than a year after buying the Roxbury house), Calder made his first works for the outdoors, ranging in height from five- to nine-feet tall.[10] *Red and Yellow Vane* (fig. 3) and *Red, White, Black and Brass* (pp. 84, 87) were agile constructions with mobile elements atop tripod legs that could be firmly embedded in the soil. Made from materials typically used for indoor works, and buoyant in stature, they were unable to tolerate strong winds, so Calder had to bring them indoors when the weather dictated. *Steel Fish,* Calder's first welded work for the outdoors, was more resilient, with rods of a larger gauge. "I have made a number of things for the open air," Calder recounted in *The Painter's Object.* "All of them react to the wind, and are like a sailing vessel in that they react best to one kind of breeze."[11] By the end of 1936, Calder had completed two private commissions for outdoor works, among them the twenty-two-foot-tall *Well Sweep* (1936) for the Greek Revival home of collector James Thrall Soby (remodeled by architectural historian Henry-Russell Hitchcock) in Farmington, Connecticut.[12] At the time, Soby was an advisor to Arthur Everett "Chick" Austin, Jr. at the Wadsworth Atheneum in Hartford, Connecticut, and a major supporter of Calder's work.

Like *Two Spheres* and the Parisian abstractions that came before, *Red and Yellow Vane* and *Steel Fish* were entirely nonobjective. Calder titled the works after their completion with a vague description of their form, a common practice for the artist. In *Steel Fish,* the large steel shape for which the work was likely named carries broad implications, having appeared in various manifestations in his abstract work from the early 1930s. As the artist wrote around this time, describing how art can be realized, "Spaces, volumes, suggested by the smallest means in contrast to their mass, or even including them, juxtaposed, pierced by vectors, crossed by speeds. Nothing at all of this is fixed."[13] In 1935, a similarly abstract shape appeared in an etching entitled *Grandeur-Immense* (fig. 4), the title of which refers

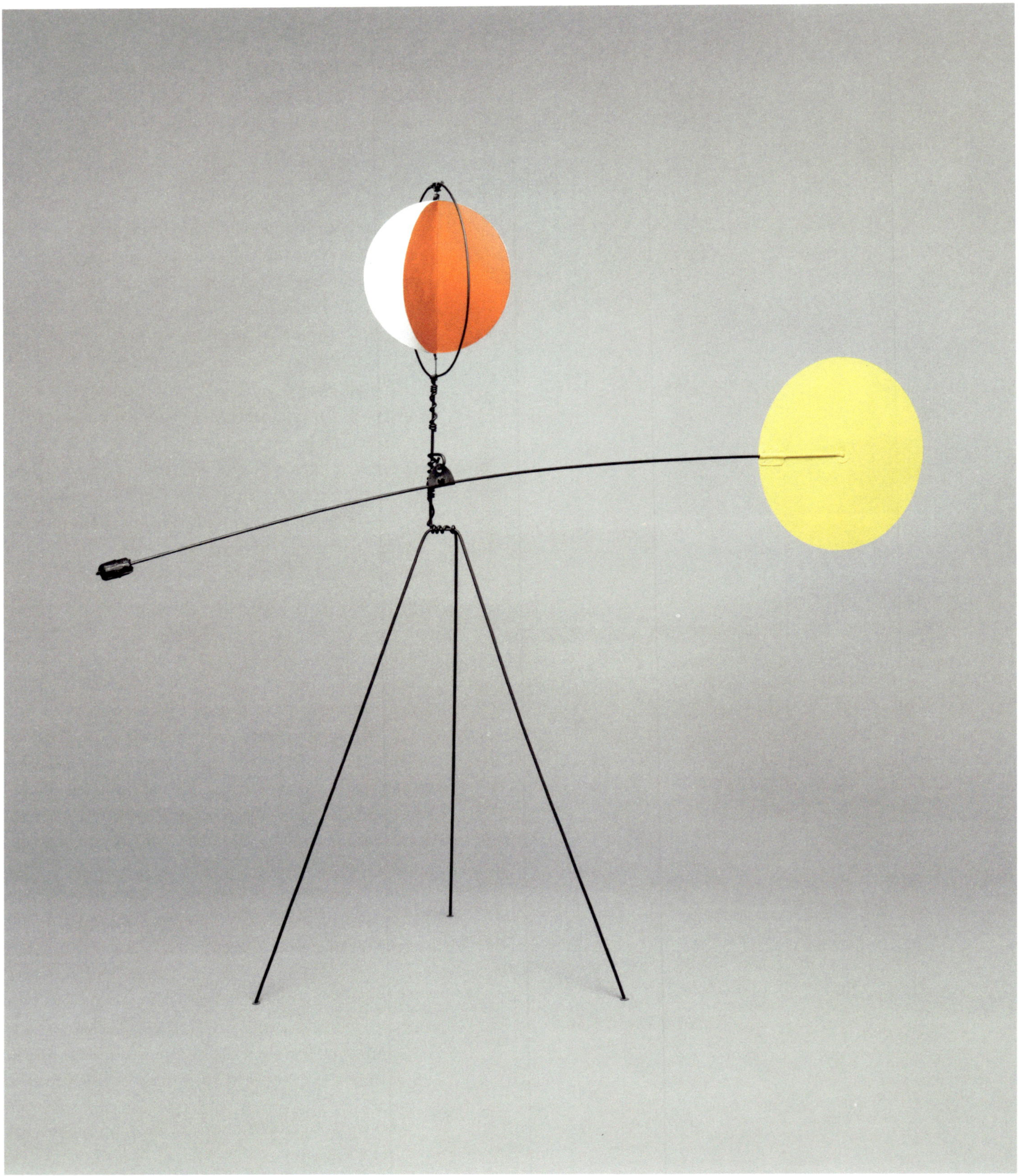

Fig. 3 *Red and Yellow Vane* (1934). Sheet metal, rod, wire, lead, and paint, 69 × 80 × 28 in. (175.2 × 203.2 × 71.1 cm). Calder Foundation, New York. Promised Gift of Holton Rower.

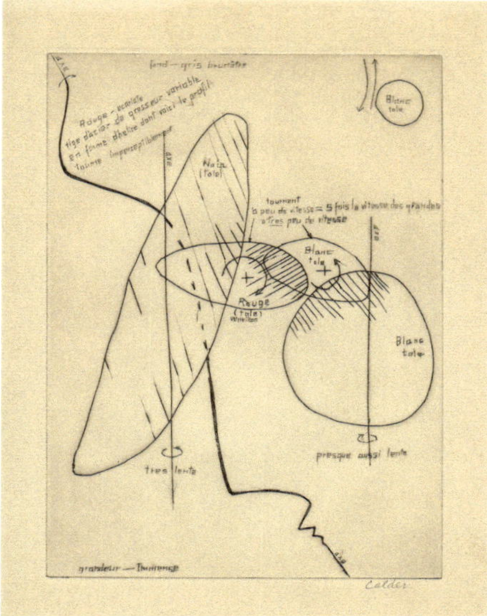

Fig. 4 *Grandeur-Immense* (1935). Drypoint etching, plate: 10 ½ × 7 ¾ in. (26.7 × 19.7 cm).

not only to an idea of scale but also evokes traditional notions of the sublime.[14] Far from a traditionalist, however, Calder expressed nature's totality in his sculpture not by adding layer upon layer (in the manner of an eighteenth-century allegorical landscape), but by a method of simplification, at once bold and succinct. By reducing the seen, Calder illuminates the unseen, giving prominence to relationships over things, to immateriality over materiality, to the energetic forces that open new fields of experience.

"Just as Calder's wire sculpture, predominately two-dimensional at the outset, came to suggest transparent volumes," wrote art historian and curator James Johnson Sweeney, "such large-scale, free-swinging mobiles as the *Steel Fish* now began to describe, with gestures like a dancer, volumes in space."[15] The summer Calder created *Steel Fish,* he brought the gestures of dance into the outdoors by collaborating with choreographer Martha Graham. Visiting her at Snake Hill Barn near Stamford, Connecticut, he enlarged what he described as a "ballet-object," or a kinetic theatrical maquette without dancers (a concept that began back in Paris in spring 1933). "I tried it [in] the open air, swung between trees on ropes," Calder wrote in *The Painter's Object,* "and later Martha Graham and I projected a ballet on these lines. For me, increase in size—working full-scale in this way—is very interesting."[16] The project was a prelude to Graham's *Panorama* (1935), which premiered the following summer in Bennington, Vermont, and featured Calder's mobiles. Calder and Graham also collaborated on *Horizons,* which premiered in February 1936 at the Guild Theatre in New York City, for which Calder made six mobiles or "visual preludes."[17] Just a week before this, Calder debuted his kinetic decor for Erik Satie's symphonic drama *Socrate* (commissioned by composer Virgil Thomson and Chick Austin) during the First Hartford Music Festival at the Wadsworth Atheneum.

A number of photographs from this period capture Calder in the process of installing his outdoor works in Roxbury, highlighting the elemental landscape. In one picture from 1934, taken by Soby, Calder stands next to *Steel Fish* on the hill behind the farmhouse, with its large steel form waiting to be "crossed by speeds" (fig. 5). Swiss photographer Herbert Matter also photographed Calder assembling *Five Rods and Nine Discs* (1936), a fifteen-foot-tall standing mobile that the artist made for his property. In a few of these images, the expansive *Steel Fish* can be seen in the background (fig. 6). Like *Red and Yellow Vane* and *Red, White, Black and Brass, Five Rods and Nine Discs* was anchored in the soil; its mobile element hung from a post made from pipes of decreasing diameter, suggesting a divining rod of sublunary forces. What Matter's photographs capture are pivotal moments in the trajectory of Calder's career, moments in which he surrenders his control as an artist to the unseen forces of nature. "A landscape doesn't demand from the spectator his 'understanding', his imputations of significance, his anxieties and sympathies," writes Susan Sontag. "It demands, rather, his absence."[18]

14 *Grandeur-Immense* (1935) was created for Anatole Jakovki's *23 Gravures de Arp, Calder, Chirico, Erni, Ernst, Fernández, Giacometti, Ghika, González, Hélion, Kandinsky, Léger, Lipchitz, Magnelli, Miró, Nicholson, Ozenfant, Picasso, Seligmann, Taeuber-Arp, Torres-García, Vulliamy, Zadkine* (Paris: Editions G. Orobitz et Cie, 1935). The portfolio was made to finance Jakovski's ultimately unrealized *24 Essais,* on the same artists plus Marcel Duchamp.

15 Sweeney, "Introduction," *Alexander Calder,* exh. cat. (New York: Museum of Modern Art, 1943), 42, 45.

16 Calder, "Mobiles," 64, 67. For an in-depth examination of Calder's projects with Martha Graham and also his participation in the First Hartford Music Festival, see Perl, *Conquest of Time,* 481–91.

17 For details on Calder's performance-related projects, see Alexander S. C. Rower, "Select Chronology," in *Alexander Calder: Performing Sculpture,* exh. cat. (London: Tate, 2015), 212–25.

18 Susan Sontag, "The Aesthetics of Silence," *Styles of Radical Will* (New York: Farrar, Straus and Giroux, 2002), 16. Originally published in 1969.

Living and working in the open air instigated a groundbreaking working process for Calder. By 1936, he realized that making mistakes on a large scale was as expensive as it was unproductive, so he began creating maquettes or scale models. The first of these was a thirty-five-inch-tall model for *Devil Fish* (1937), which translated to a five-and-a-half-foot-tall sculpture or "stabile" (as these stationary works were named by Jean Arp in 1932). Another was *Ex-Octopus* (maquette, 1936, p. 91), a seventeen-inch-tall model that was enlarged to around six-feet tall, (but not until three decades later). As he later conceded in his 1943 manuscript *À Propos of Measuring a Mobile,* "The admission of approximation is necessary, for one cannot hope to be absolute in his precision."[19] Calder's acceptance of approximation contributes to the aliveness of his stationary works. Depending on our perspective, his stabiles, with their fluid and organic curves, assume a new face at each turn, their elements unfolding in perpetuity as if in a state of continual becoming.

The maquette for *Ex-Octopus,* along with *Devil Fish* and its model, premiered in *Calder: Stabiles & Mobiles* at Pierre Matisse Gallery, New York, in winter 1937, the artist's third solo show with the legendary dealer since 1934. Here, he installed a number of maquettes at the feet of *Big Bird* (1937) with the intention of enticing patrons to commission large-scale sculptures for their gardens (fig. 7). In spring 1940, in what was his fifth solo show at Matisse's gallery, Calder premiered *Black Beast* (1940, fig. 8, pp. 98, 99), an angular, menacing stabile that stood at nearly fourteen-feet wide and nine-feet tall. Seventeen years later, Calder made *Black Beast II* (1957) in a heavier material — using a thick gauge iron plate — for the courtyard of architect Eliot Noyes' home in New Canaan, Connecticut. As the artist recalled in his autobiography, it was *Black Beast* and *Devil Fish,* along with the standing mobile *Spherical Triangle* (1938), that counted as "the forerunners of the big stabiles to come."[20]

Calder's entire oeuvre is marked by dramatic shifts in media, style, and scale, and his early inventions in Roxbury were no exception. Just as the open air encouraged an increase in size in his outdoor works, it also instigated a lightness of form in his indoor creations. *Starfish* (1934, fig. 9) was among the earliest manifestations of the hanging mobiles that Calder made in Roxbury. While it formally recalls *Cône d'ébène* (1933, fig. 10), the last of Calder's hanging mobiles made in Paris, it is strikingly different in execution and sensibility. *Starfish* is refined, complex, and more sophisticated in its tension with gravity, whereas *Cône d'ébène* is coarse and lumbering, made of solid ebony. In other works from around 1934, Calder

19 Calder, "À Propos of Measuring a Mobile," manuscript, Calder Foundation archives, 1943.

20 Calder, *Autobiography,* 179, 254.

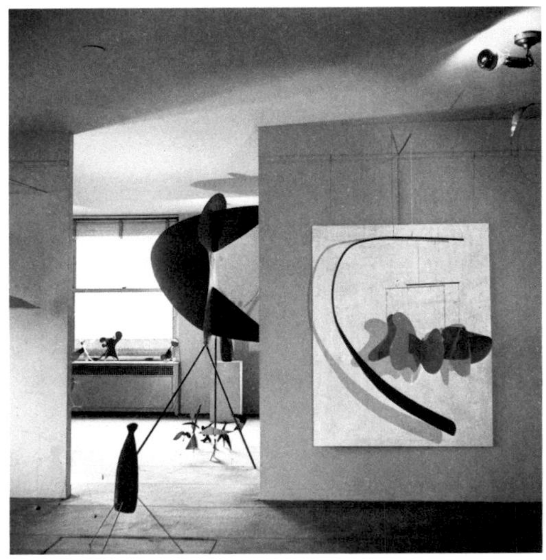

Fig. 7 Installation photograph showing *Ex-Octopus* (maquette, 1936), *Calder: Stabiles & Mobiles,* Pierre Matisse Gallery, New York, 1937. Photograph by Herbert Matter.

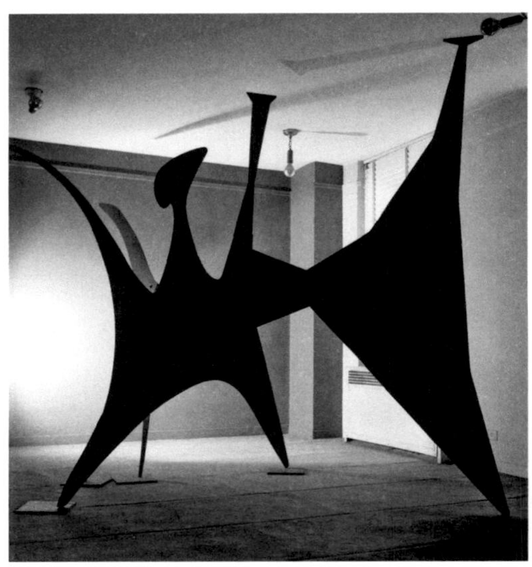

Fig. 8 Installation photograph showing *Black Beast* (1940), *Calder,* Pierre Matisse Gallery, New York, 1940. Photograph by Herbert Matter.

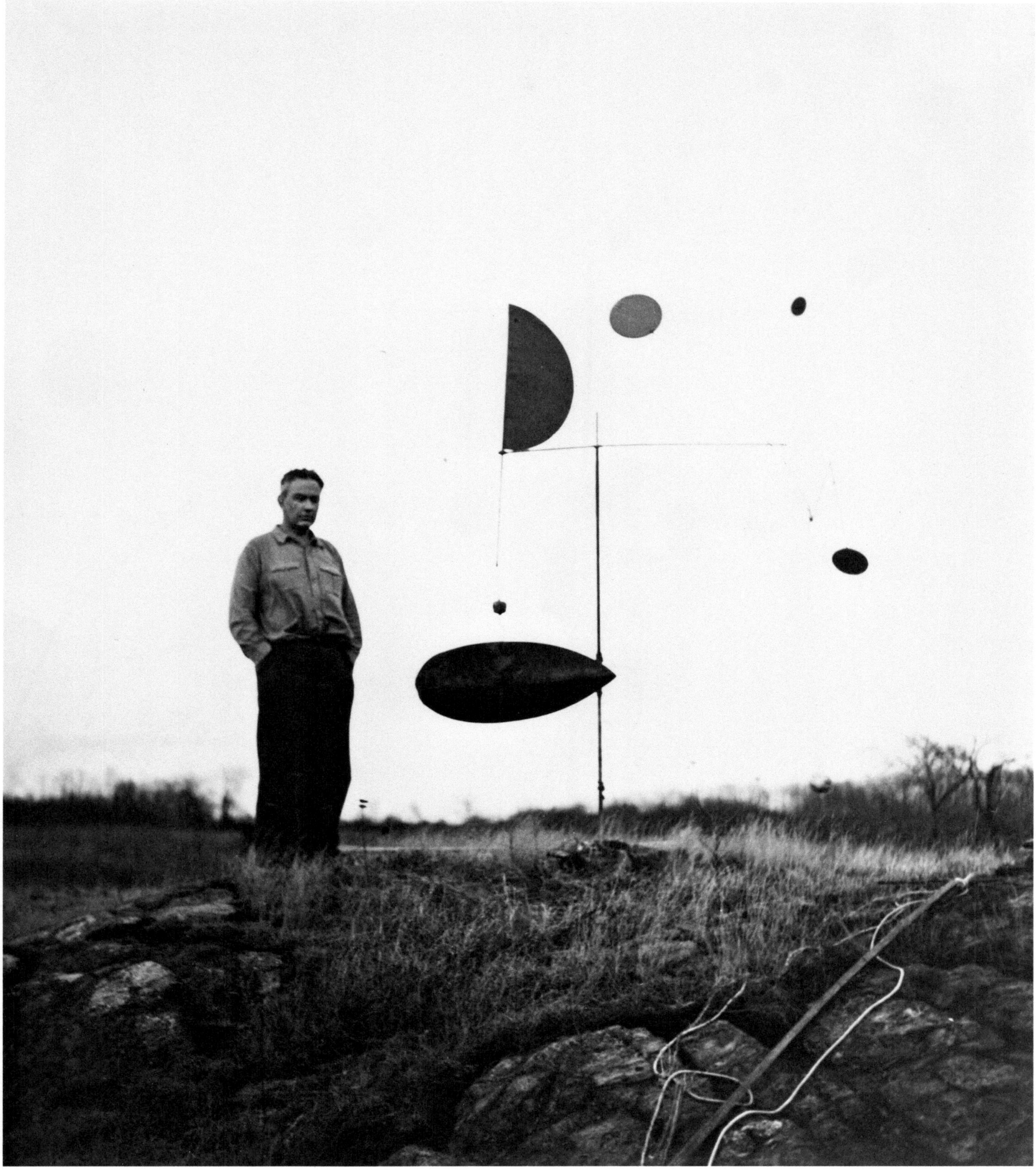

Fig. 5 Calder with *Steel Fish* (1934), Roxbury, 1934.
Photograph by James Thrall Soby.

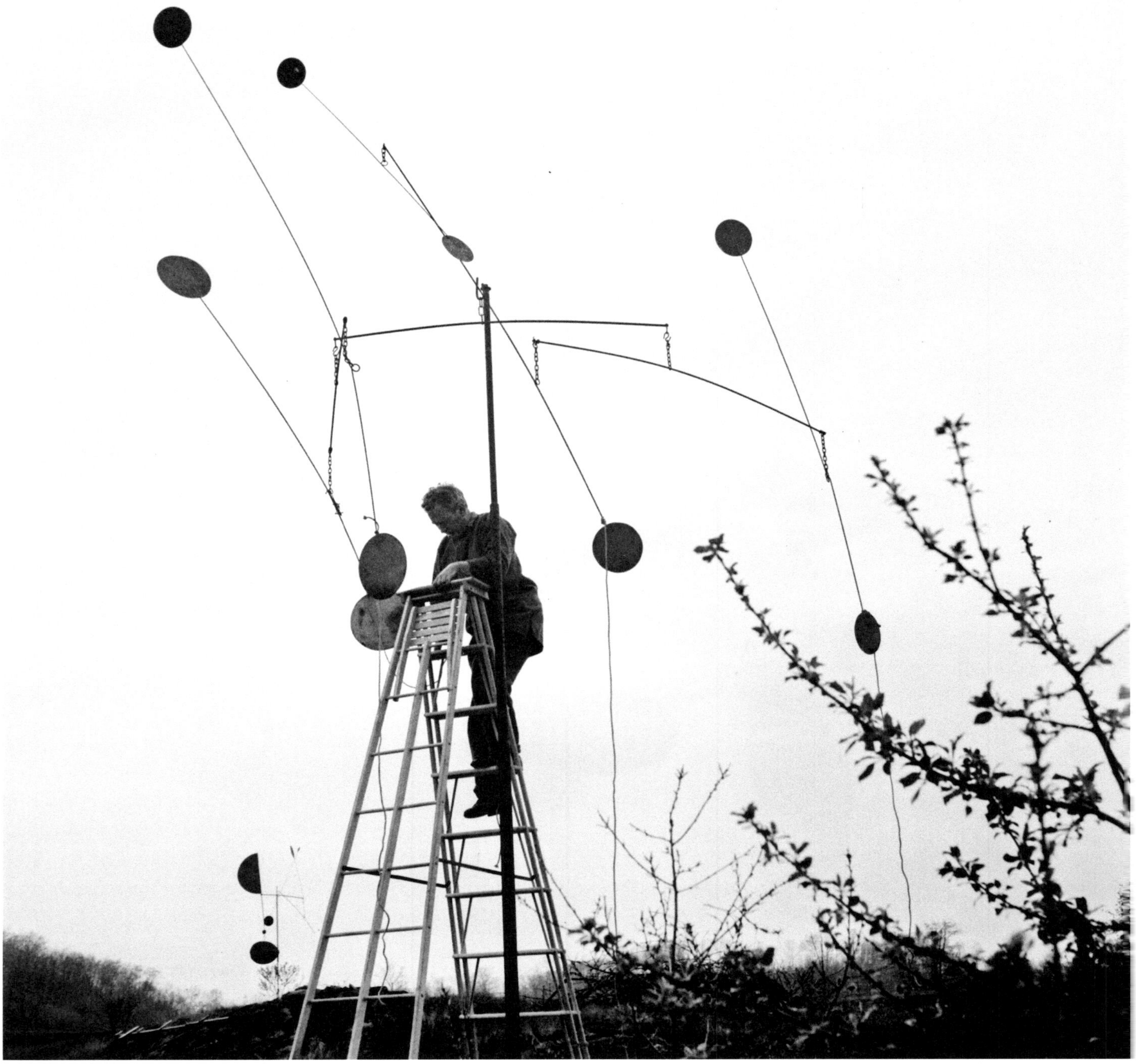

Fig. 6 Calder assembling *Five Rods and Nine Discs* (1936), Roxbury, 1938 (*Steel Fish* [1934] is pictured in the distance). Photograph by Herbert Matter.

suspended delicate, energy-dense wooden elements from strings, allowing for greater movement. The lighter Calder's mobiles became, the more unpredictable the expanse of their dimensions and the character of their motions.

For *Starfish,* Calder carved directly into wood, a practice he began in the mid-1920s in New York with his figurative works. He often used wood in his abstract sculptures of the 1930s, such as *Untitled* (1935, p. 78), for which he reckoned with the grain to make forms at once agile and exotic. Seven years later, when sheet metal was in short supply during World War II, Calder went so far as to destroy one of his conventional wood sculptures from 1929 (entitled *The Crowd*) in an act of extreme recycling, so that its ebony pieces could serve as the basis for his "Constellations" (so-named by Sweeney and Duchamp). These abstract wood and wire sculptures premiered in 1943 in what would become Calder's last show with Matisse: *Calder: Constellationes.* "They had a suggestion of some kind of cosmic nuclear gases—which I won't try to explain," Calder recalled. "I was interested in the extremely delicate, open composition."[21] *Untitled* (1945, pp. 85, 87, 89), which includes a variation on an ovoid-like form as a unifying force in resonance with *Steel Fish*, postdates his foray into the Constellations.

Calder always had a deep affinity for humble materials (his *Cirque Calder* was crafted from a wide spectrum of them), and he expanded upon this interest in Roxbury in surprising ways. Having stumbled upon a dumping ground used by previous homesteaders, Calder began to make mobiles with shards of colored glass, bits of broken pottery, and pieces of metal that could be set in motion by the slightest breath of air. In a work such as *Tines* (1943, p. 85), which includes tines snapped off a pitchfork, as well as the stem of a broken wine glass, Calder engaged luminous and sonorous energy. The mobile not only reflects and refracts light, but its elements collide at surprising moments, creating delicate pinging sounds. The frequencies of light and sound that reverberate in *Tines* give new meaning to Calder's conviction that a "mobile in motion leaves an invisible wake behind it, or rather, each element leaves an individual wake behind its individual self."[22] Even after the direct act of experience is over, the mobile does not cease its work on us.

Writing on Calder's development in Roxbury, Sweeney remarked: "Little by little, calculated forms gave way to forms suggested by the material — a lump of wood, a piece of bone — till finally the materials employed seemed scarcely touched by tools."[23] Nowhere is Calder's intuition of material more astonishing than in *Apple Monster* (1938, pp. 84, 86, 87), an object made from the fallen branch of an ancient apple tree at Roxbury that the artist turned upside down and modified to create a Surrealist personage. The energy emanating from this work is twofold: it is at once a relic of the Roxbury property and an object that gives us insight into the artistic act of seeing. As Brazilian art critic Mário Pedrosa intimated, "[Calder] was able to draw from wood as if moved by some divine sense or mysterious faculty for intimate communication with things, his hands deprived of any tool, like those of a magician."[24] In its untitled sister sculpture from that year — nicknamed "Vertebra Monster" by Calder Foundation employees — Calder incorporated a cow vertebra which he had found on the property (p. 85). Perched atop the sculpture's back is a progeny of spheres that vibrate when activated, creating a contrapuntal value that harkens back to some of his earliest abstractions from Paris, among them *Croisière* (1931).

21 Calder, in H. Harvard Arnason and Ugo Mulas, *Calder* (New York: Viking, 1971), 202.

22 Calder, "À Propos of Measuring a Mobile."

23 Sweeney, "Introduction," 40.

24 Mário Pedrosa, "Tension and Cohesion in the Work of Calder," *Mário Pedrosa: Primary Documents,* eds. Glória Ferreira and Paulo Herkenhoff (New York: Museum of Modern Art, 2015), 255.

25 Plato's *Philebus,* section 51c, quoted in Alfred. H. Barr, Jr., *Cubism and Abstract Art,* exh. cat. (New York: Museum of Modern Art, 1936), 14.

26 Duchamp, *Collection,* 52.

27 Notably, Calder was known to repurpose etching plates, as evidenced in the copper tray derived from an unused etching for the 1948 special edition of *Selected Fables* by Jean de La Fontaine, illustrated on page 83.

28 For further context, see Robert Penn Warren, "A Poem of Pure Imagination: An Experiment in Reading," *The Rime of the Ancient Mariner* (New York: Reynal and Hitchcock, 1946), 70.

Another sculpture from this tribe, *Praying Mantis* (1936), was exhibited in Alfred H. Barr, Jr.'s *Fantastic Art, Dada and Surrealism* at the Museum of Modern Art, New York in 1936. Calder was also represented in Barr's *Cubism and Abstract Art* mounted the previous spring at the museum. In his remarks on abstract art for the accompanying catalog, Barr quoted Plato's *Philebus:*

> I will try to speak of the beauty of shapes, and I do not mean, as most people would think, the shapes of living figures, or their imitations in paintings, but I mean straight lines and curves and the shapes made from them, flat or solid, by the lathe, ruler and square... These are not beautiful for any particular reason or purpose, as other things are, but are always by their very nature beautiful, and give pleasure of their own quite free from the itch of desire.[25]

Coincidentally, Plato's statement not only resonates with what Calder said about *Two Spheres* in 1932 ("This has no utility and no meaning. It is simply beautiful."), but also appears in what Duchamp wrote about Calder's work in 1949, published the following year in the *Collection of the Société Anonyme:* "In their treatment of gravity, disturbed by gentle movements, [the mobiles] give the feeling that 'they carry pleasures peculiar to themselves, which are quite unlike the pleasures of scratching', to quote Plato in his *Philebus.*"[26]

Although Calder did not intentionally align his work with the ideals of Surrealist automatism, there is something automatic in his immediate way of creating, as expressed in these works from 1938. Calder was also drawn to the energetic dimensions of single-line drawing, and Coleridge's *The Rime of the Ancient Mariner,* published in the first edition of *Lyrical Ballads* in 1798, counted among his projects. This poem, supposedly inspired during Coleridge's walks through Somerset's Quantock Hills, was a favorite of the Surrealists, with its supernatural descriptions of "the sky and the sea" all but capsizing a boat and its inhabitants. The 1946 special edition included 29 single-line etchings by Calder, among them seascapes and setting suns that hark back to Calder's fabled experience off the coast of Guatemala.[27] What Robert Penn Warren wrote about the meaning of a poem in his accompanying essay for *The Rime of the Ancient Mariner* could very well apply to the mobile: "We may say that the reader does not interpret the poem but the poem interprets the reader. We may say that the poem is the light and not the thing seen by the light. The poem is the light by which the reader may view and review all the area of experience with which he is acquainted."[28] Perhaps the sublime lies not in an object itself—in the greatness of measurable dimensions—but in the nature of the mind's immeasurable response.

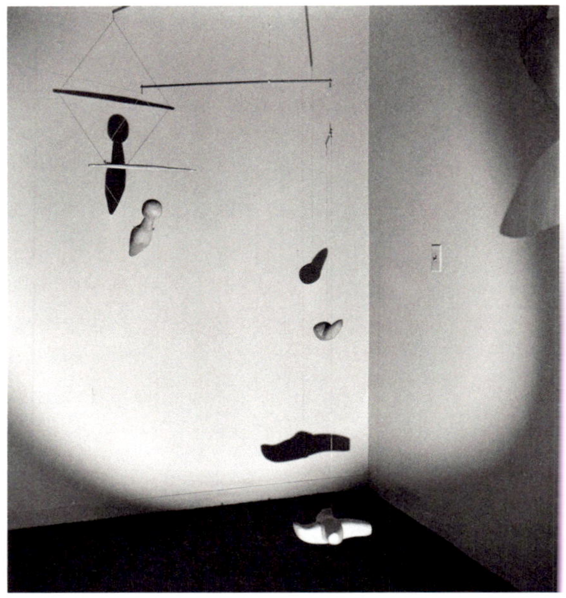

Fig. 9 Installation photograph showing *Starfish* (1934), *Calder: Stabiles & Mobiles*, Pierre Matisse Gallery, New York, 1937. Photograph by Herbert Matter.

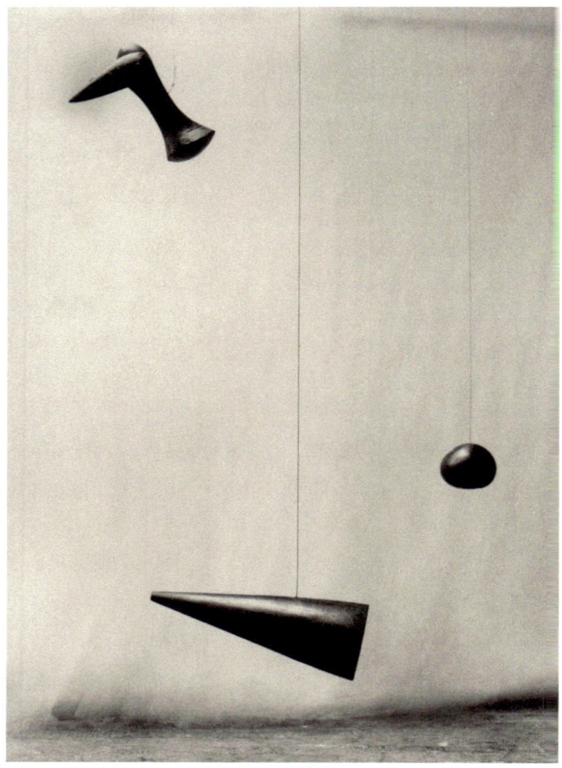

Fig. 10 *Cône d'ébène* (1933), 1933. Photograph by Marc Vaux.

In October of 1938, Calder began building a "vast and unencumbered" studio space on the side of a hill near his Roxbury home on the foundations of the old dairy barn, which was completed the following spring.[29] At twenty-five by forty-feet, with a roof that peaked at thirty-two feet, the studio was a large reservoir that engaged a sense of continuity between art and nature. "It did not stay unencumbered for long," wrote Calder, and it soon overflowed with all manner of mobiles, stabiles, standing mobiles, and paintings, as evidenced by Matter's photographs from 1941 (fig. 11).[30] An excerpt from André Masson's handwritten poem "L'Atelier d'Alexander Calder" touches upon the incalculable synthesis of earth, light, sound, and time that reverberated throughout the space:

> One green day you saw a red bird / in pursuit of a yellow bird; / you know that we are bound to nature / that we belong to the earth. / Hung from the studio's rafters, / in the streaks of light a gong sensitive to the caprices of air / is struck only with the greatest caution / With the step of a dove it rings: what hour does it sound?[31]

Notably, Calder encouraged Rose and André Masson to relocate to Connecticut during the war years, along with Yves Tanguy and Kay Sage. Masson's poem, which the artist wrote in Calder's studio while sleeping on the studio bed, attests to the profundity of their friendship, Calder having been pivotal in resolving the artist's displacement during the war. Marc Chagall, David Hare, Hans Richter, and Arshile Gorky were among some of the other artists who settled near Calder's home in Litchfield County, and he also hosted a number of Surrealist exiles, among them André Breton. By the mid-1940s, Calder had rebuilt the bohemian community from his Paris years in Roxbury, Connecticut.

The landscape's profound impact on Calder continued to expand in the years to come. His mobiles and standing mobiles became increasingly sophisticated, from the constantly shifting states of *Untitled (Mobile with N Degrees of Freedom,* 1946, pp. 100, 102, 103) to the punctured voids in *Red Maze I* (1954, p. 59) and *Untitled* (1954, p. 94), expressing thresholds of presence and absence. His stabiles, too, continued to grow, not only in experiential complexity but also in size. By the 1960s, he was making sculptures of a colossal scale, among them *La Grande vitesse* (1969), the first sculpture to be funded by the public art program of the National Endowment for the Arts, for which he made a 1:5 intermediate maquette (pp. 105, 114). For Calder, art and nature remained deeply interrelated aspects of the great dimension of experience. "Not extractions," he wrote, "but abstractions. Abstractions that are like nothing in life except in their manner of reacting."[32]

29 Calder, *Autobiography,* 177.

30 Ibid.

31 André Masson, "L'Atelier d'Alexander Calder," handwritten poem, 1942. First English translation in *Calder,* exh. cat. (New York: Buchholz Gallery/Curt Valentin, 1949); revised translation in *Calder* in *Connecticut,* ed. Eric M. Zafran, exh. cat. (New York: Rizzoli, 2000), 16.

32 Calder, "Comment réaliser l'art?", 6.

Susan Braeuer Dam is Director of Research and Publications at the Calder Foundation, where she has served as associate editor on a number of seminal publications that include *Calder Jewelry* (Calder Foundation, 2007) and *Calder by Matter* (Cahiers d'Art, 2013). Recent articles by Dam have appeared in *Calder in France* (Cahiers d'Art, 2015), *Calder and Picasso* (Almine Rech Gallery, 2016), and *Calder: Monumental* (Denver Botanic Gardens, 2017).

Following:

Fig. 11 *Apple Monster* (1938) and *Black Beast* (maquette, 1939), Roxbury studio, 1941. Photograph by Herbert Matter.

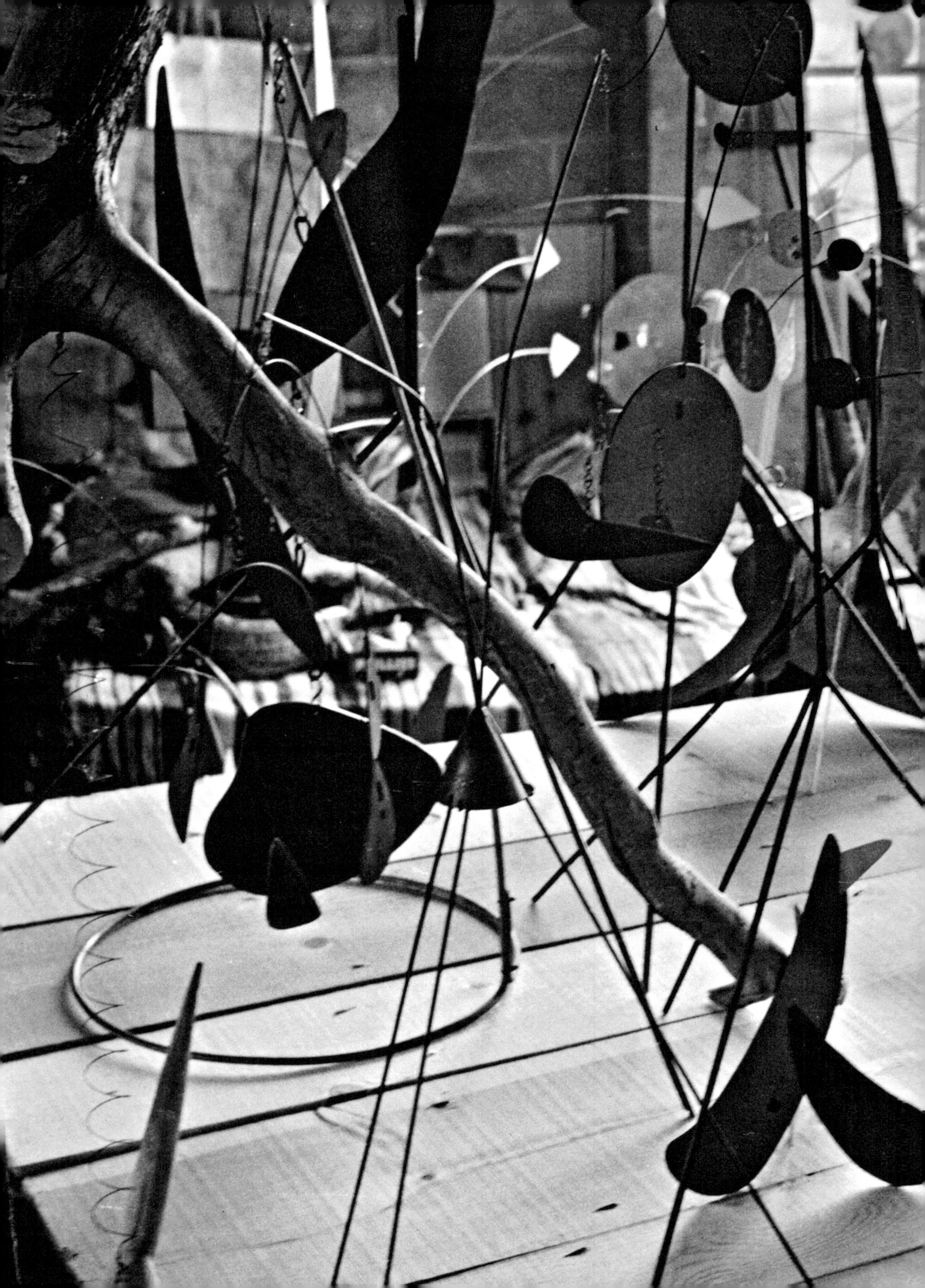

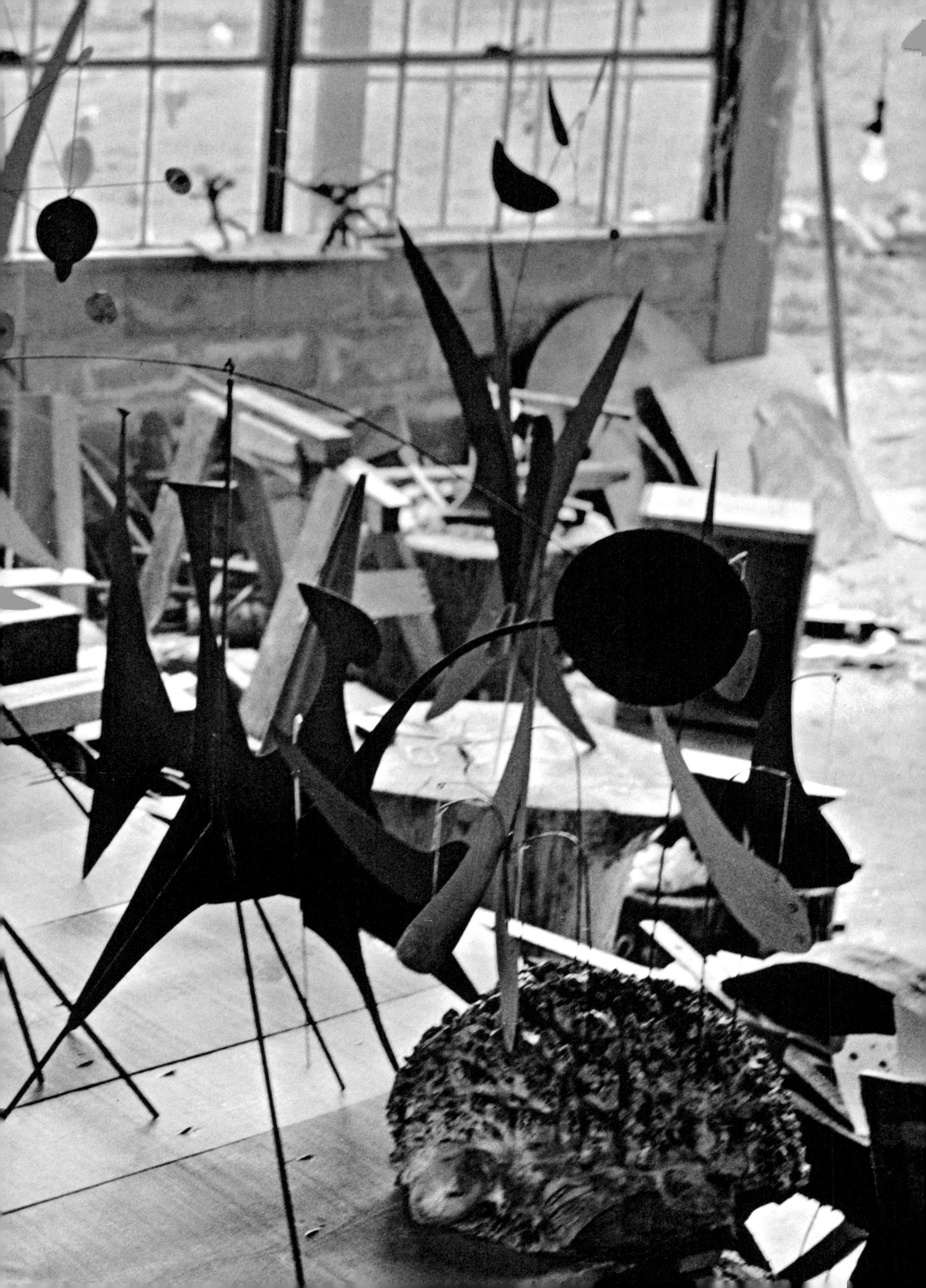

MORE THAN BEAUTIFUL

POLITICS AND RITUAL IN CALDER'S DOMESTIC ITEMS

JESSICA HOLMES

Alexander Calder once recalled an incident that occurred between him and his wife Louisa shortly after they married. The two were living in Paris and had decided to hire a live-in cook. Louisa set out to furnish a spare bedroom for the new employee, with items including a broc and washbasin. Describing the distaste he felt towards her purchase, Calder mused, "A broc is a beautiful thing of conical shape, tall and slender — and instead she had bought a pitcher, fat and dumpy, while the basin had a flat bottom ... I feel that if one accepts things which one does not approve of, it is the beginning of the end ... Bad taste always boomerangs."[1] Scandalised by the offending items, Calder destroyed them, driving a spike through each, despite Louisa's protest that he wouldn't "see these things anyway, because they'll be in the cook's room."[2]

In the decade since I first recounted it in my essay *A Broc is a Beautiful Thing: Calder's Domestic Treasures*[3] (2007), I've mulled this story over countless times, thinking about how Louisa once wrote to her mother before she and Calder married of the artist's "tremendous originality, imagination and humour," which she declared, "appeal to me very much and which make life colorful and worthwhile."[4] How alarming it must have been for the newlywed to see her jocular husband fly into a rage over a seemingly inconsequential pair of objects. What caused such a vehement reaction in Calder?

This rare display of ferocity may seem surprising coming from an artist known for his good nature (although Calder's surviving family confirms that privately he was often far less amiable), however, the recollection is illuminating. Calder's aesthetic rigor and commitment to solid design underlie his demeanor. The artist demanded perfection from the tools and objects that surrounded him, and so, rather than give in to using deficient mass-manufactured goods, his frequent solution was to make superior versions with his own hands. For every mobile, every monumental public sculpture, every wire portrait for which he is renowned, there is also a humble ashtray, a pragmatic folding table, or an electric toaster that is also Calder-devised. Most of these inventions were constructed for personal use. Louisa Calder and the couple's two daughters, Sandra and Mary, also benefited from Calder's ingenuity: a baby rattle (p. 74), a set of repurposed teacups, and a bacon fork much beloved by Louisa all attest to this. Calder's domestic items were often beautiful, but all were primarily conceived to be functional and sturdy. His striking ingenuity in the creation of these objects had its roots in his marvelous output of early toys, which treated humor as an intellectual pursuit, and also, of course, his famous *Cirque Calder*, an assemblage of objects made from found and recycled articles and other proletarian materials. Filtered through the lens of these early achievements, Calder's household objects take on a fresh significance.

The essence of Calder's politics can be found in these humble pursuits. Calder could be demonstrably political when moved by dire or extreme situations. His contribution of *Mercury Fountain* to the Spanish Pavilion at the 1937 World's Fair in Paris, which was displayed alongside Picasso's *Guernica* in support of the Spanish Republic (which was at the time under siege by Franco's Fascists), is an early testament to this, as is his participation in anti-Vietnam protests during the 1960s. So too is his signature on the New Year's advertisement he and Louisa

1 Alexander Calder, *Calder: An Autobiography with Pictures*, ed. Jean Davidson (New York: Pantheon Books, 1966), 124.

2 Ibid.

3 Jessica Holmes, "A Broc is a Beautiful Thing: Calder's Domestic Treasures" in *Simplicity of Means: Calder and the Devised Object*, exh. cat. (New York: Jonathan O'Hara Gallery, 2007) 5–23. The present essay is a reconsideration and expansion on themes established in this prior essay.

4 Louisa James to Louisa Cushing James, 1930, Calder Foundation archives.

took out in the *New York Times* in 1966, on behalf of the organization SANE (The Committee for a SANE Nuclear Policy), where they contended:

> A New Year, New World. Hope for: An end to hypocrisy, self-righteousness, self-interest, expediency, distortion and fear, wherever they exist. With great respect for those who rightly question brutality, and speak out strongly for a more civilized world. Our only hope is in thoughtful Men—Reason is not treason.[5]

Despite these public declarations of his political position, Calder's work rarely displayed an overtly political perspective, unlike the work of his contemporaries such as André Breton or Hans Bellmer, for instance. However, Calder's handmade, recycled, or modified utilitarian objects—which were part and parcel of the Calder family's everyday life—manifest his staunch commitment to a personal politics that is, when examined, impossible to separate from a broader worldview. The domestic items are unequivocal solutions to everyday problems the artist might have encountered as he went about his daily life. Also embedded into the creation of these items is the personal significance Calder placed on ritual endeavors above commercial aims. Writing of Calder's mobiles, Alex J. Taylor remarked that, "Like automated appliances...Calder's 'invention' served as another kind of manifestation of 'Yankee ingenuity'...and provided the cultural correlate of high-tech novelties promised by American abundance."[6] However, I maintain the opposite: Calder's household objects eschew the rampant capitalism that came to define American political and cultural life in the twentieth century, and in fact highlight the pragmatic philosophy Calder espoused, less in words, but rather, in the very way he lived and worked.

The pitcher and basin are not the only instances where mass-market design raised Calder's ire to the point of destruction. The remnants of a manufacturing stamp in the metal uncovered during recent conservation of the baby rattle (c. 1935, p. 74) Calder made for his infant daughter show that it was made from a piece of Tiffany silver. Likely given to Calder and Louisa as a wedding gift, the artist saw no need for a piece of futile, decorative silver, even one with the label of an extravagant jeweler. So he broke it down and refashioned it into a plaything for his baby, alchemically suffusing the Tiffany silver with a purpose. Into his middle age and beyond, when the artist had achieved enough success that he had the means to live quite comfortably (even grandly if he had chosen), Calder maintained his rustic lifestyle, complete with useful utensils and tools he fashioned or modified himself. For Calder, his self-made items functioned in a superior way to the more readily available, store-bought alternatives.

Calder's predilection for original thought manifested itself from childhood, and his mechanical inclination was evident from a young age. As a small boy, his parents left him and his older sister Peggy with family friends in Philadelphia for an extended period while they traveled across the country by train to the American Southwest, seeking treatment for his father's ailing health. Calder remembered later, "I took my parents' departure and our new surroundings as a natural course of events. Mother wrote to us about being able to see the locomotive when the train ran around a curve. There was a mechanical element in this picture which interested me, I suppose."[7] What is most remarkable is that even in the face of this potentially

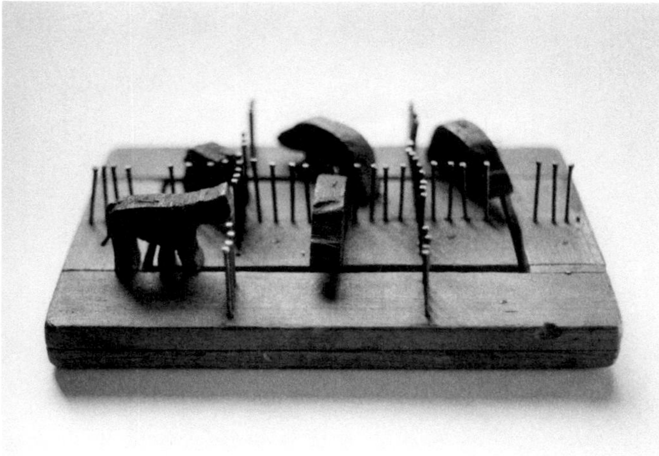

Fig. 1 *Animal Zoo Puzzle* (c. 1911), 1965. Photograph by Antonio Violich.

traumatizing event, Calder's intellectual curiosity prevailed. Indeed, he often made good use of his inventive nature to create toys and games for himself and Peggy. When he was eight years old, Calder and his family moved to Pasadena, California. Given the basement of their house to use as his workshop, Calder discovered his facility with tools and materials. He later remembered that his parents were supportive of his early endeavors, noting that, "Mother and father were all for my efforts to build things myself—they approved of the homemade."[8] Besides crafting jewelry for his sister's dolls from bits of wire he found in the streets, he constructed other ingenious toys and contraptions. A neighbor who fought a losing battle with slugs in the garden received a homemade slug-killer, for example. "I made him a two-pronged fork out of wire with a trigger ejector with which he could demolish the slugs at his ease."[9] Even more sophisticated was a small puzzle game (fig. 1) given by Calder to his father as a birthday gift around 1911:

> A small wooden rectangle was divided into six pens by fourpenny nails. A tiger, a lion, and three bears, all suitably painted, were fastened into slots so that they could be moved from pen to pen. The challenge was to clean the pens without having two animals in the same pen at once (thus avoiding bloodshed).[10]

Calder constructed all of the game's parts—hammering the nails into the block and carving the little sliding animals. Made entirely from items he was able to find around the house or on the street, the advanced level of planning and strategy behind the innovative game is impressive by any standards. At the time of its creation, Calder was not yet twelve years old.

Graduating from Stevens Institute of Technology in Hoboken, New Jersey, in 1919, Calder nurtured these early interests, undertaking a degree in mechanical engineering. For several years afterward, he assumed a nomadic existence, bouncing from job to job. He had no problem finding engineering work, but little of it proved stimulating to him. Then, in 1922, while working at a logging camp in Washington State as a timekeeper, Calder spontaneously asked his mother, who was living in New York, to send him a set of oil paints. She obliged, and he began to paint the surrounding landscapes. Something resonated and shortly thereafter, he quit his engineering job and returned to New York to become an artist.

5 Calder and Louisa Calder, "1966: A New Year, New World," *New York Times*, 2 January 1966.

6 Alex J. Taylor, "Unstable Motives: Propaganda, Politics, and the Late Work of Alexander Calder," *American Art* 26, no. 1 (Spring 2012), 31.

7 Calder, *Autobiography*, 15.

8 Calder, *Autobiography*, 21.

9 Calder, *Autobiography*, 38.

10 Margaret Hayes Calder, *Three Alexander Calders: A Family Memoir* (Middlebury, VT: Paul S. Eriksson, 1977), 42.

When Calder arrived, he enrolled in drawing and painting classes at the Art Students League, at first thinking that he might become a painter. Living in a cheap cold-water flat on a student's budget, he took to hand-making whatever necessities he lacked. Calder had no watch or clock in the tiny but sunny apartment he rented on Fourteenth Street, so he made himself a working sundial out of wire (fig. 2). In the form of a rooster, this astonishing object and pragmatic device (sadly no longer extant) is Calder's earliest known wire sculpture.

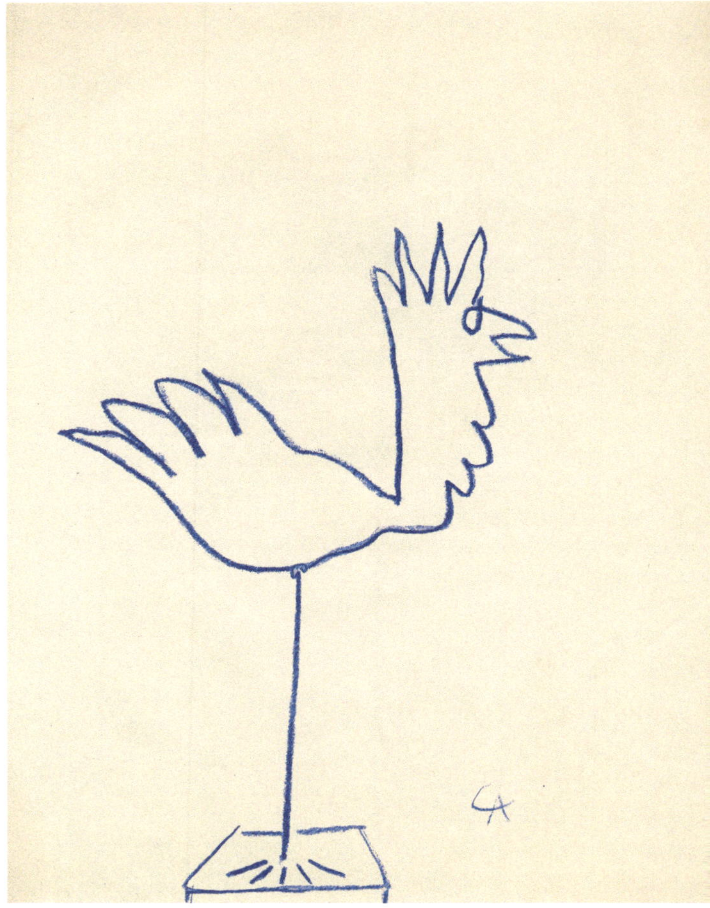

Fig. 2 This drawing of Calder's 1926 wire sundial was illustrated in his 1966 autobiography. *Rooster Sundial* (1965). Ink on paper, 9 × 8 in. (22.9 × 20.3 cm).

Calder soon found a job as a freelance illustrator for the *National Police Gazette*, and for the next several years sketched dozens of line drawings for the magazine. In 1925, the *Gazette* sent Calder to cover the Ringling Bros. and Barnum & Bailey Circus. In the early twentieth century, the circus still enjoyed huge popularity as adult entertainment. At the time, it was not merely an amusement for children, but an intellectual diversion that spurred public dialogue and commentary. "I spent two full weeks there practically every day and night,"[11] Calder noted, over which time he became intimately familiarised with the spectacle. He studied every detail meticulously, paying particular attention to "how the rigging was actuated" and "the spatial relationships within the tent."[12] This experience served him when he departed for Paris the following year—having been recommended to the city by "everyone who had been there"[13]—for it was there that the *Cirque Calder* was born. In the mid-1920s, Paris was the undisputed capital of the art world, and Calder—still thinking of himself primarily as a painter—believed his work would advance there. He arrived in the summer and began work on his celebrated *Cirque*. He was familiar with the types of movement performed by the various troupers and animals and began to create diminutive, moving figures whose actions were based on what he had seen at Ringling Brothers. The miniature players were fabricated from cloth, wood, found objects, and most importantly, wire, a material both structurally sturdy and pliable.

Cirque Calder (fig. 3) is a feat of imagination. Composed of hundreds of pieces, it includes every circus performer in small scale: trapeze artists with articulated limbs, a ring-master who brings a megaphone up to his mouth to shout to the crowd, a dog that flips, a horse that gallops—these characters all existed in *Cirque Calder* just as they did in the live circus. Calder soon became the toast of the Parisian avant-garde, presenting elaborate, two-hour

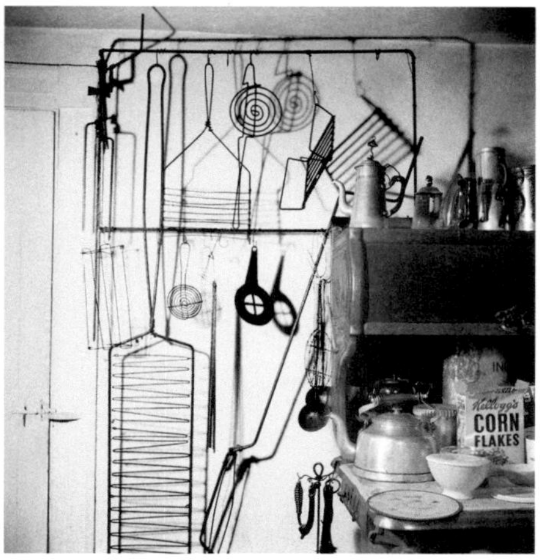

Fig. 4 Rack with grills and utensils (c. 1935–45), Roxbury house kitchen, 1950. Photograph by Herbert Matter.

performances in which each of the figures played a role. Soon, his friends were bringing their friends to see this groundbreaking piece of performance art. Enthusiasts marveled at the production's mechanical intricacy and also at the way these mechanics still yielded to chance, just like life. *Cirque Calder* was not a mere replica of a circus—it was an *actual* circus, existing on its own terms. Legrand-Chabrier, the influential Parisian cultural critic, observed:

> Here is a model assembly of a circus tent, a surprising and complicated flying trapeze apparatus with three trapezes that permits, by the play of a wire manoeuvred by a finger, and not obligatorily, to make two trapezists of cork bodies joined to wire arms and legs execute the same tricks as our flying trapezists of flesh and blood. All this combined and balanced according to the laws of physics in action such that it allows the miracles of circus acrobatics.[14]

Calder met Louisa aboard a ship, on one of the several transcontinental voyages of his early career. They married in early 1931 in Concord, Massachusetts, and spent most of the next two years living in Paris. Upon their return to the United States in 1933 and, after borrowing a little money from a friend and drawing on a life insurance policy, the Calders put a down payment on their first home, a dilapidated farmhouse in Roxbury, Connecticut. "Limitation was the source of invention,"[15] Calder's son-in-law Jean Davidson once wrote of the artist, which may partially explain the impetus for the countless early housewares and furniture Calder developed for their use. As is often the case after the purchase of a first house, finances were tight and "the place needed everything—plumbing, heating, electricity, the works," Calder's biographer, Jed Perl has noted.[16] With these specialized undertakings requiring professional oversight (and therefore a certain amount of money), Calder, with his can-do spirit, often simply made himself the things he and Louisa needed in the early years of home-ownership. The beauty of these objects was never compromised by functionality, and their functionality was never inhibited at the expense of form.

Photographs of the Calder kitchen in the Roxbury house attest to the artist's prodigious output. One image of the kitchen (fig. 4) shows "a room that looks...almost more like a fantasy of a country kitchen than an actual place to prepare and consume meals."[17] A large wall rack displayed a wide range of hand-made cooking devices, including grills to hold and cook food, an example of which is included in the exhibition (p. 69), fashioned in a variety of sizes. Another rack was devoted to utensils: serving spoons and forks, not unlike the oversize aluminum measuring spoons and fanciful *Figa* fork (c. 1948, p. 70) shown here. Even the cabinets in the Roxbury kitchen are Calder-made, some of the earliest and most substantial of his kitchen creations.

> Our furniture and effects had come from Paris in six or seven large cases made out of some North European white wood. Out of one of these, I made a corner cupboard for the new kitchen, in which to hang pots and pans. Later on, after the fire, I made another cupboard... and for that one I used a large case which came with some of my jewelry back from the Museum of Modern Art...I also housed in the legs of the sink and put a hook of my own manufacture on the door, in the middle.[18]

11 Calder, *Autobiography*, 73.

12 Alexander S. C. Rower, *Calder Sculpture* (New York: Universe Publishing, 1988), 7.

13 Calder, *Autobiography*, 76.

14 Legrand-Chabrier, "Un petit cirque a domicile," *Candide*, no. 171, 23 June 1927. Translation courtesy Calder Foundation, New York.

15 Jean Davidson, "Human Shape," in *Autobiography*, rev. ed. (1977), 6.

16 Jed Perl, *Calder: The Conquest of Time: The Early Years: 1898–1940* (New York: Alfred A. Knopf, 2017), 442.

17 Hilton Kramer, "Toys, Trivets and Serving Trays," *New York Times* Magazine (17 October 1976), 70.

Following:

Fig. 3 Calder with *Cirque Calder* (1926–31), 1929. Photograph by André Kertész.

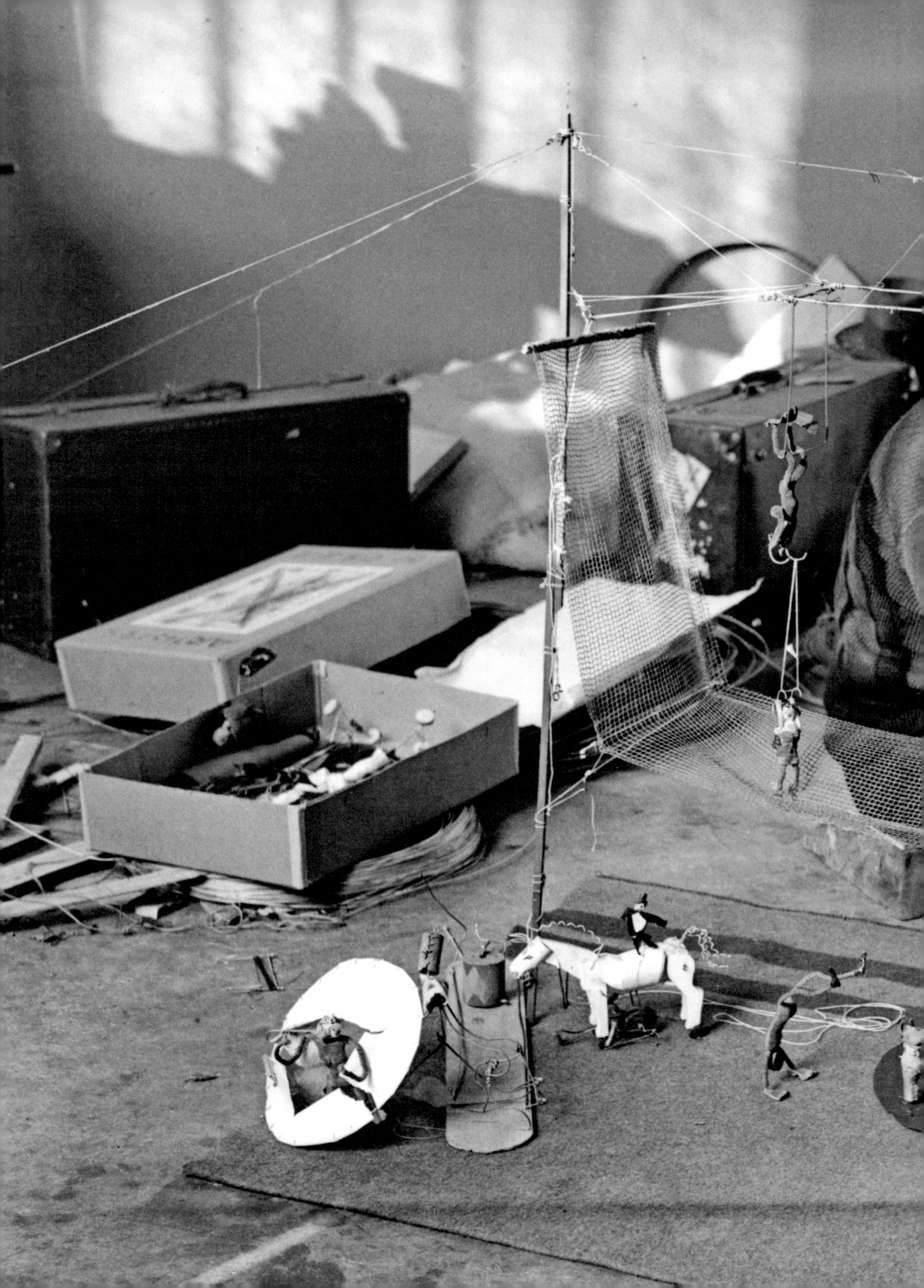

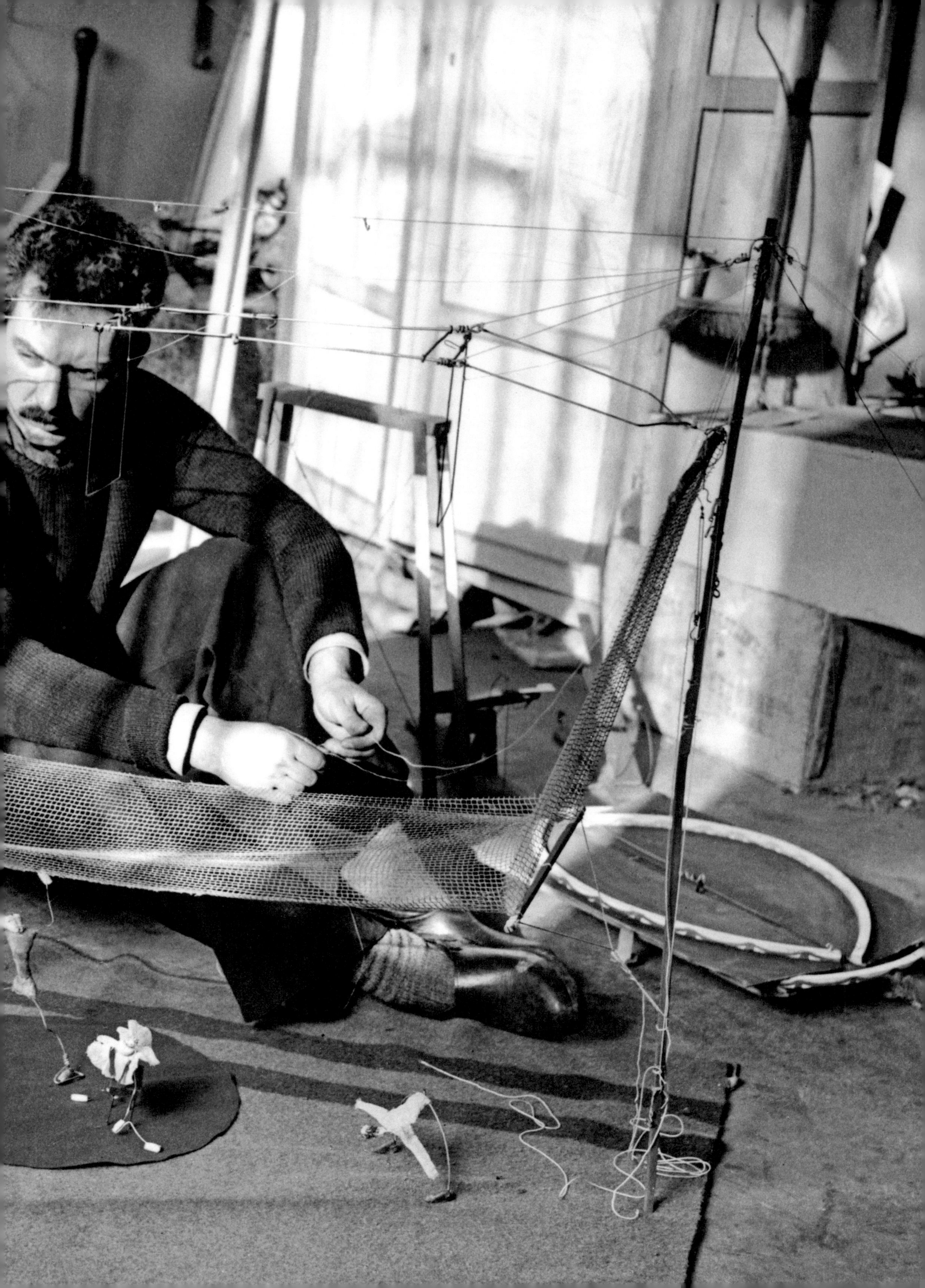

Calder was also inclined towards making improvements on his creations. This was a common process for the artist: to make an object, study its design, and then revise it, with amendments made in the next attempt. It was in this ritualistic way that Calder eventually invented his first mobile—its movements driven entirely by the breeze—after initially experimenting with the creation of motor-driven kinetic sculpture. The earliest known free-hanging mobile, *Small Sphere and Heavy Sphere* (1932/33) is largely comprised of repurposed objects. The mobile consists of two spheres, each suspended on its own line from a horizontal rod hanging from the ceiling (fig. 5), and encircled by a variety of found objects, such as a discarded tin can, empty glass bottles, and a small, wooden crate. When the larger sphere, made of iron, is swung, it causes the smaller, lighter-weight sphere to oscillate freely, creating an unpredictable cacophony of noises. Eventually, mobiles—usually made from sheet metal and wire—would become Calder's most celebrated invention.

Small Sphere and Heavy Sphere, in its utilization of reused items, relates not only to later mobiles like *Tines* (1943, p. 85)—whose elements are composed of found detritus—but also to Calder's more unassuming domestic objects. For instance, Calder devised a superb dinner bell (fig. 6, pp. 70, 75) from a Mexican wine goblet that had lost its stem and assorted pieces of glass. With the colorful shards swinging from wire looped around the waist of the glass, the bell might at first seem too fragile to summon anyone to a supper table; but it is surprisingly assured and luminous in tone, its dangling elements evoking Calder's mobile sculptures. Likewise, even in their lean years, the kitchen toaster—an inexpensive, commercially abundant object—was an item the Calders probably could have afforded for their home. But Calder believed his visualization of a toaster was stronger than that of a mass-produced one, which led him to develop toasters of his own conception. One design includes an ingenious "warming plate" upon which toasted slices of bread could rest, melting the butter via the heat generated by the machine below (p. 76). He eventually made five different toasters, each having a similar basic framework but minor variations in design and function. This system of working was not dissimilar from that of his late career, when he employed this process of re-working, even during the creation of his massive public sculptures. As Alexander S. C. Rower noted:

> Sometimes a 1:10 scale model would be made and then a 1:5 model would be constructed. Wind tunnel testing was employed to confirm the stability of the form...Calder himself approved the plans for any changes, and he continually refined his sculptures using aesthetic solutions to the structural problems... At each step, Calder designed and redesigned his original composition, altering shapes, materials, and balances as it suited him.[19]

Whether a monumental stabile soaring above a public plaza or a domestic item intended for personal use, the artist's procedural rigor remained constant.

Deeply embedded in these processes is Calder's solemn accedence to ritual, not in the strictly religious sense but rather in the way certain habitual activities, performed with reverence, become divine. As ritual studies scholar, Catherine Bell has written, "Activities that are merely routinized are not the best examples of the ritual-like nature of invariance unless they are also concerned with precision and control."[20] In *Alexander Calder: From the Stony River to the Sky*, the installation of Calder's household objects in specialized groupings and domestic tableaux allude to the significance of drinking coffee, smoking a cigarette, and

18 Calder, *Autobiography*, 147.

19 Alexander S. C. Rower, "Calder in Nature," *Calder: Storm King Art Center* (Mountainville, NY: Storm King Art Center, 2003), 15–16.

20 Catherine Bell, *Ritual: Perspectives and Dimensions* (Oxford: Oxford University Press, 1997), 150.

21 Ron Padgett, *Collected Poems* (Minneapolis: Coffee House Press, 2013), 389.

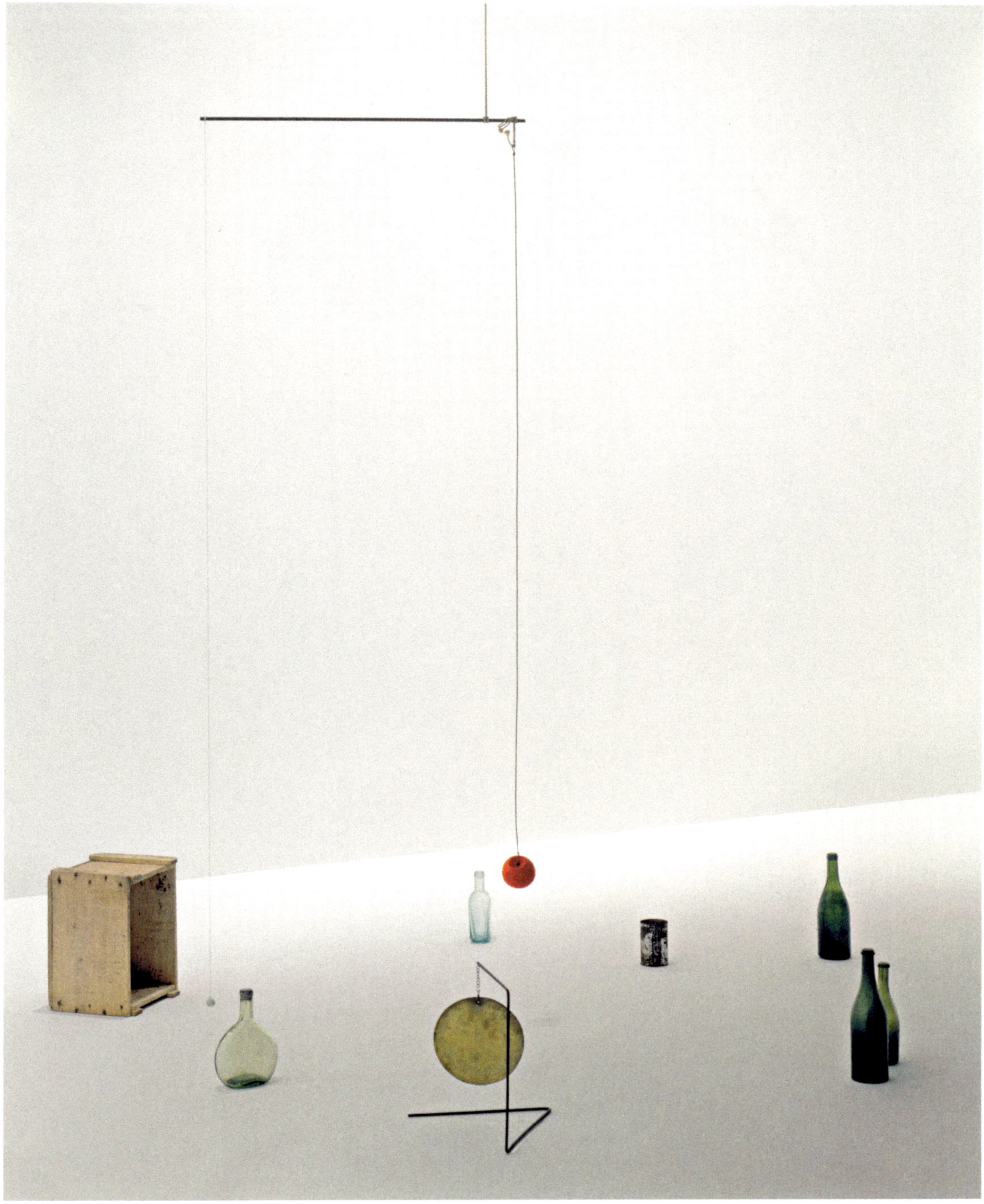

Fig. 5 *Small Sphere and Heavy Sphere* (1932/33). Cast iron, wood, cord, thread, rod, paint, and impedimenta; height: 125 in. (317.5 cm), dimensions variable. Calder Foundation, New York. Mary Calder Rower Bequest, 2011. Photograph by Jerry L. Thompson.

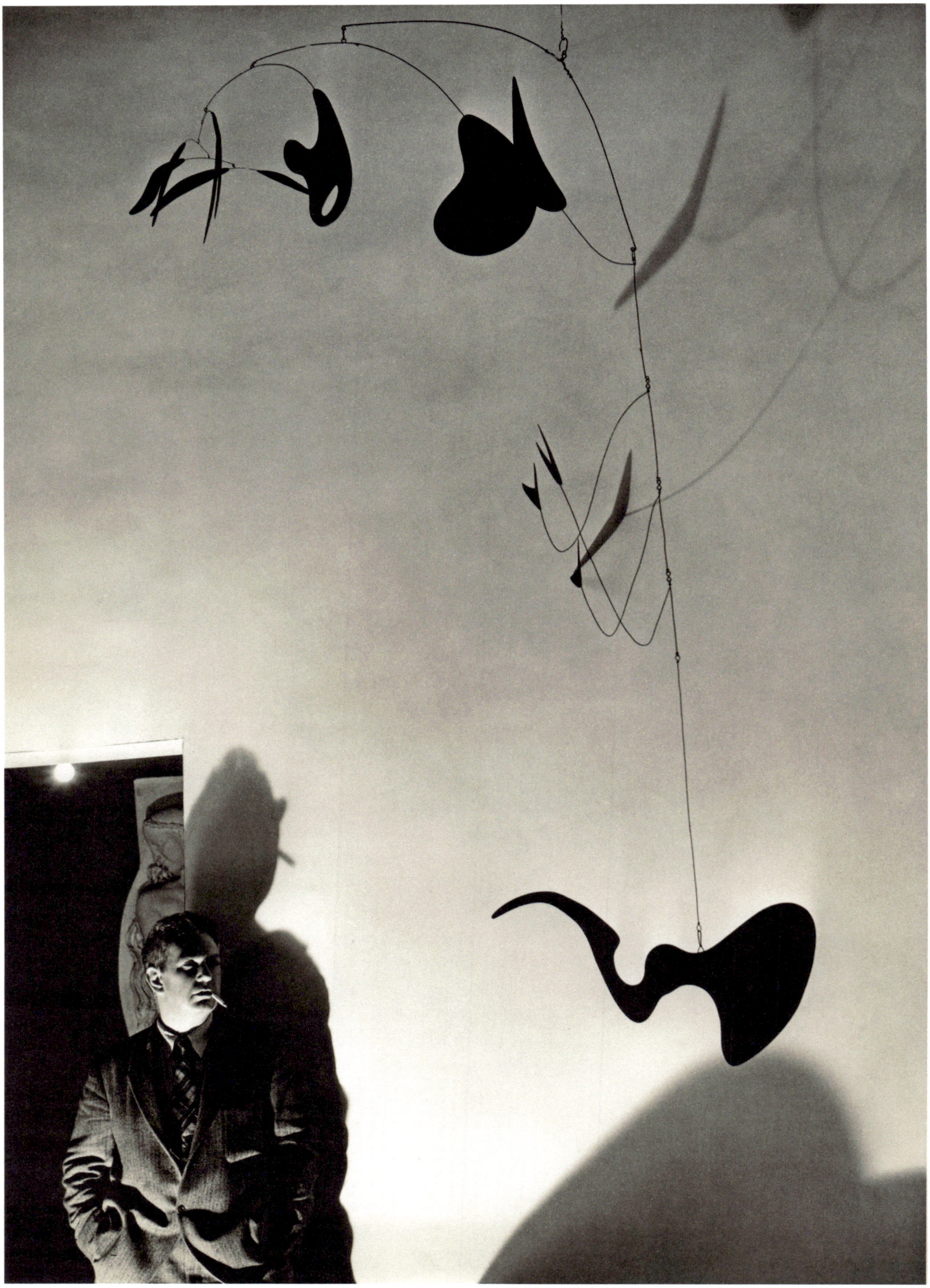

Fig. 8 Calder with *Eucalyptus* (1940), 1940. Photograph by André Kertész. Calder Foundation, New York.

22 Stanley William Hayter, "Alexander Calder at Paris," in *Homage to Alexander Calder*, Gualtieri di San Lazzaro, ed. Special issue of *Xxe siècle Review* (Paris), 1972.

playing chess as acts of ritual rather than as simple, routine undertakings. Each of these activities is one in which Calder not only partook but made an intrinsic part of his life. By performing them ceremoniously, Calder imbued a personal life force into the handmade objects he used to accomplish these rituals, elevating them from plebeian household items into hallowed totems.

"The morning coffee. I'm not sure why I drink it. Maybe it's the ritual / of the cup, the spoon, the hot water, the milk, and the little heap of / brown grit, the way they come together to form a nail I can hang the day on," wrote poet Ron Padgett.[21] And so it was with Calder. Early in Calder and Louisa's marriage, when the couple were still living in Paris, Calder devised a contraption that allowed him to have his morning coffee in bed. As artist and friend of the Calders Stanley William Hayter describes:

> The kitchen was on the *soupente* level up a short stairway from the studio in which was his bed. An elaborate machine with two wires issued from the kitchen on which a species of cradle carried the coffee pot. By dint of hauling on one string the gas could be lit under the percolator; another string turned it off and then the coffee could be carried on the wires down to the side of the bed without Sandy having to get up. I think it was his wife Louisa…who told me that should the apparatus fail to function Sandy would get up, repair it, return to bed and continue the whole routine.[22]

Even this early in his domestic life, the observance of morning coffee was so primary that Calder preferred to spend his leisurely morning hours before beginning the bustle of the day improving the device that allowed him his ritual as he envisioned it, rather than simply pouring the coffee and returning to bed. Later on, the Calder's house in Roxbury, not being a loft, made replicating this device impossible, but the same obsessive care still went into making and improving the coffee items that were in service to the family during their decades living in the home. The coffee-making apparatus itself was actually a store-bought item, a Moka pot based on the classic Italian design (p. 83). The Calder's pot seems to have been badly fashioned so that the coffee grinds tended to slip out of the pot when the coffee was being poured. Likewise, the knob that held the lid closed grew hot along with the rest of the metal pot, which made holding the lid closed near impossible. Rather than buying a better pot, Calder improved upon the design of the existing one. Two elegant twists of wire became the solution to coffee-pouring troubles: one affixed to the handle pushed down on the lid when pressed, keeping the grind bucket held fast within the container, while the other looped upwards from the hot knob to prevent singed fingertips. As any serious coffee aficionado knows, the receptacle into which the drink is poured matters—and

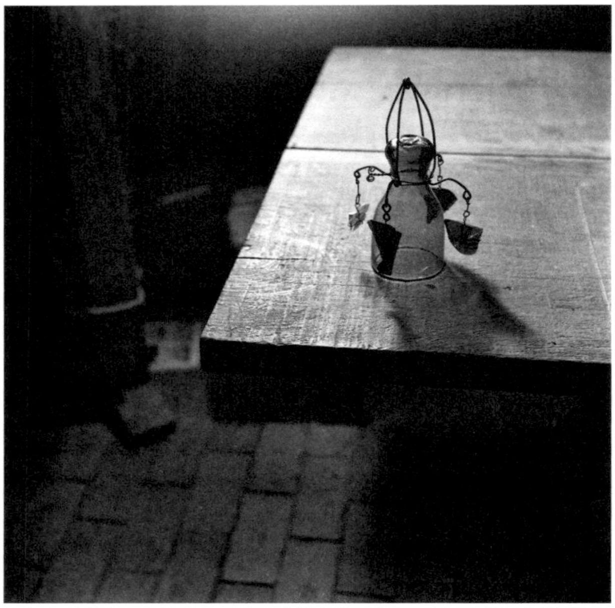

Fig. 6 Dinner bell (c. 1942), Roxbury house “big room,” 1950. Photograph by Herbert Matter.

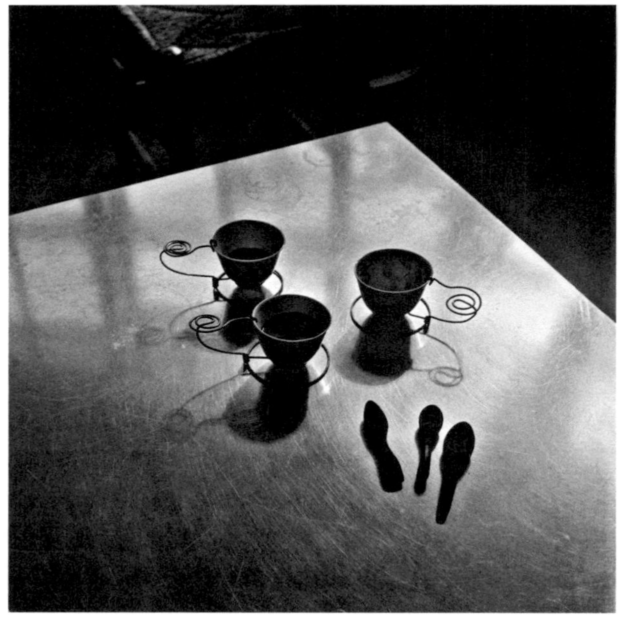

Fig. 7 Chinese teacups converted by Calder to espresso cups with brass wire zarfs and ebony spoons (c. 1935–40), Roxbury house “big room,” 1950. Photograph by Herbert Matter.

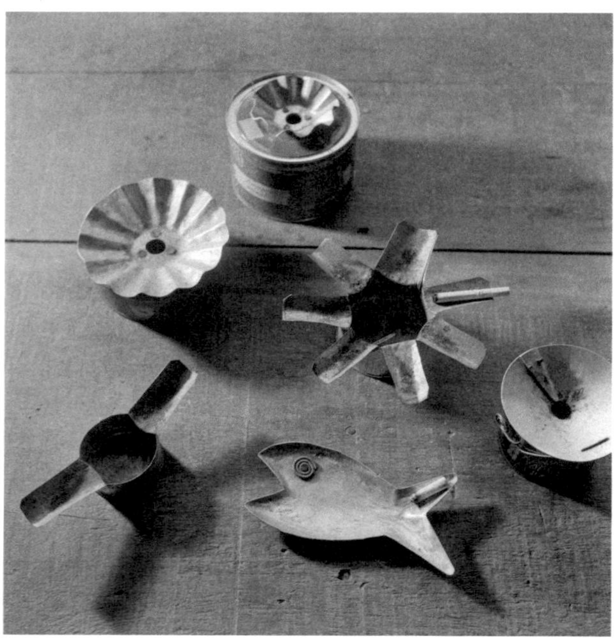

Fig. 9 Recycled tin can ashtrays and a fish ashtray (c. 1935–50), Roxbury house “big room,” 1950. Photograph by Herbert Matter.

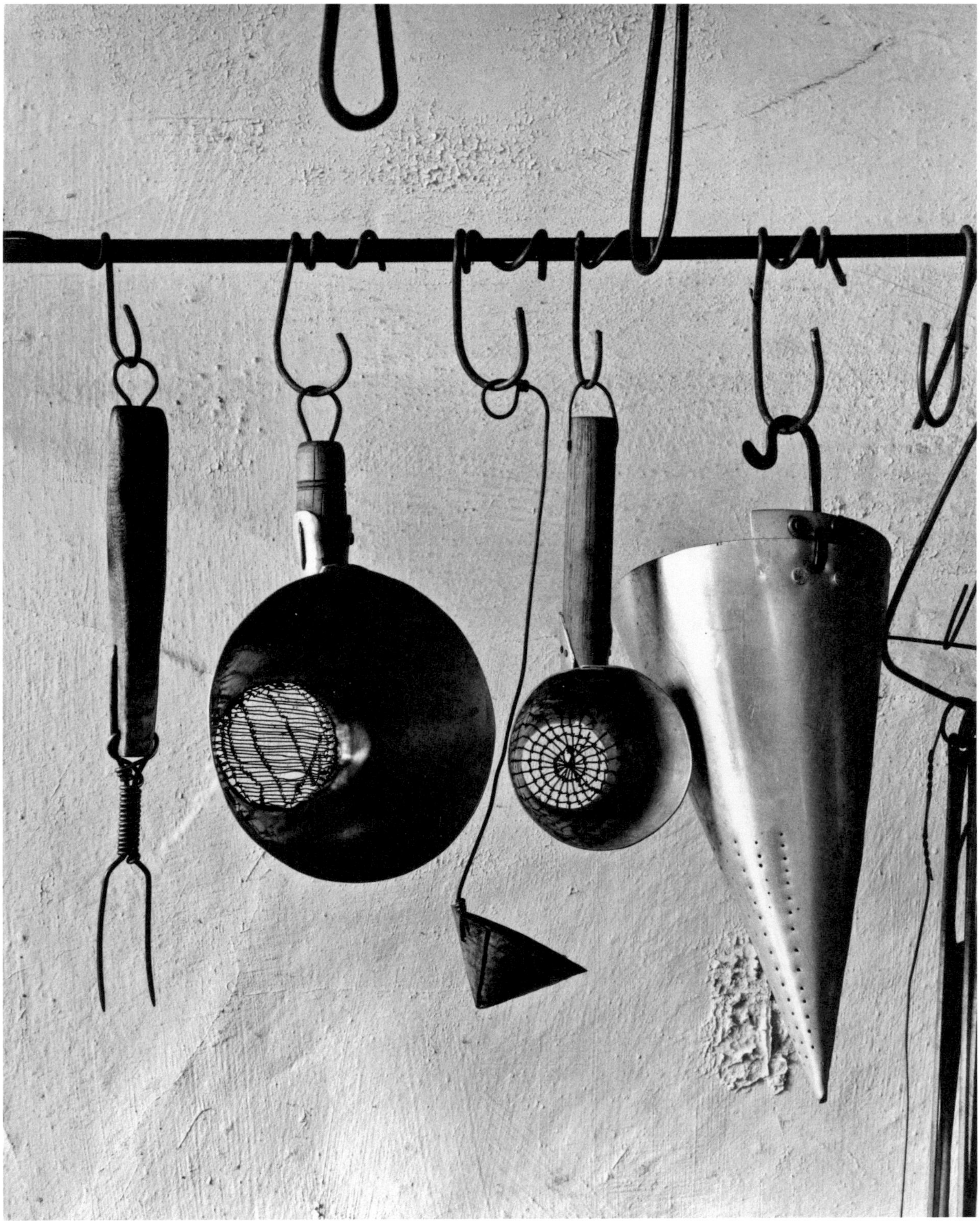

Fig. 10 Fourchette à bacon (c. 1940), passoire (c. 1940), conical scoop (c. 1940), passoire (c. 1940), and chinois (c. 1940), Roxbury, 1976. Photograph by Evelyn Hofer.

so, Calder reimagined an inexpensive set of mass-produced teacups. The original cups had no handles and were therefore difficult to hold when hot. Calder appended zarfs (fig. 7, p. 82), that, with their graceful spirals of brass wire (akin to those found in Calder's jewelry), elevated the stubby little cups into sacred drinking vessels. The serving trays, coffee spoons, creamer, and sugar scoop round out the tableaux, all pieces modified from their original, mass-produced sources (or else up-cycled from materials Calder had ready at hand). Of particular note is the copper serving tray (p. 83), derived from a series of etchings on copper plates Calder made when he illustrated the 1948 book, *Selected Fables*, by Jean de La Fontaine. The etching on this particular plate did not make the cut for the final version of the book, so Calder bent it into a tray, sparing the handsome copper from the trash.

The selection of ashtrays on display here suggests the importance of smoking for Calder as a sacrosanct ritual. Just a few generations ago smoking was an accepted social rite, and Calder himself was frequently photographed with a cigarette dangling from his lips (fig. 8). Implicit in the design of these ashtrays is Calder's desire to live with quality-made, original objects. Though crafted of simple materials—mainly emptied coffee or olive oil cans that likely would have been otherwise discarded—every ashtray is unique. One example, the animal ashtray (c. 1943, p. 78), is a Beech Nut brand coffee can repurposed into a fantastical beast with a head, tail, and eight legs, every appendage providing a discrete tray upon which to rest a cigarette, so that one ashtray could easily accommodate a party of ten. Again, rather than simply buying a number of cheap ashtrays to place around the house, Calder chose to create his own (fig. 9). Taking this inclination one step further, he not only made each one a singular object, he often improved their functionality. The American art critic John Canaday, once a visitor to Calder's home, put it thus:

> He has...solved the ashtray problem, a major annoyance in contemporary life, with a did-it-himself contraption that (a) holds the cigarette securely when it is laid down—no rolling, no dropping, no falling; (b) accommodates vast quantities of ashes in such a way that they can't blow out over the table and won't spill even if the thing falls on the floor; (c) is decorative; (d) has sentimental associative values; (e) costs only a few cents, or nothing; and (f) is therefore, disposable—although no one who has ever managed to get away with one has been known to treat it with anything but reverence.[23]

Canaday's ecclesiastical language speaks to both the mid-century importance placed on cigarette smoking as a ritual activity and also the totemic qualities with which Calder's ashtrays were imbued. Calder's chess set (c. 1944, p. 68), the centerpiece of another domestic scene installed in the present exhibition, is robust with reworked materials, its pieces constructed from a sawed-off baluster and the feet of an old sofa. One of only three sets Calder was known to have made, this one was likely created for and exhibited in the

23 John Canaday, "Mobile Visit with Alexander Calder," *New York Times Magazine* (25 March 1962), 32, 125.

24 Larry List, ed., *The Imagery of Chess Revisited*, exh. cat. (New York: George Braziller, 2005), 69, 70.

25 Canaday, "Mobile Visit with Alexander Calder," 125.

landmark 1944 exhibition, *The Imagery of Chess*, organized by Marcel Duchamp and held at the Julien Levy Gallery in New York. The roster of artists who participated in the exhibition reads like a Who's Who of modern artists (Isamu Noguchi, Marcel Duchamp, Max Ernst and Arshile Gorky to name only a few), but Calder's chess set was the most "American in spirit—large, bright and bold, but rough-hewn from whatever resources were at hand."[24] With its long historical association with battle, the game of chess enjoyed renewed popularity in the 1940s, as the world plunged deeper into the Second World War. The game resonated powerfully with many prominent artists of the day, including Calder, who was known to occasionally enjoy a round. One can easily imagine him tucked into a nook in Roxbury with a companion, seated on wooden, Calder-made chairs, hovering over a low-slung, Calder-made aluminum table, strategizing his next move by the light of a Calder-made spot lamp (p. 68). Although Calder may not have been the most devoted chess player, his friendships with artists who were—like those mentioned above, as well as others like Yves Tanguy and Kay Sage, who were his neighbors in Connecticut—attuned him to the gravity and ceremony the game could impart amongst its disciples.

Louisa Calder once declared that a two-pronged object (fig. 10)—one in the arsenal of kitchen items produced by her husband—was in fact, "the best bacon fork in the world."[25] Despite their early row over the inferior pitcher and washbasin, the two were united in their distaste for shoddy goods, and Calder's spurning of the mass-produced in favor of the handmade whenever possible. Toaster, ashtray, coffee cup: Calder produced a lifetime's worth of practical items that are mundane in name only. What Louisa and the couple's children received in return was a lifetime living in a house of magic, where a bacon fork was never simply a bacon fork. Their respect for everyday ritual grew from a mutual and deeply ingrained belief that the mass-market object, though easily acquired, was not a better solution than a common item alchemically transformed by an artist's hands. A piece of fine silver becomes a baby's plaything; a shattered wine glass becomes a dinner bell; a sheet of metal becomes a printing device and then a coffee tray. Bad taste always boomerangs, Calder said. There are politics in that.

Jessica Holmes, the former longtime Deputy Director of the Calder Foundation, has published and lectured widely on Alexander Calder's life and work. As a writer and critic, her work appears frequently in *The Brooklyn Rail*, *BOMB*, *Hyperallergic*, and numerous other publications. Find her writing and other projects at www.jessica-holmes.net.

FROM THE STONY RIVER TO THE SKY

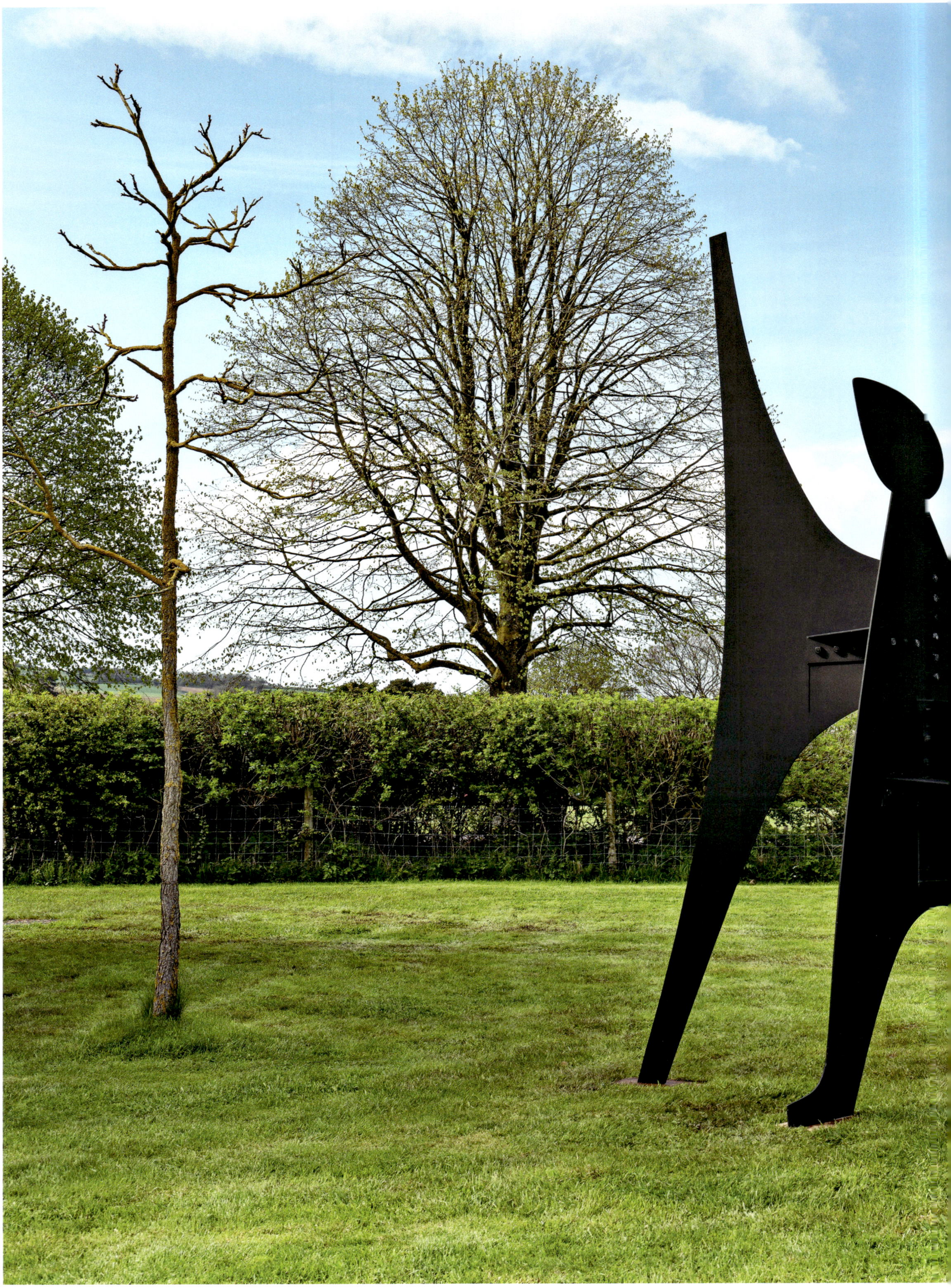

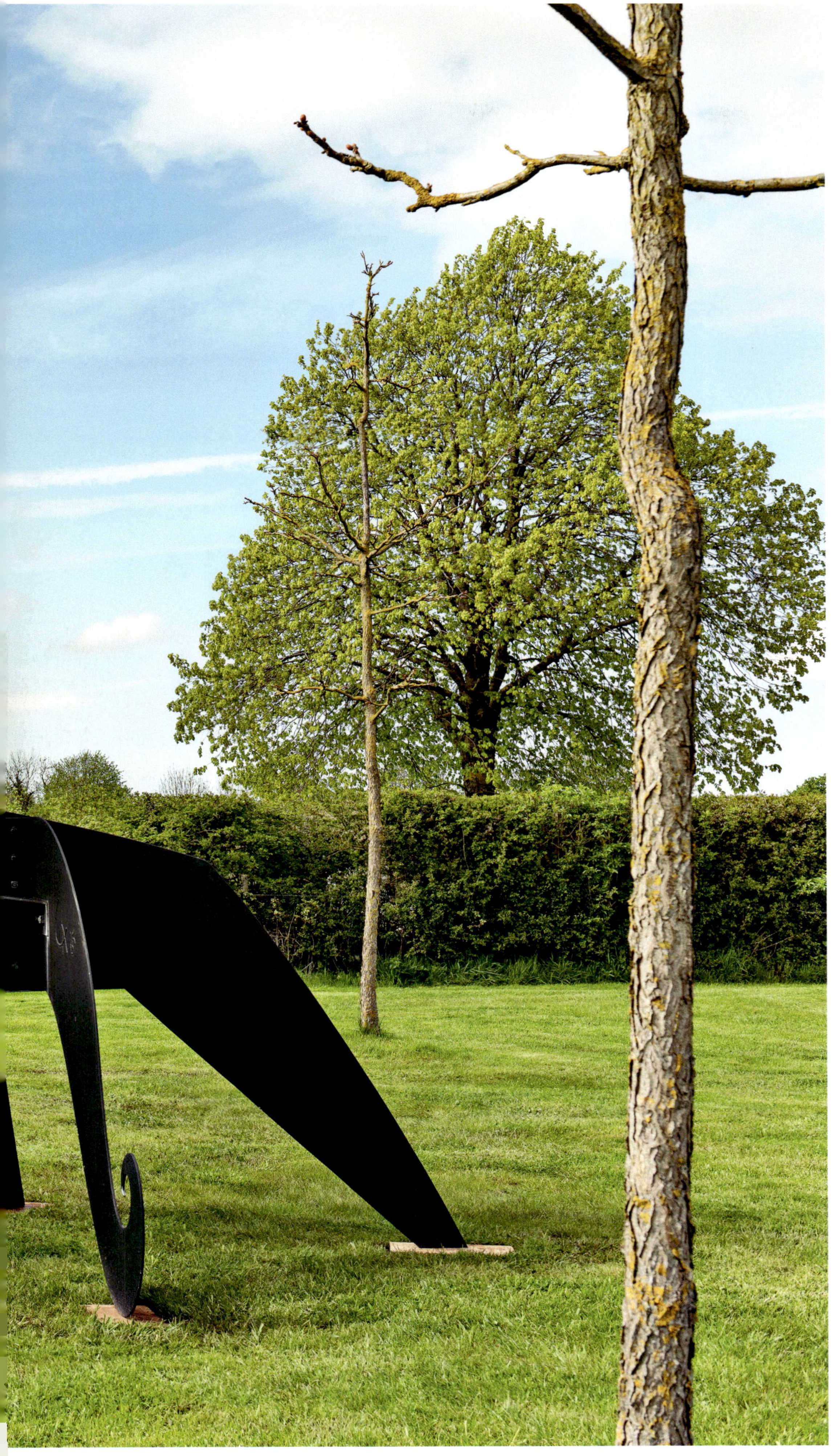

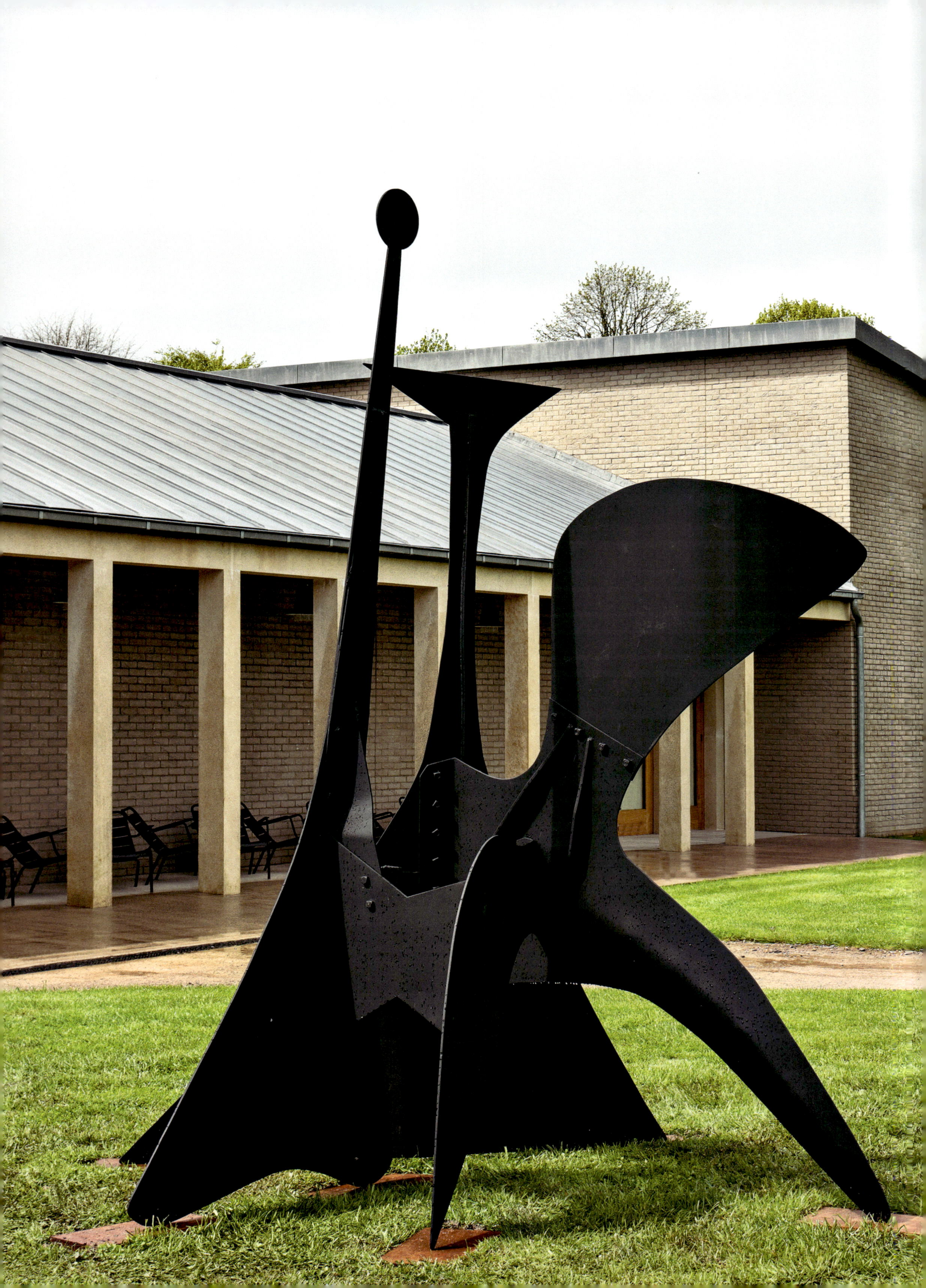

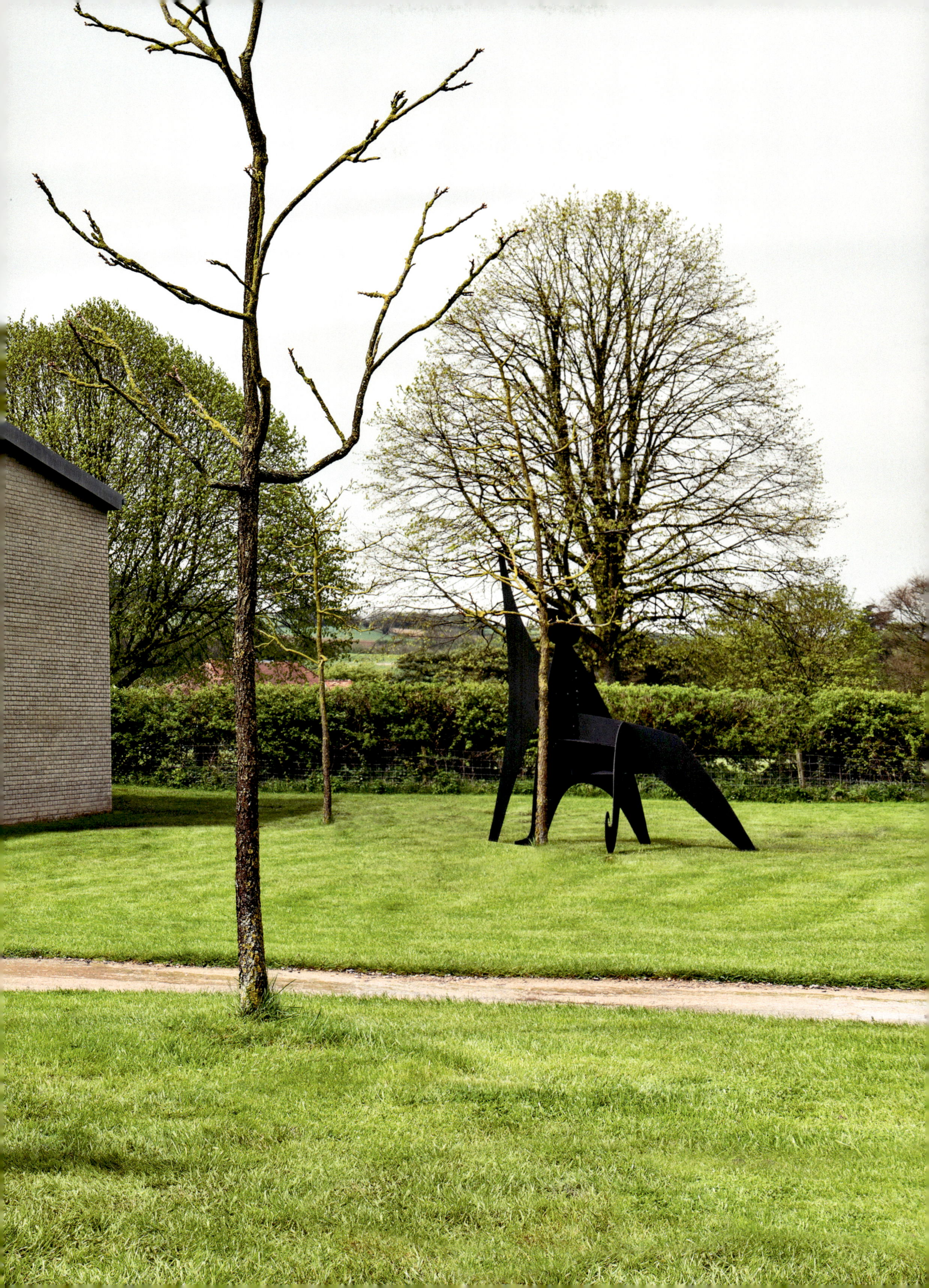

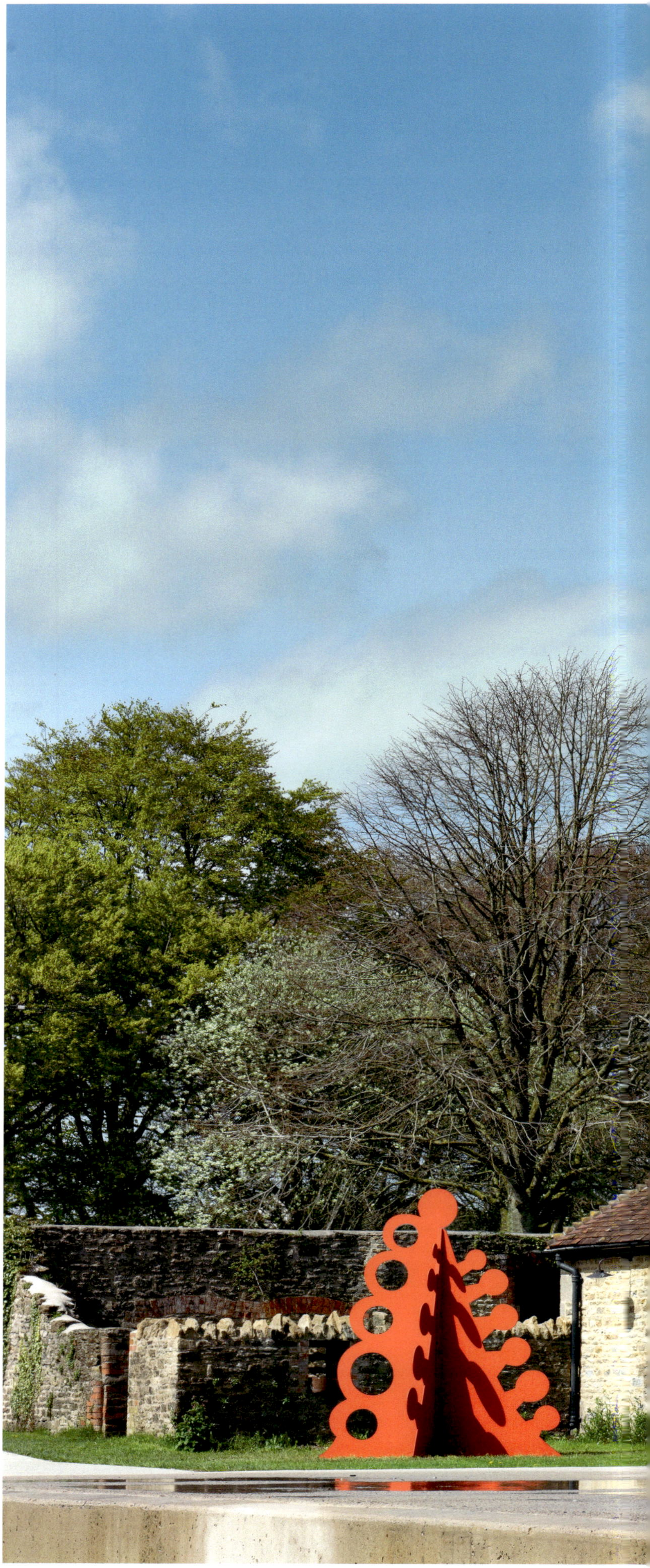

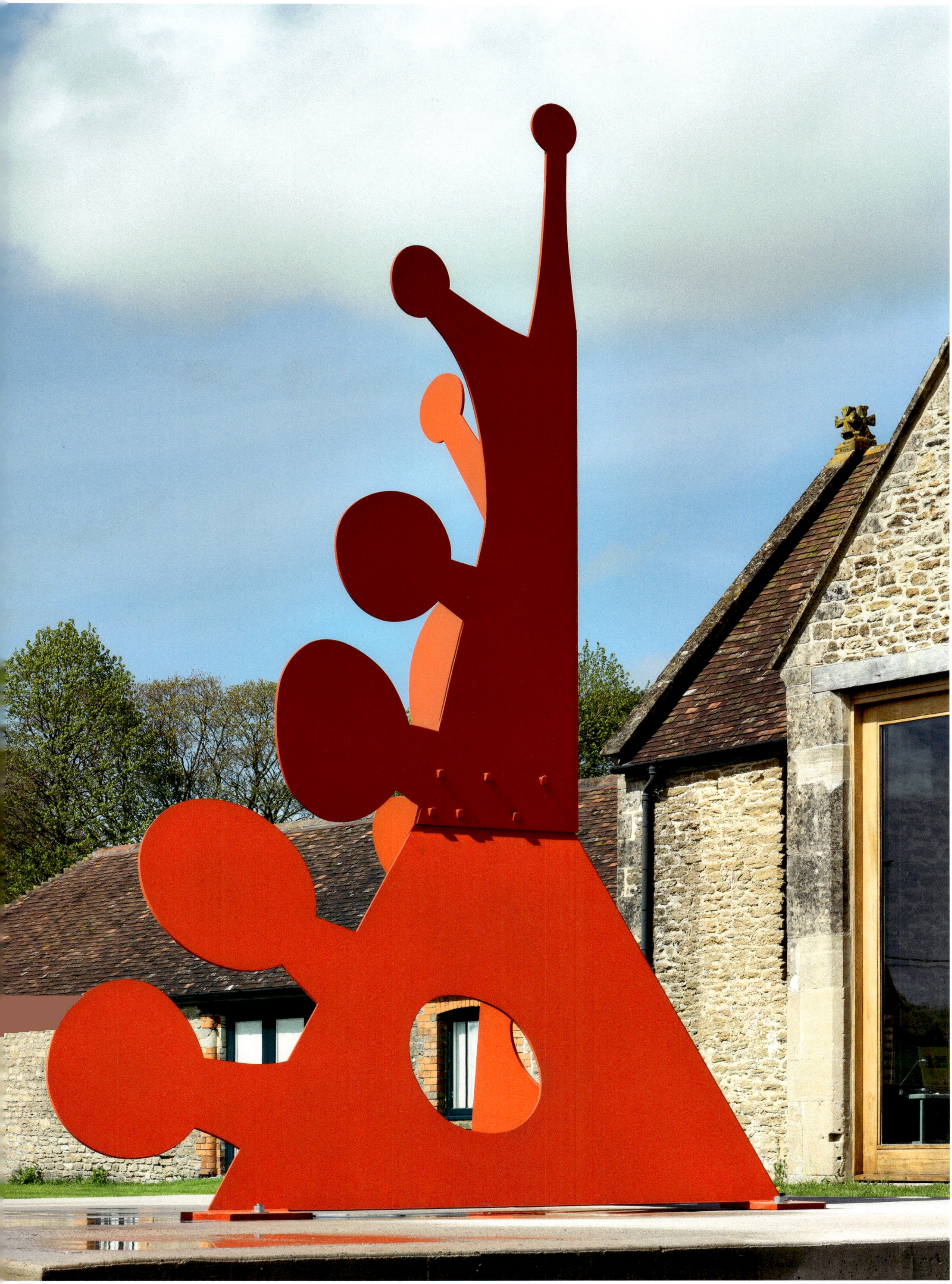

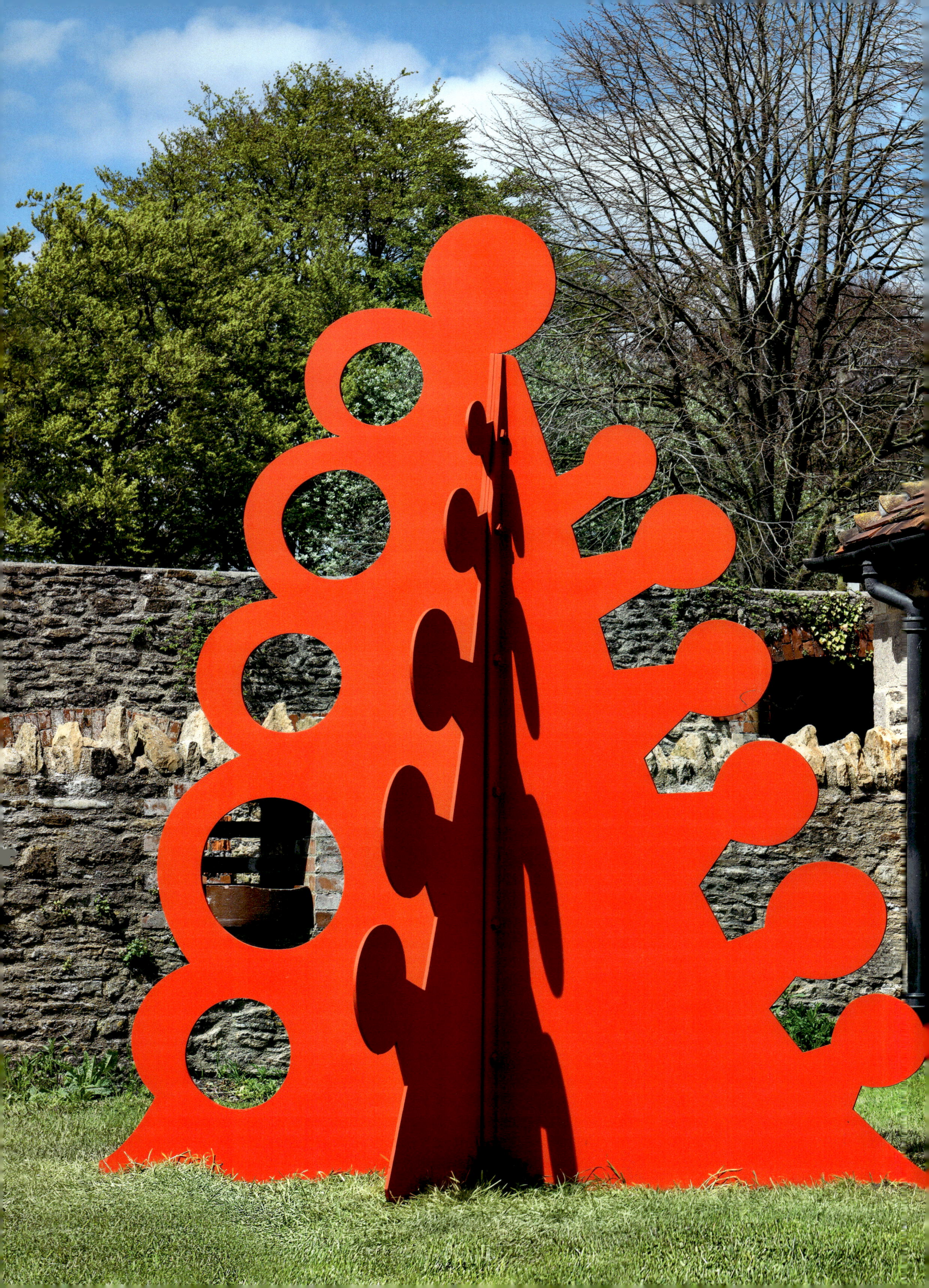

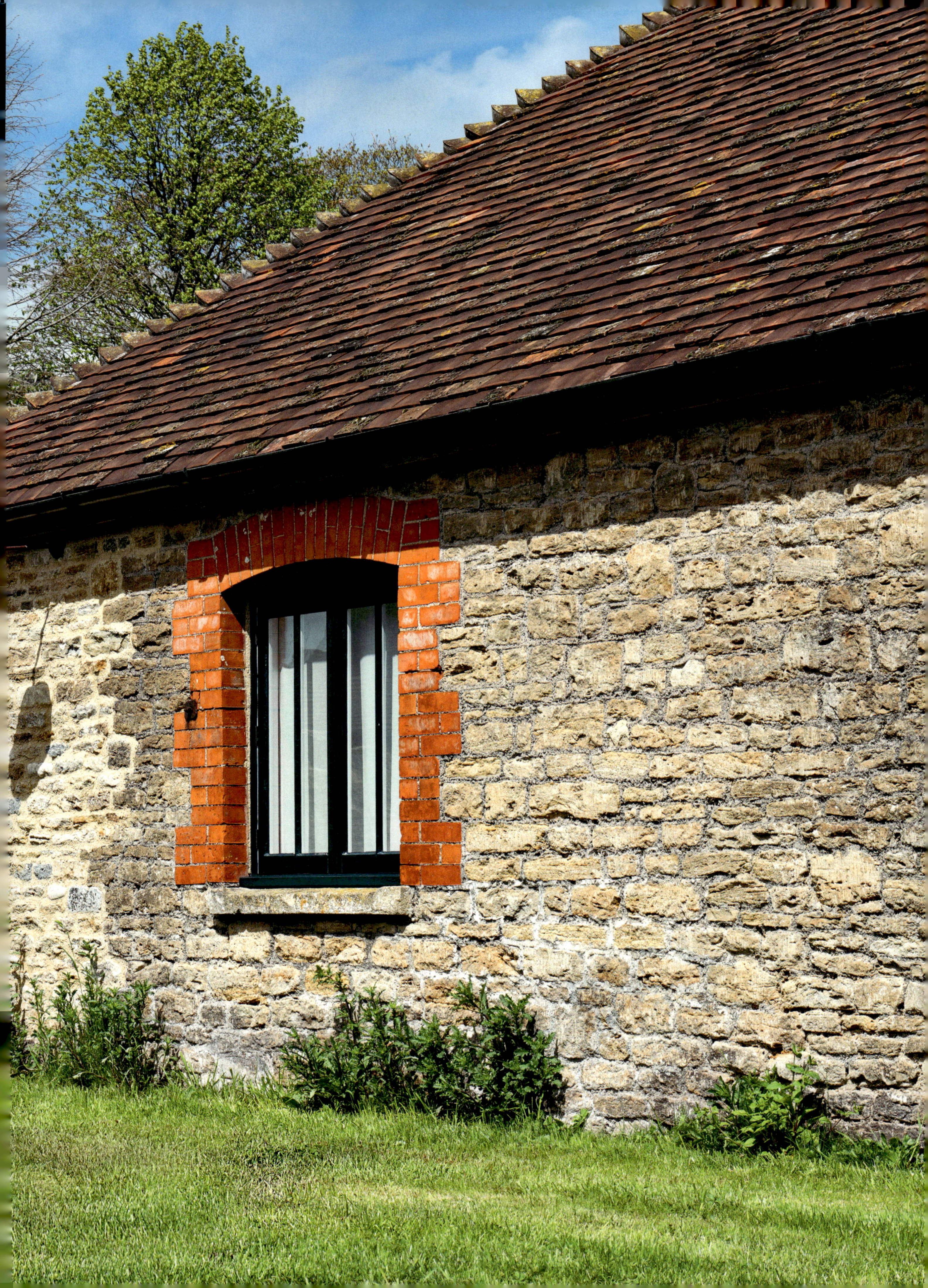

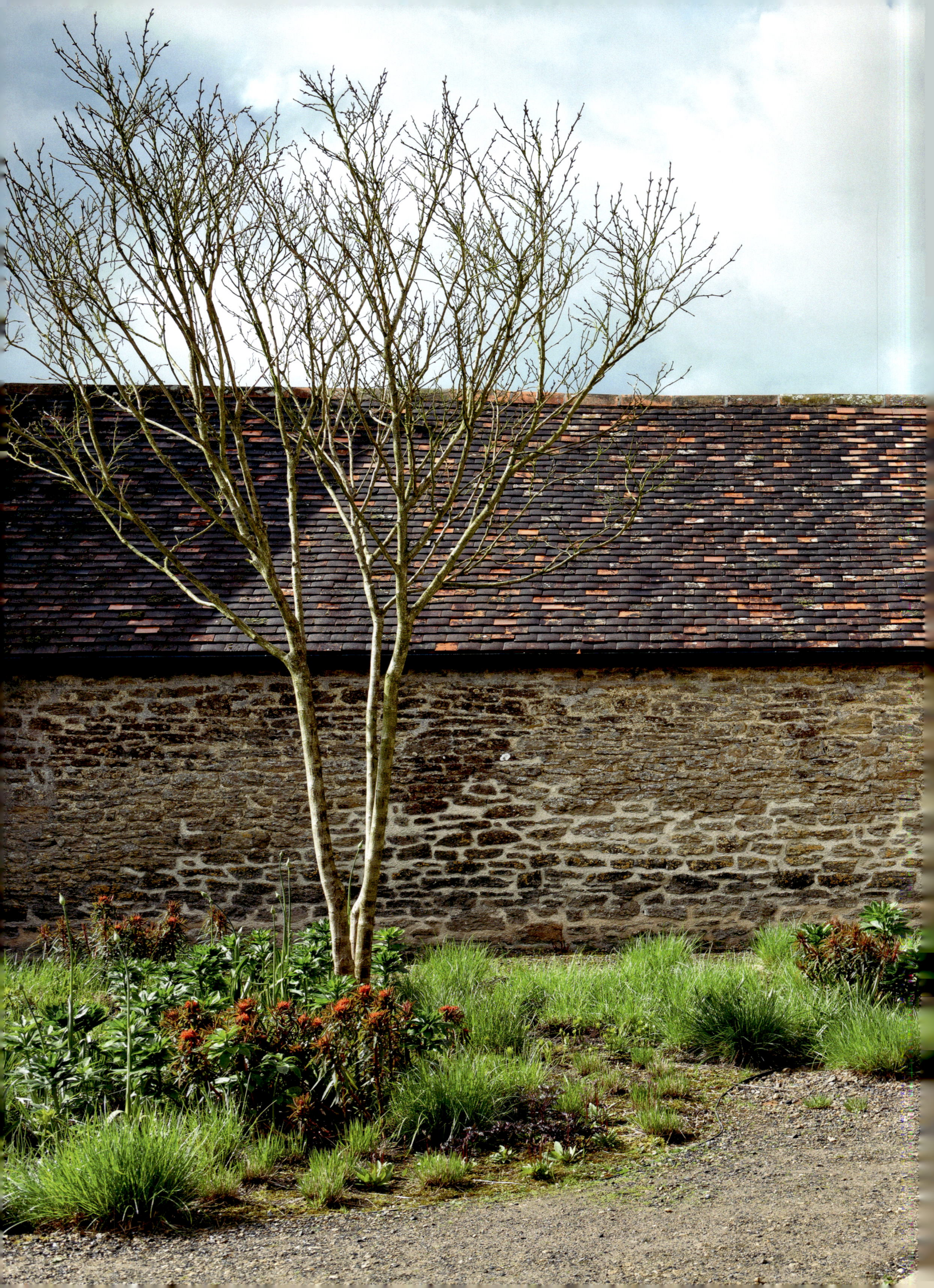

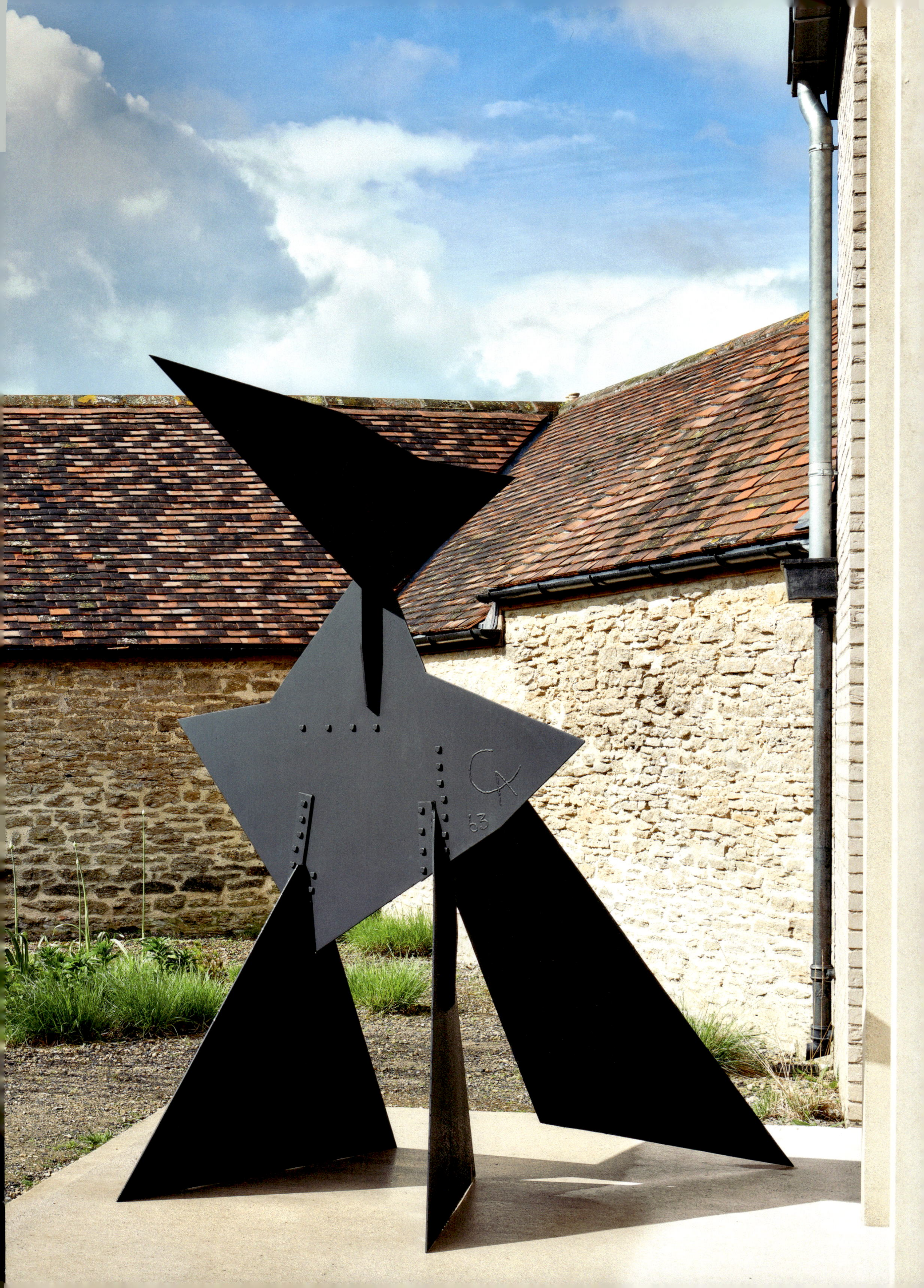
CA
63

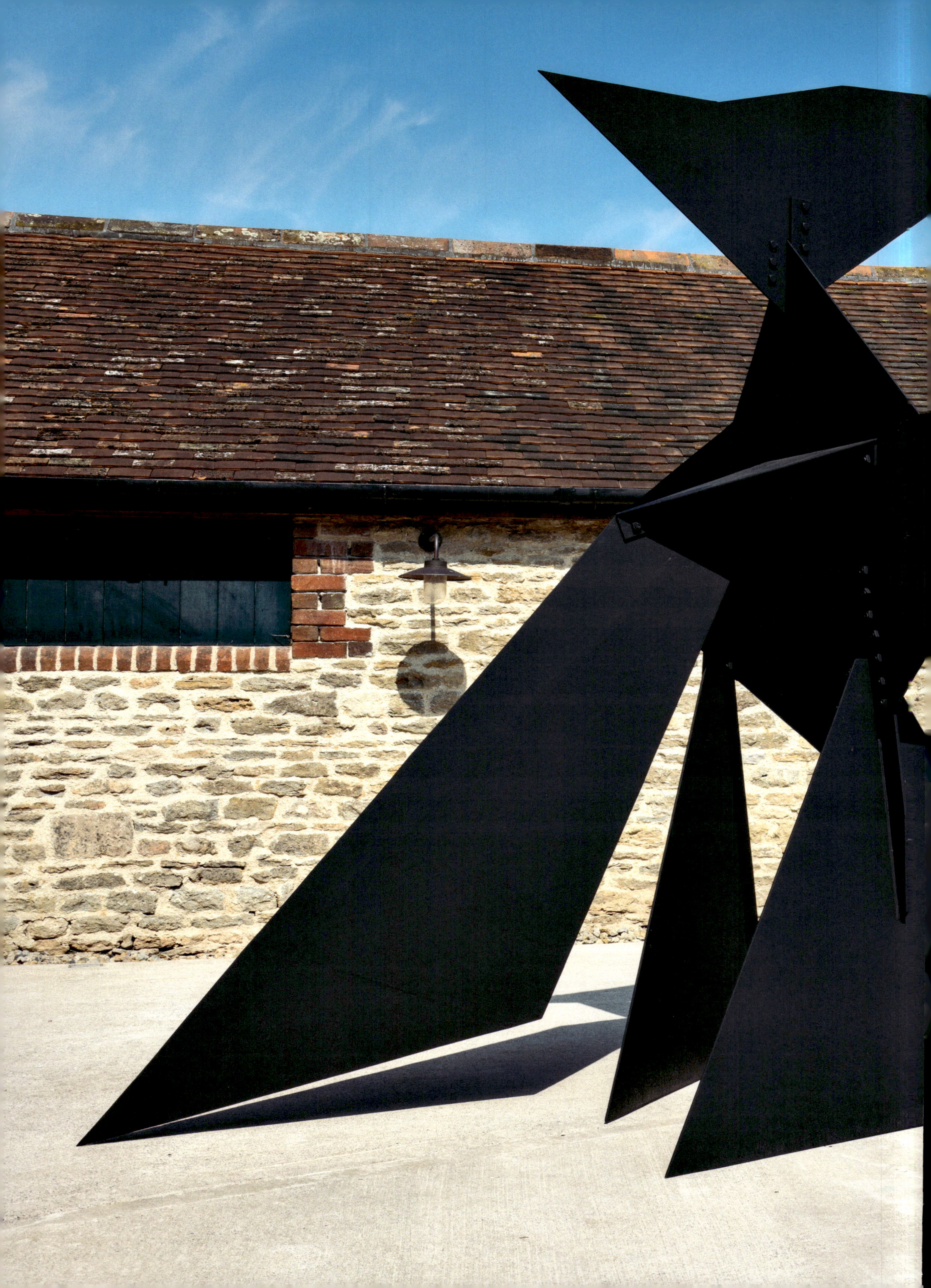

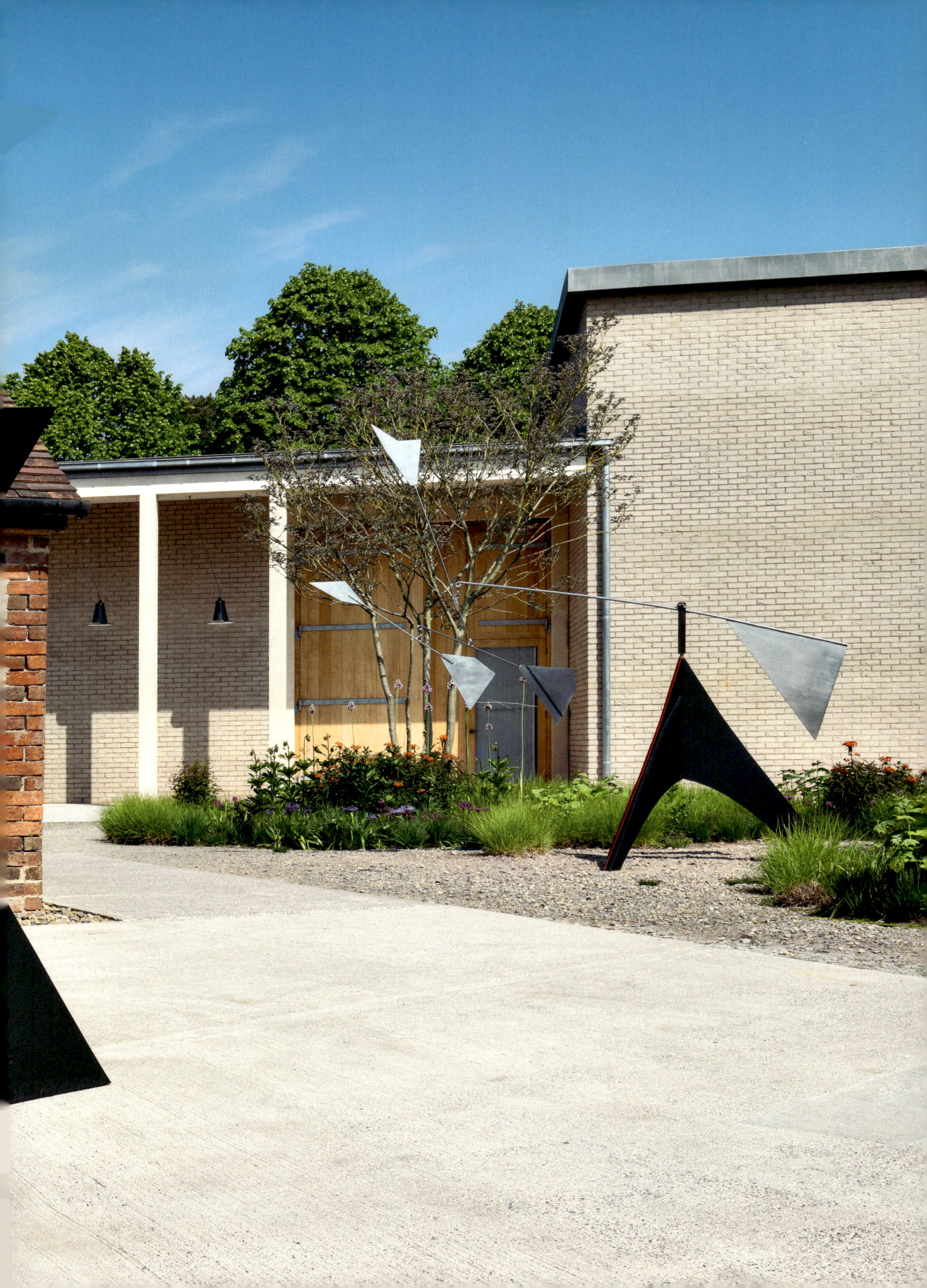

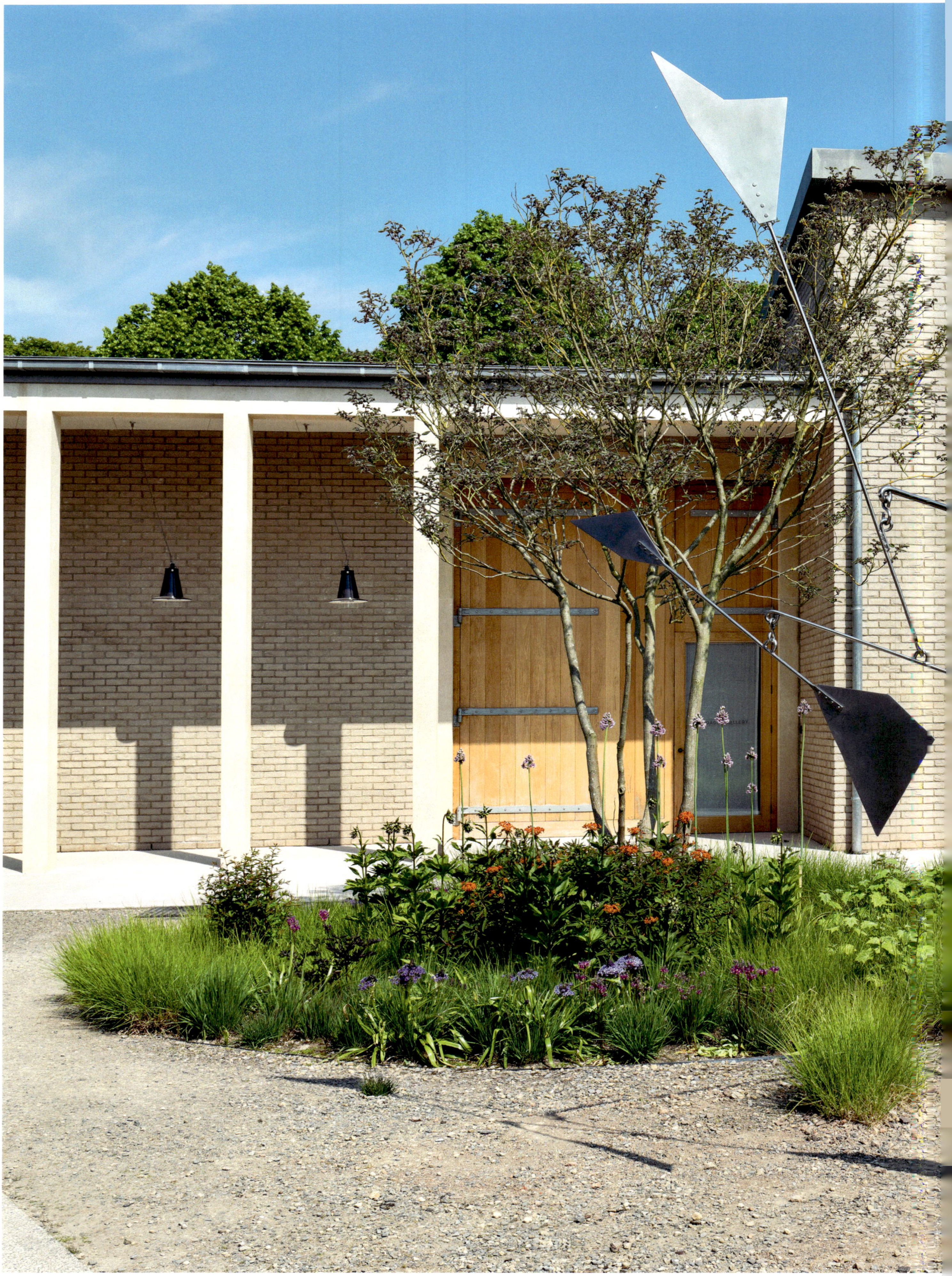

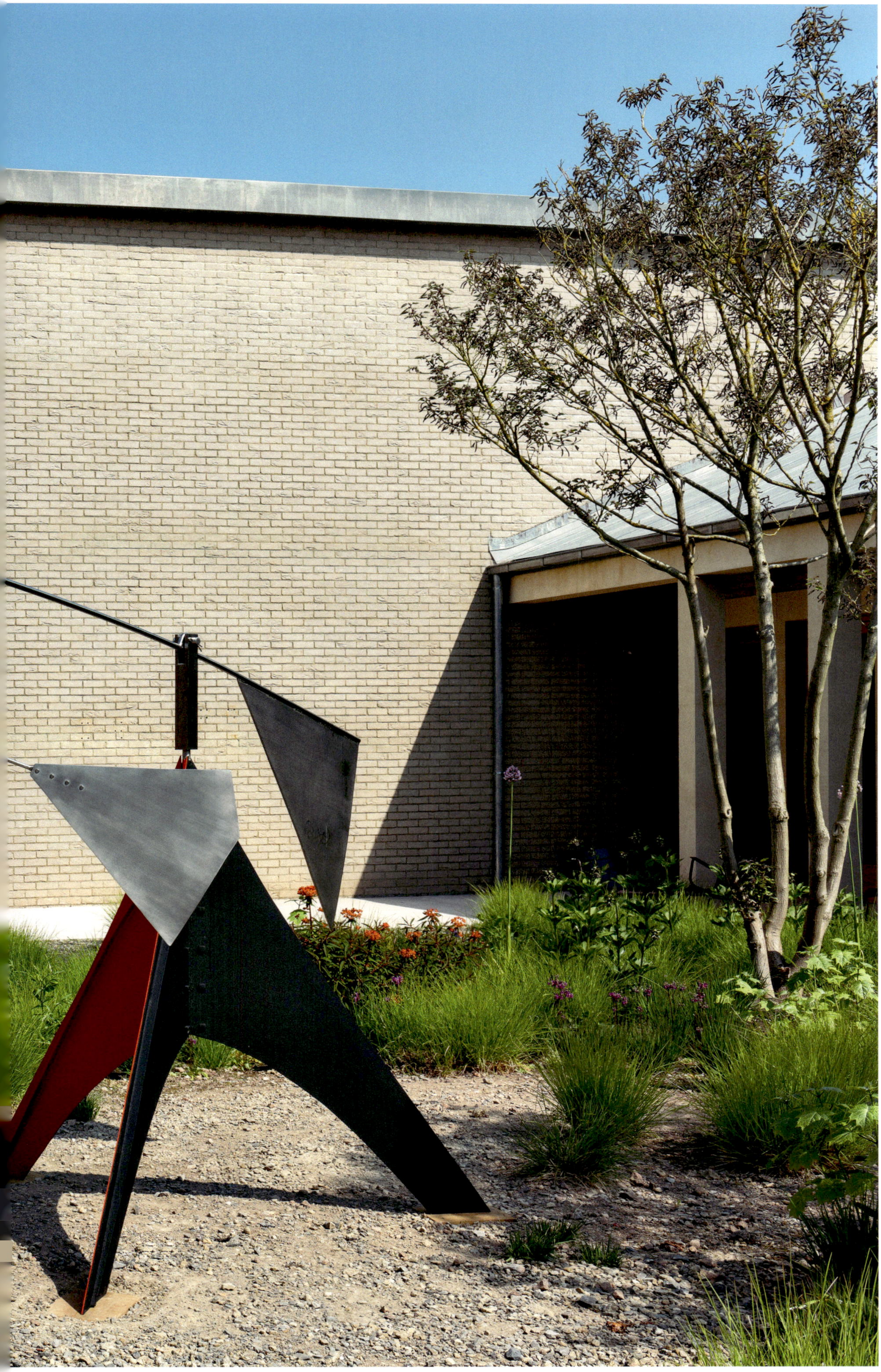

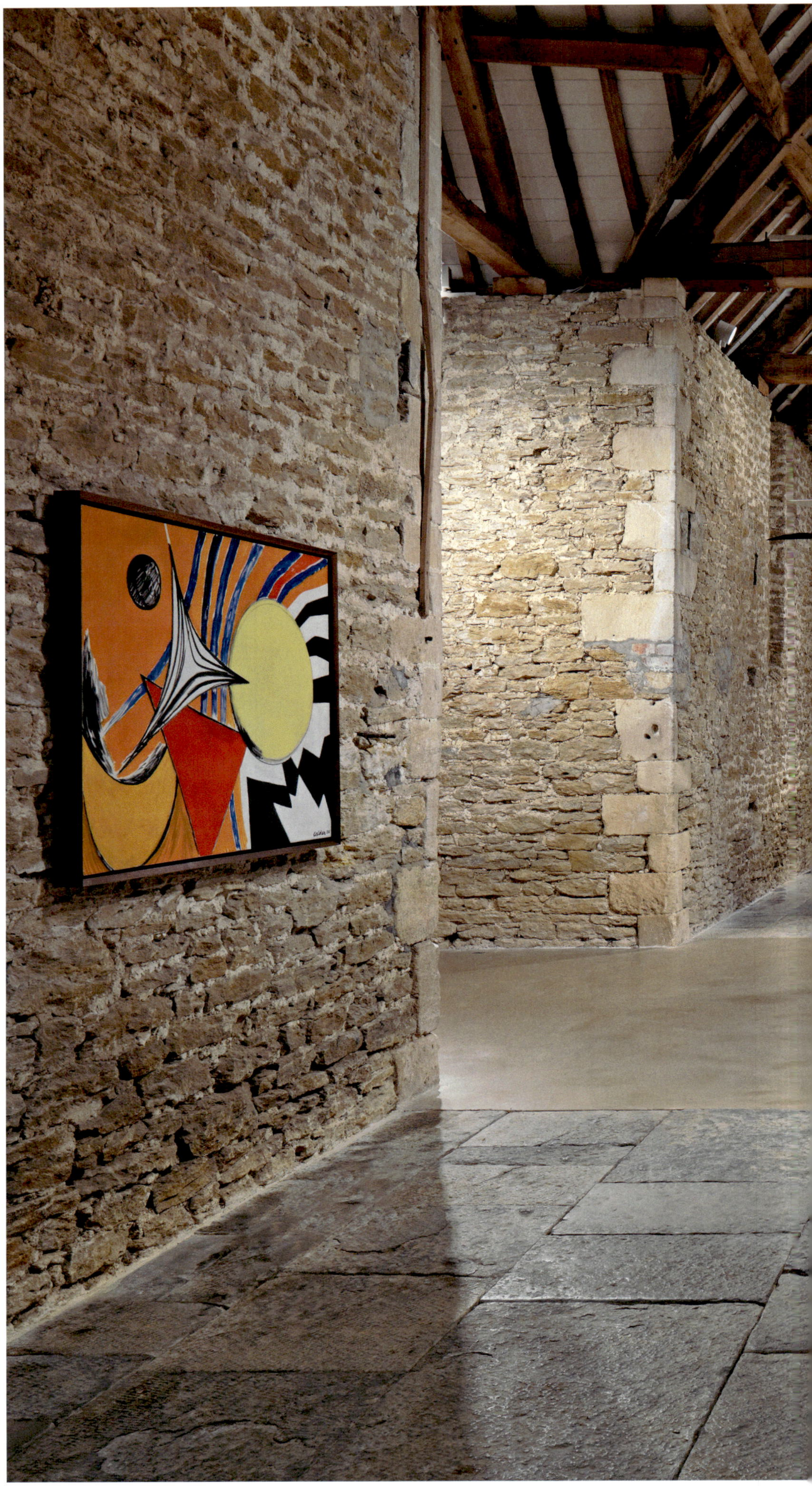

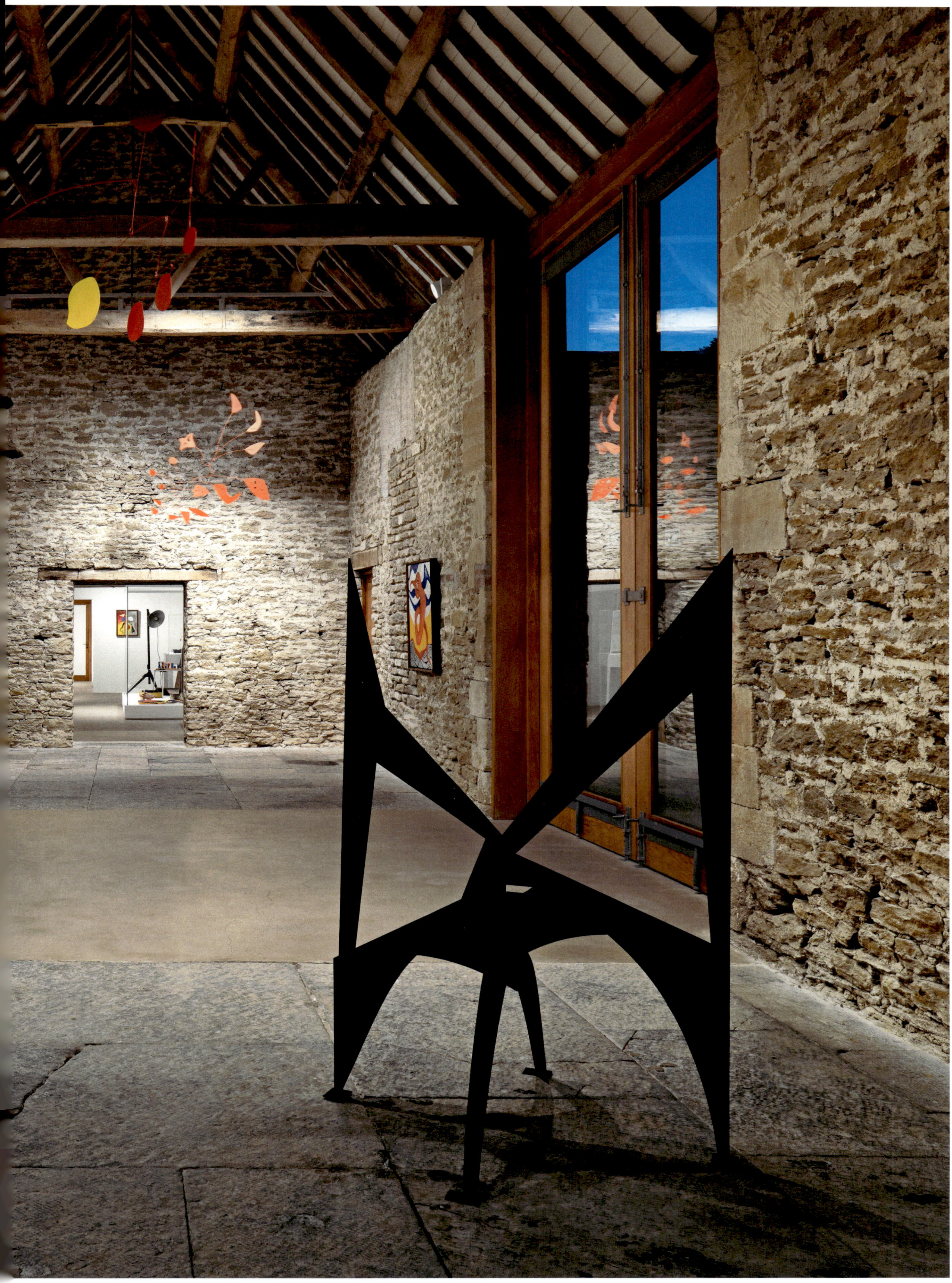

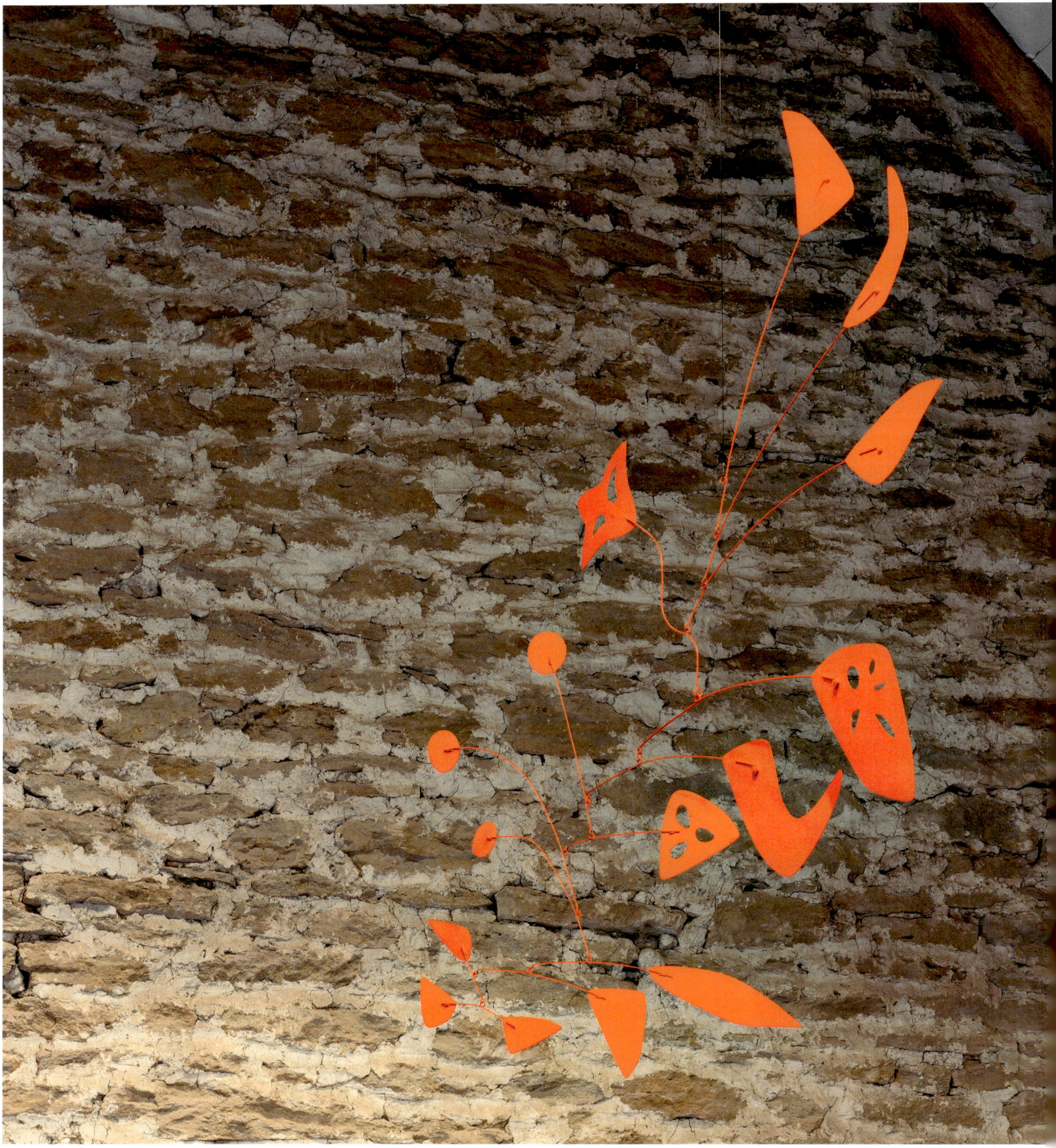

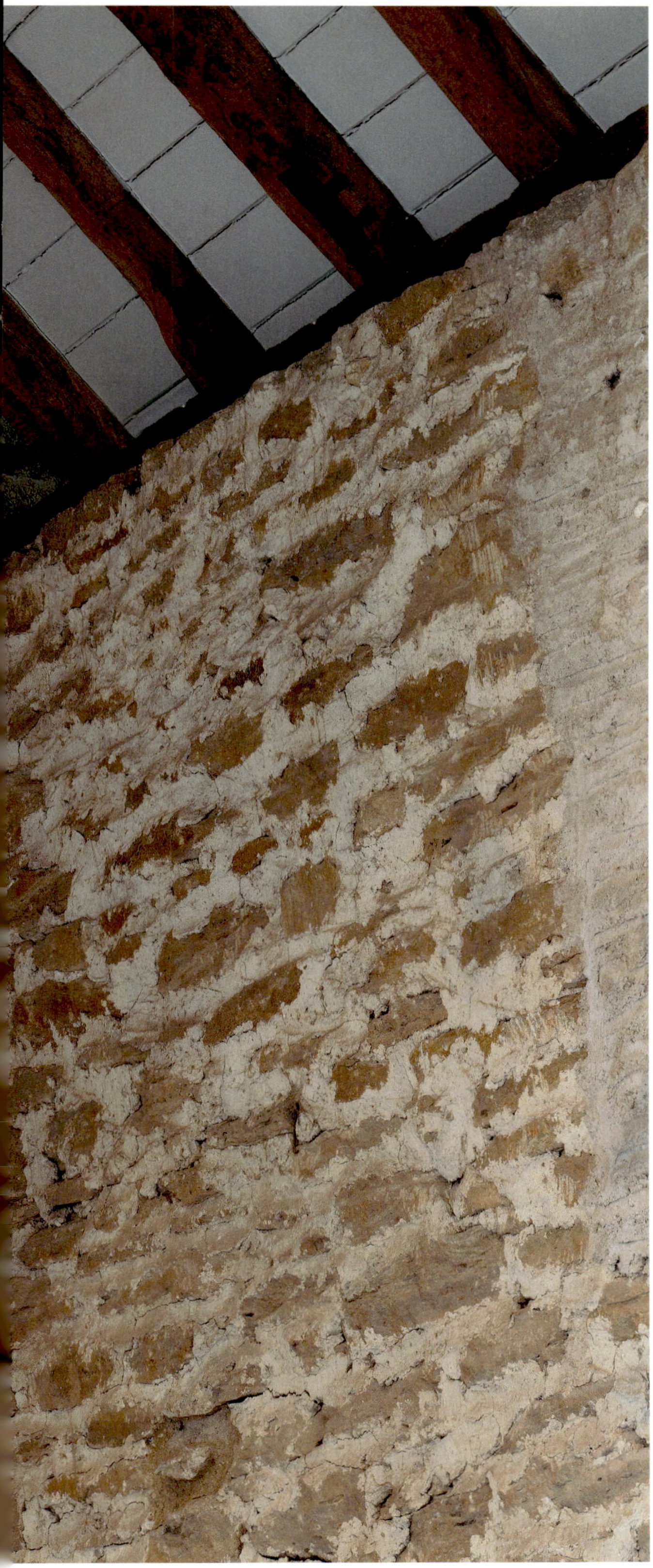

Red Maze I, 1954
Sheet metal, wire, and paint
51½ × 43 in. (130.8 × 109.2 cm)

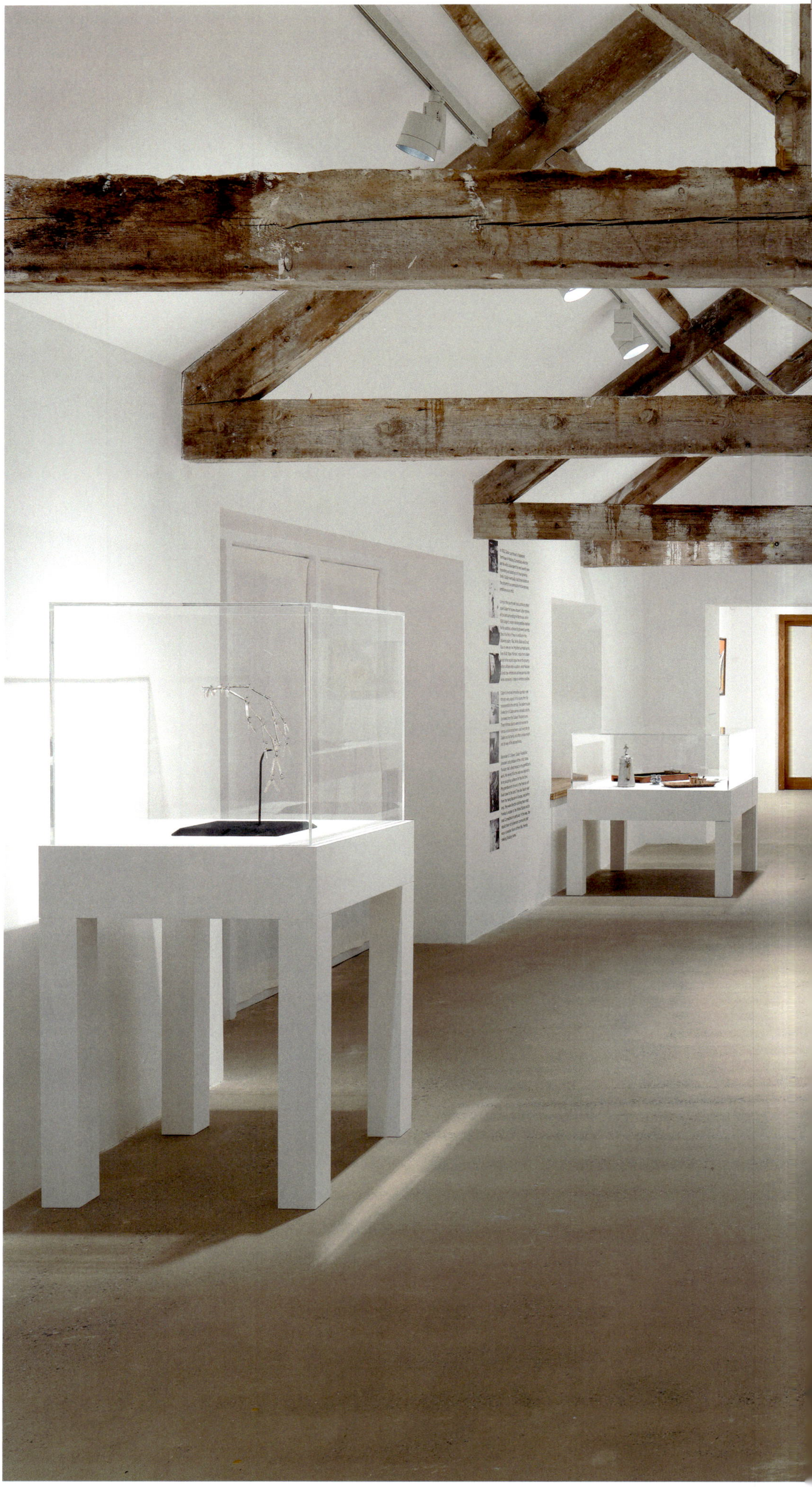

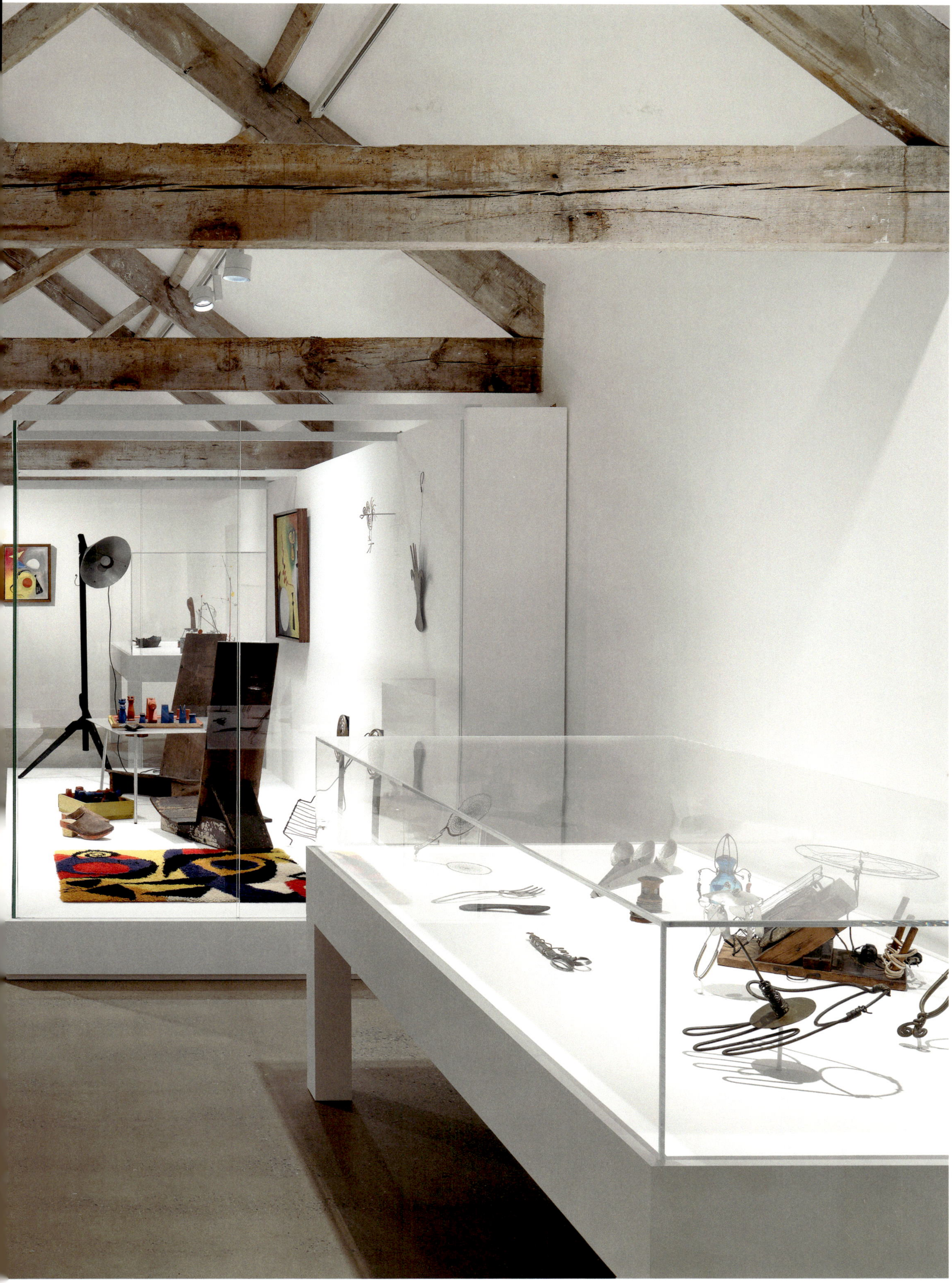

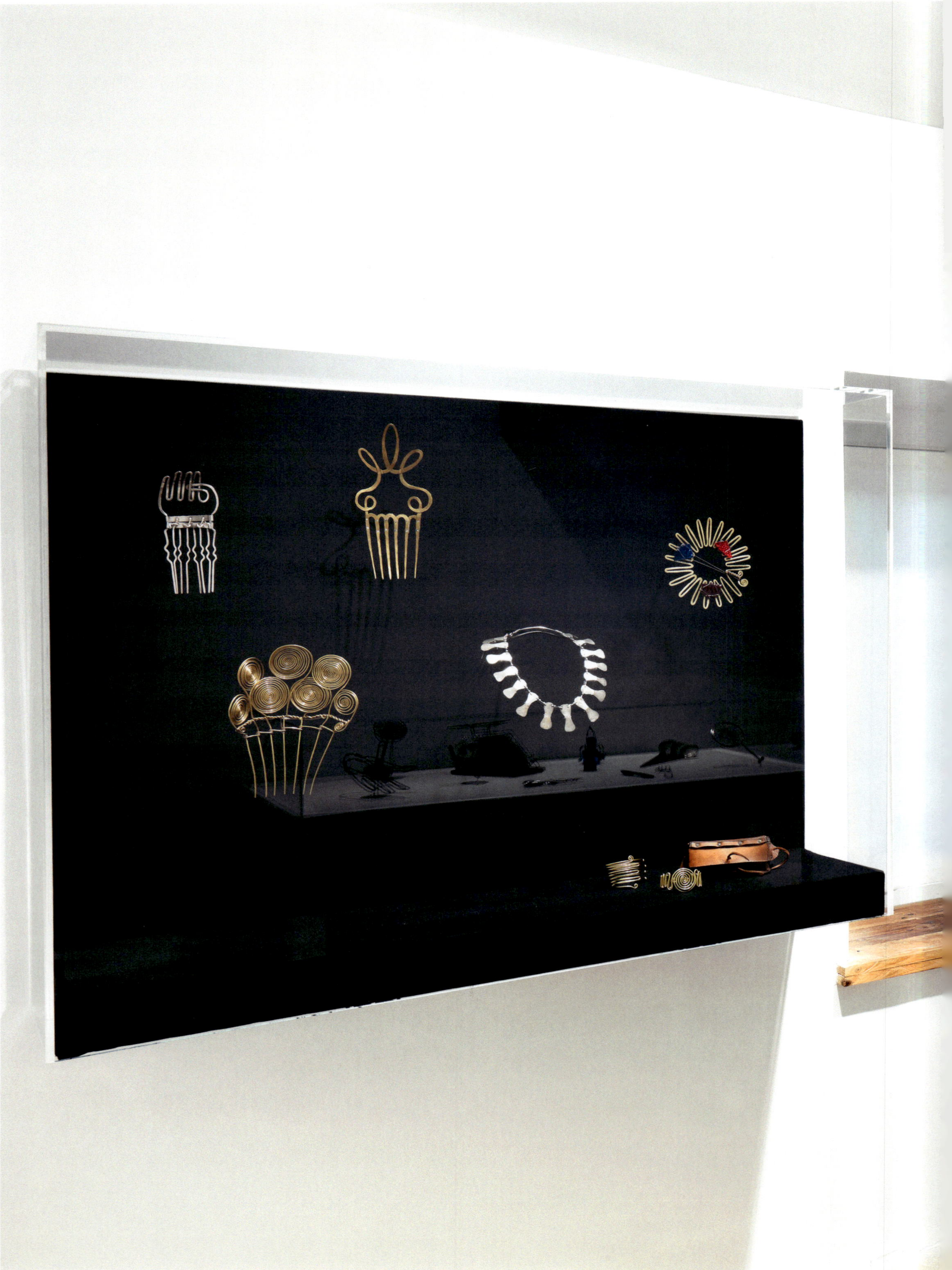

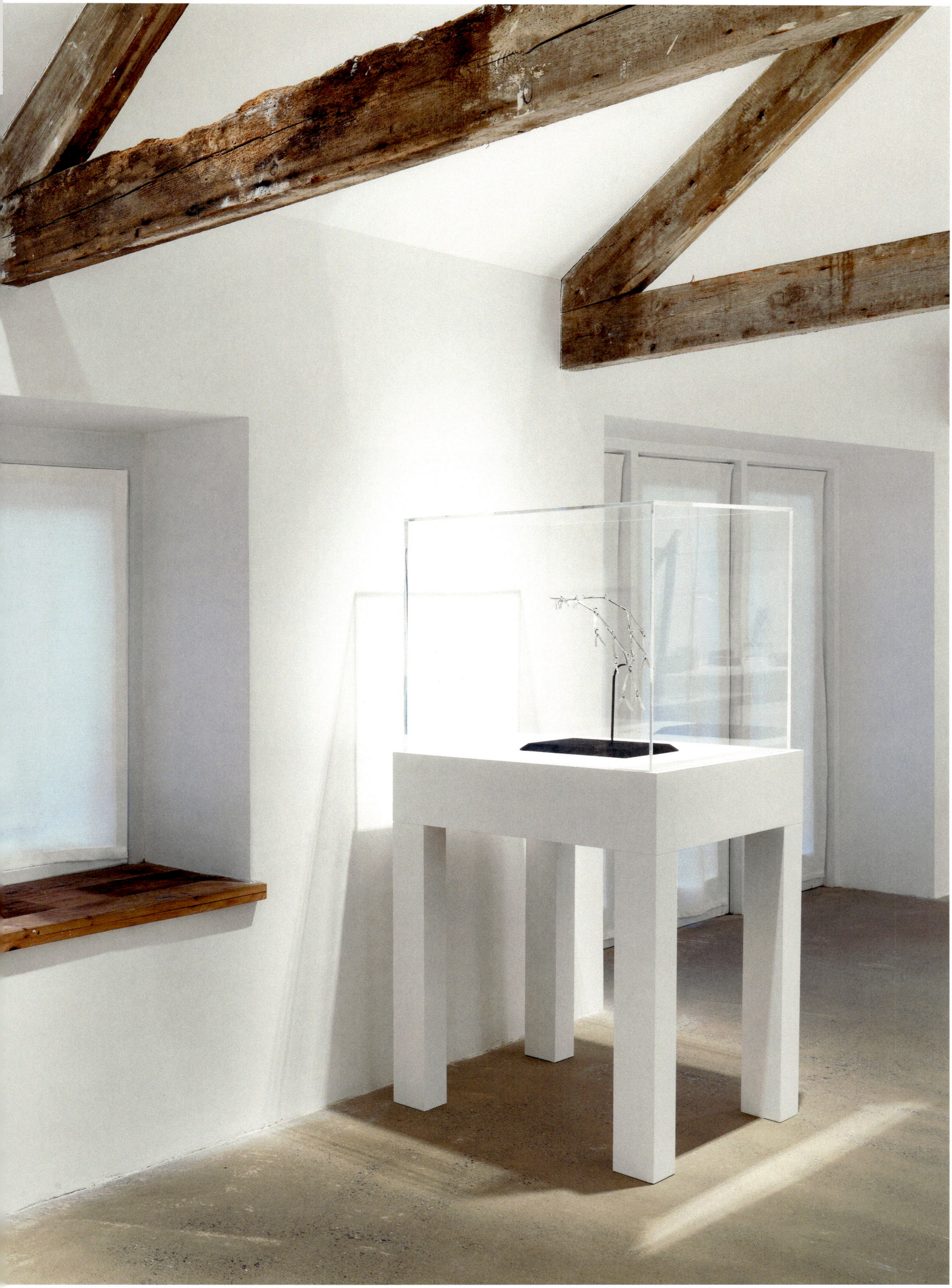

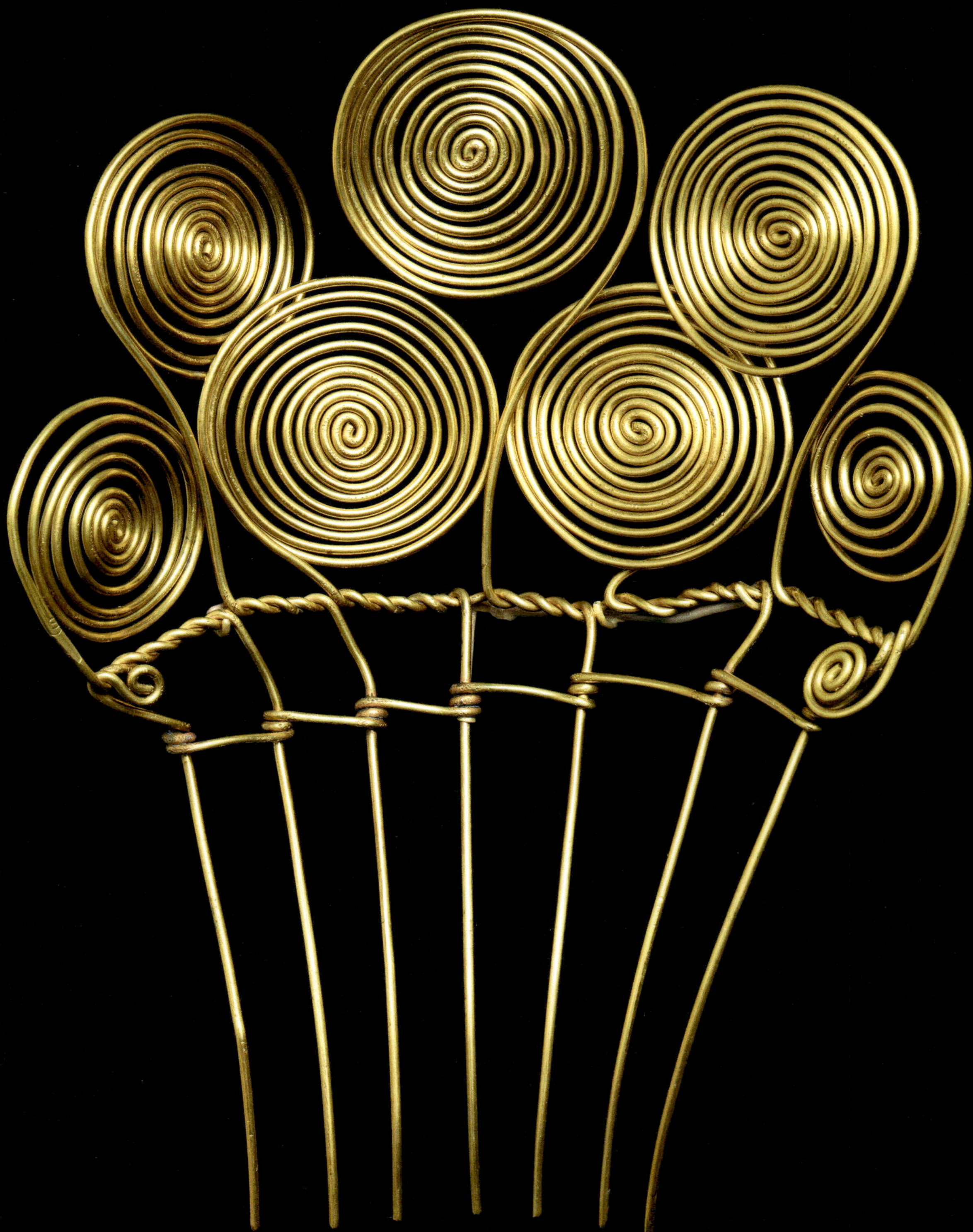

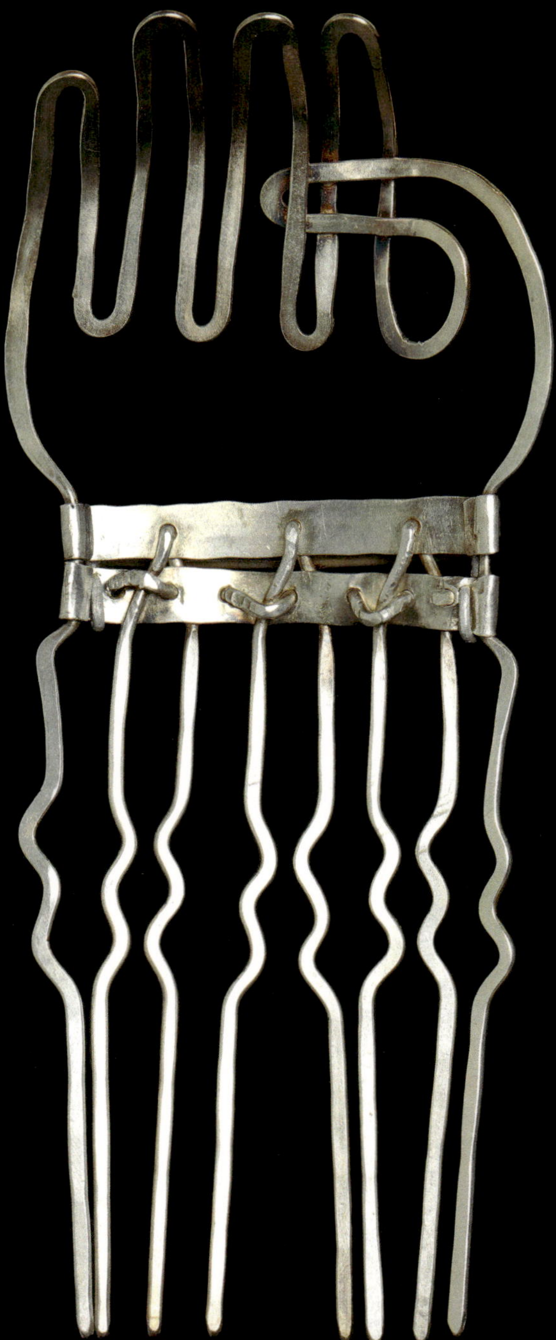

Necklace, c. 1942
Silver wire
17 × 12 in. (43.2 × 30.5 cm)

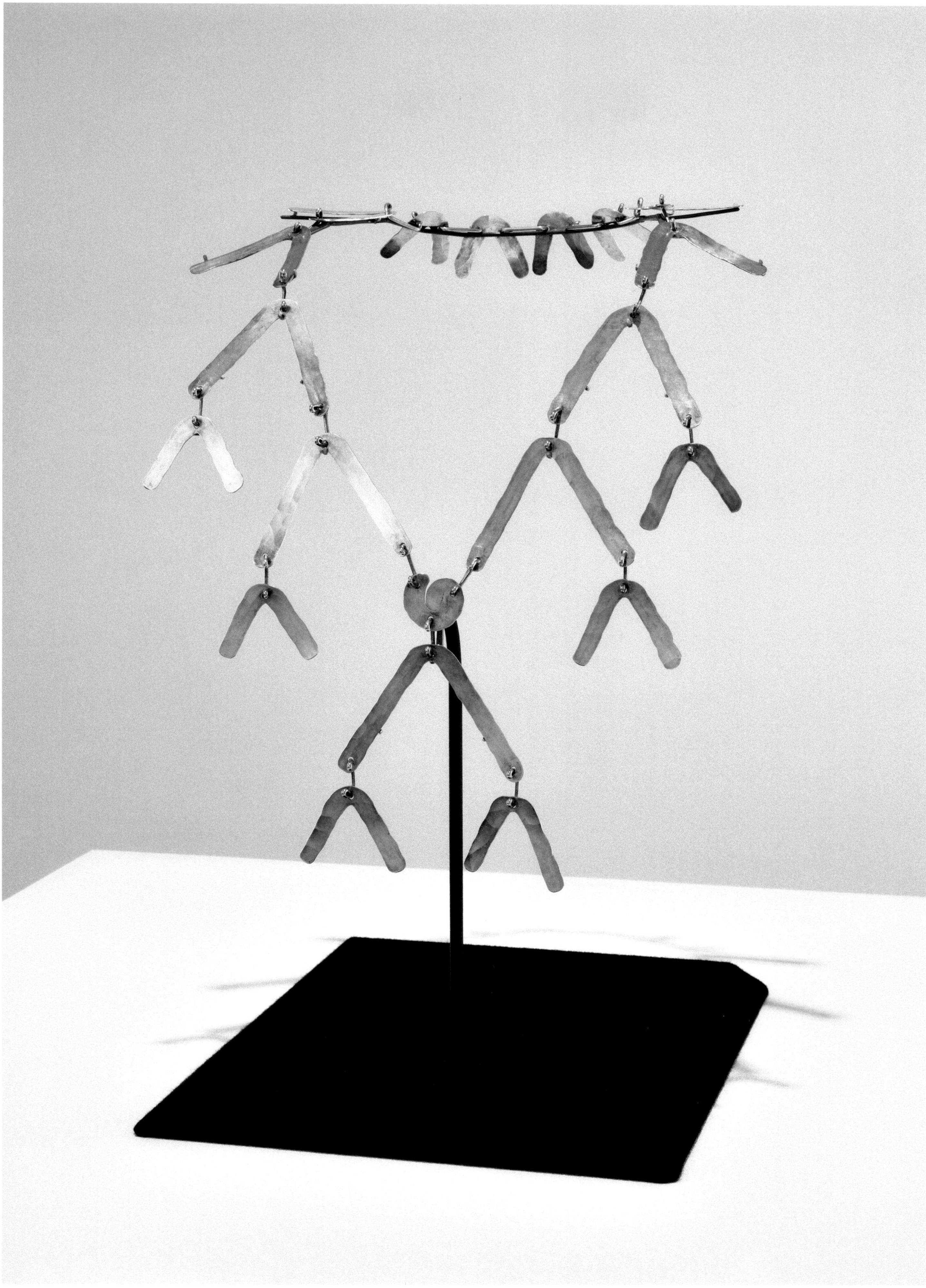

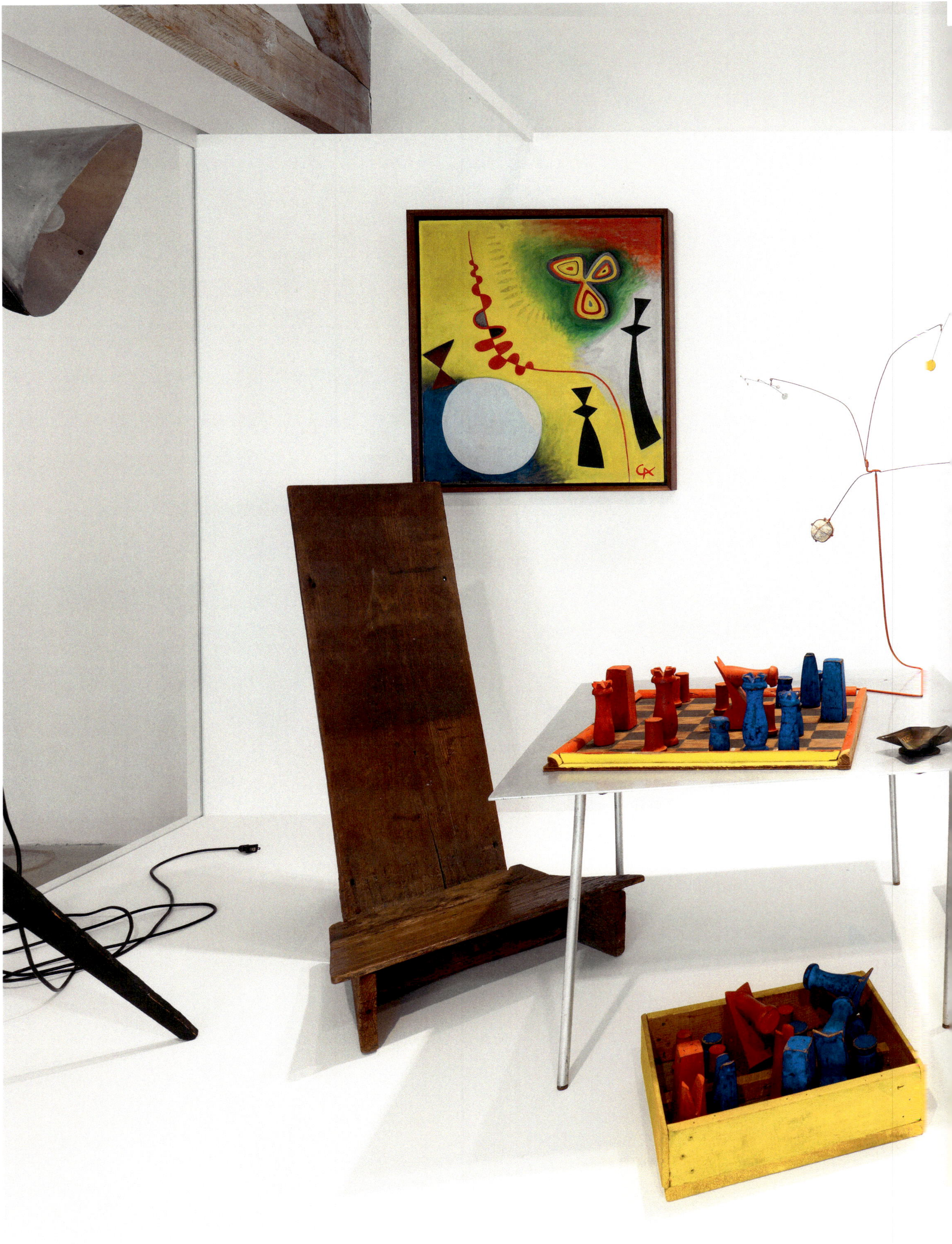

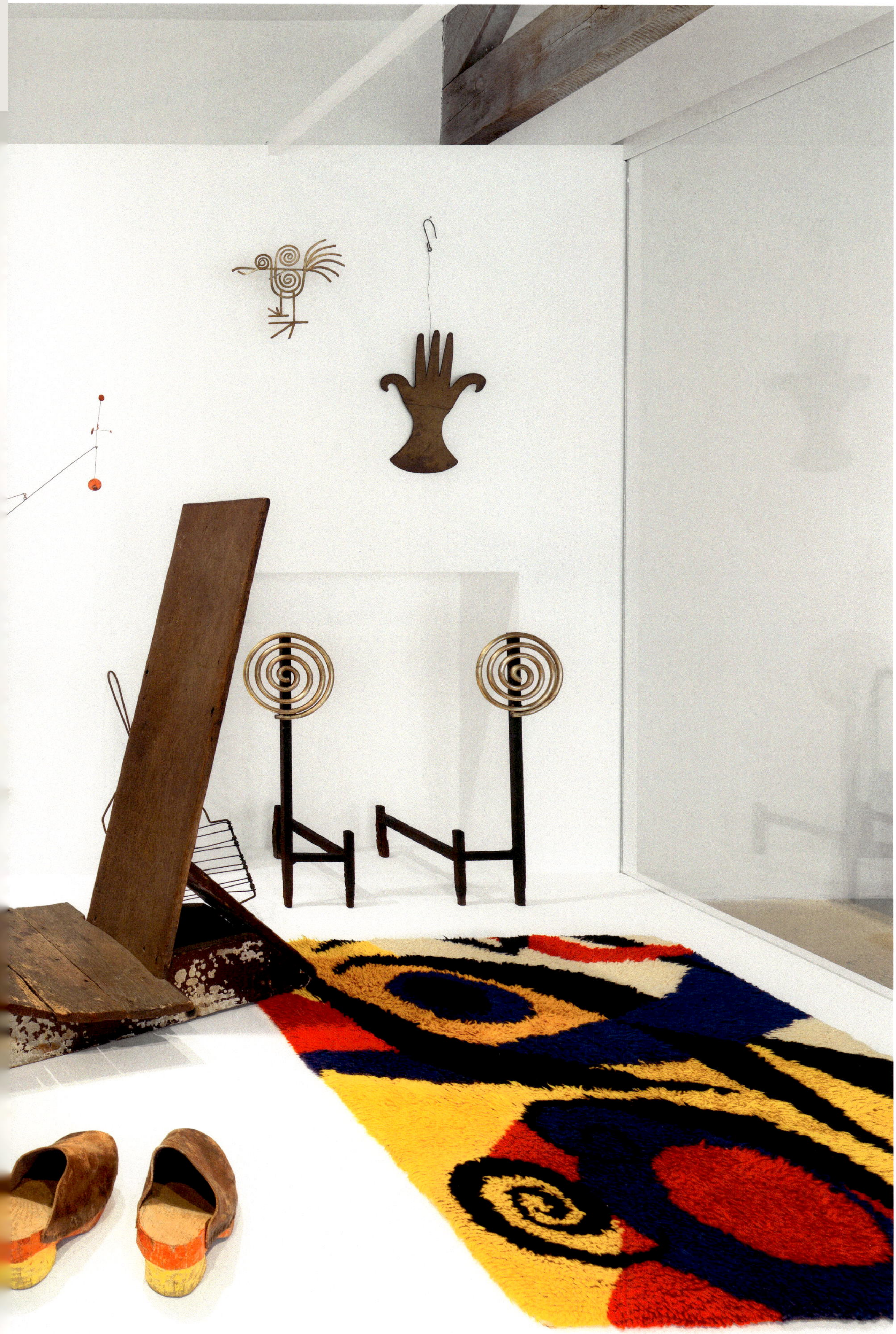

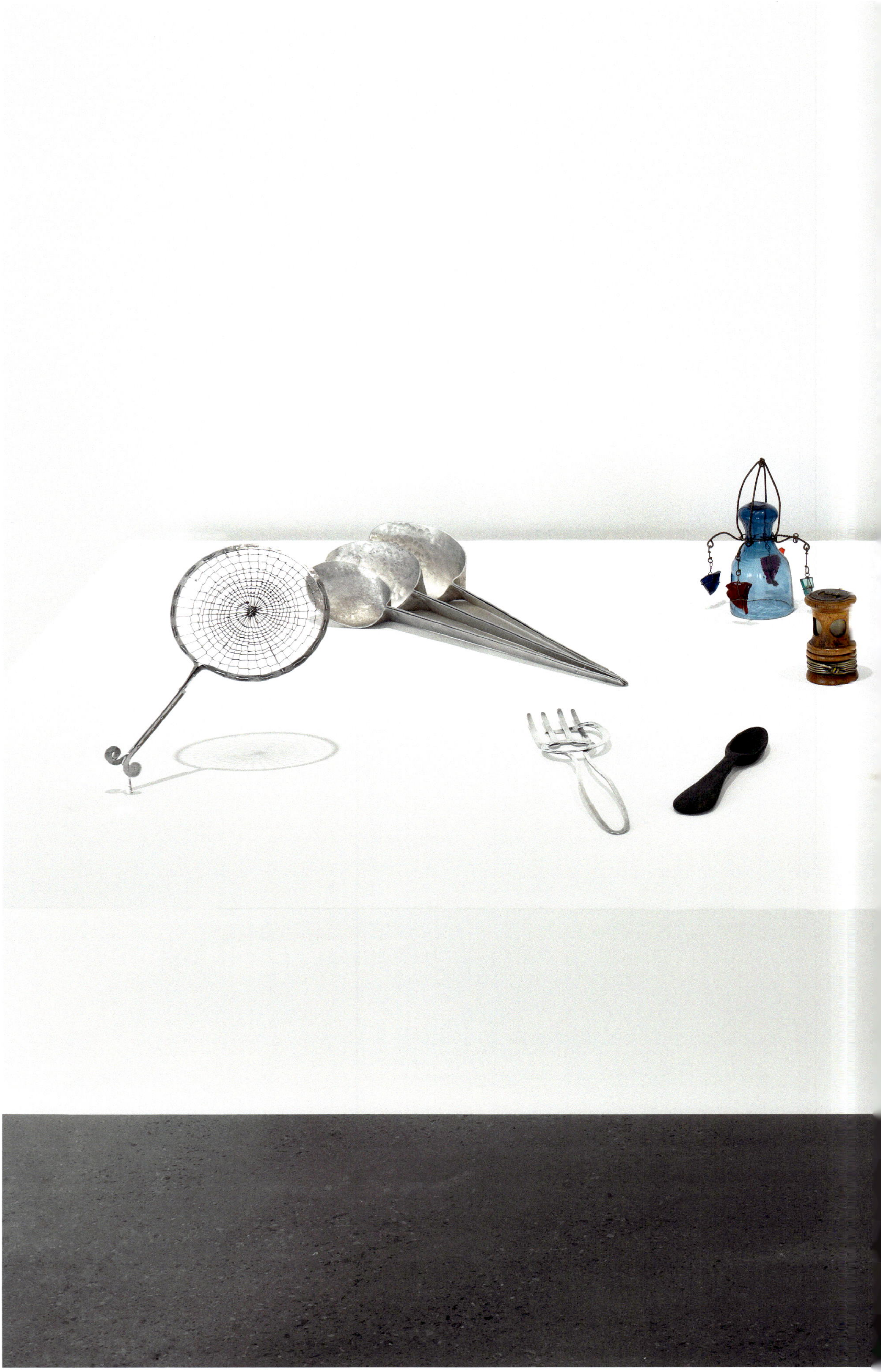

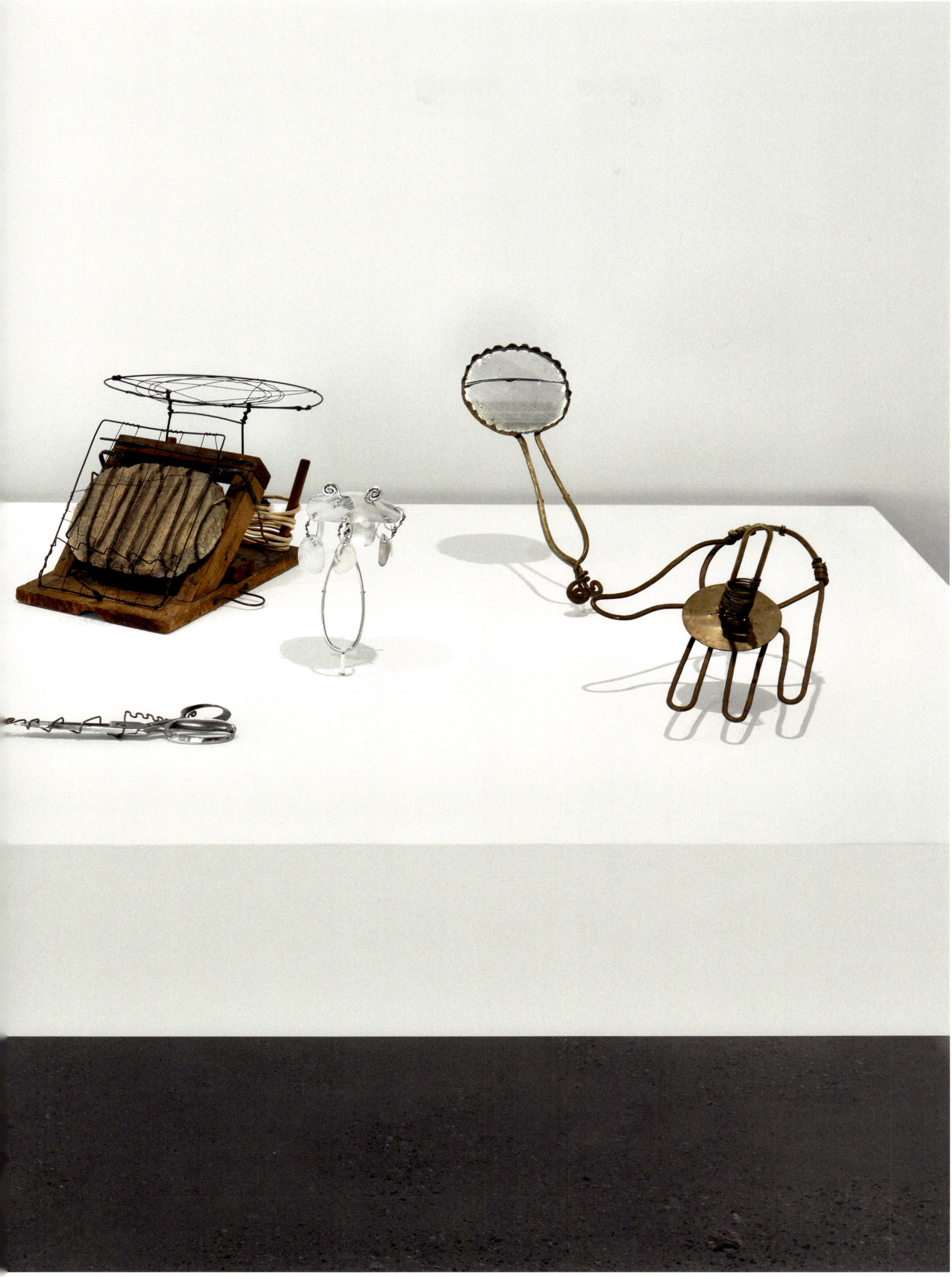

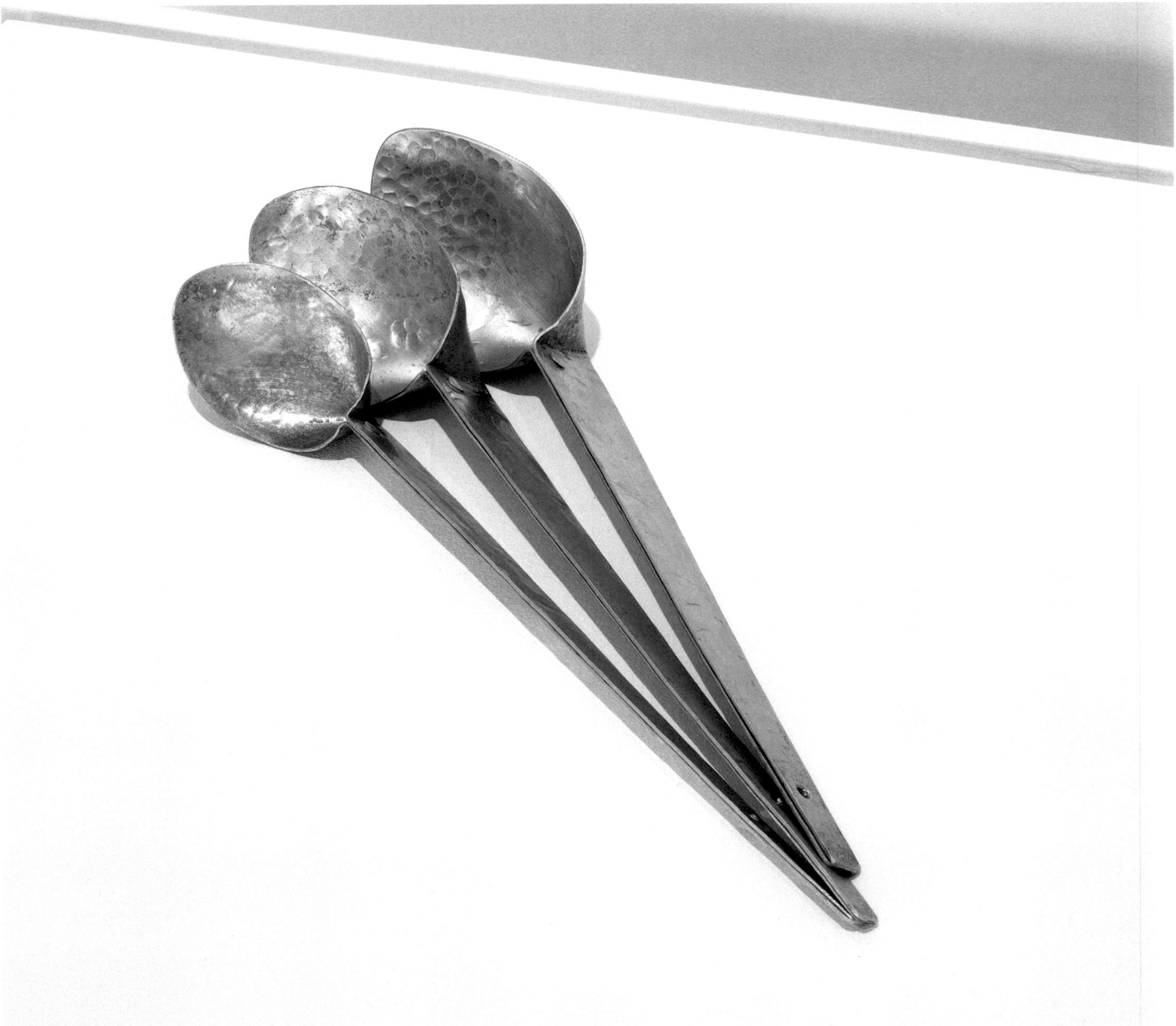

Measuring spoons, c. 1940
Sheet metal
17 × 3⅜ × 3½ in. (43.2 × 8.5 × 8.9 cm) (right)
16½ × 3⅝ × 3½ in. (41.9 × 9.2 × 8.9 cm) (middle)
16 × 3 × 3½ in. (40.6 × 7.6 × 8.9 cm) (left)

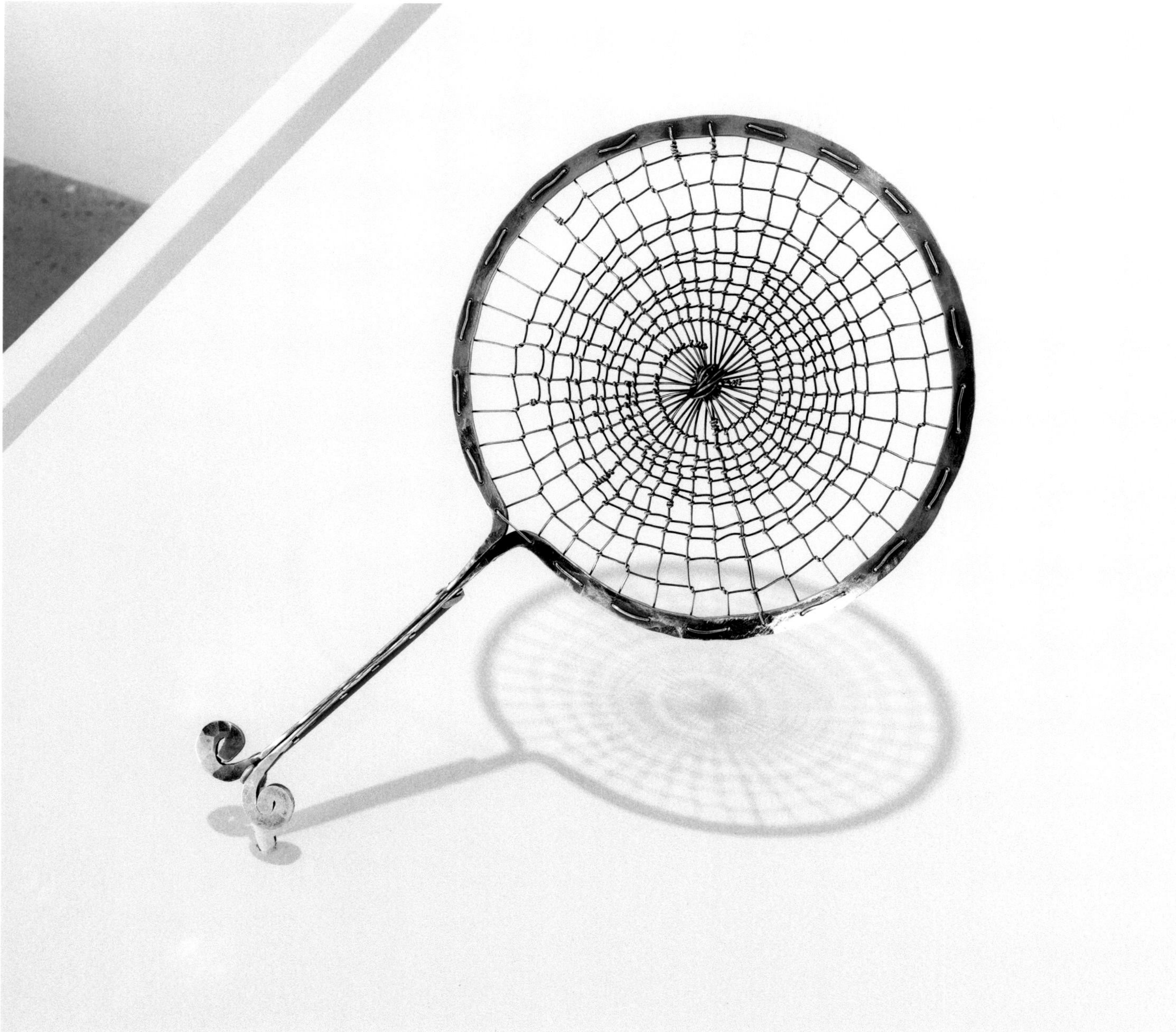

Milk skimmer, c. 1940
Silver wire
10 ⅜ × 5 ⅝ in. (26.4 × 14.3 cm)

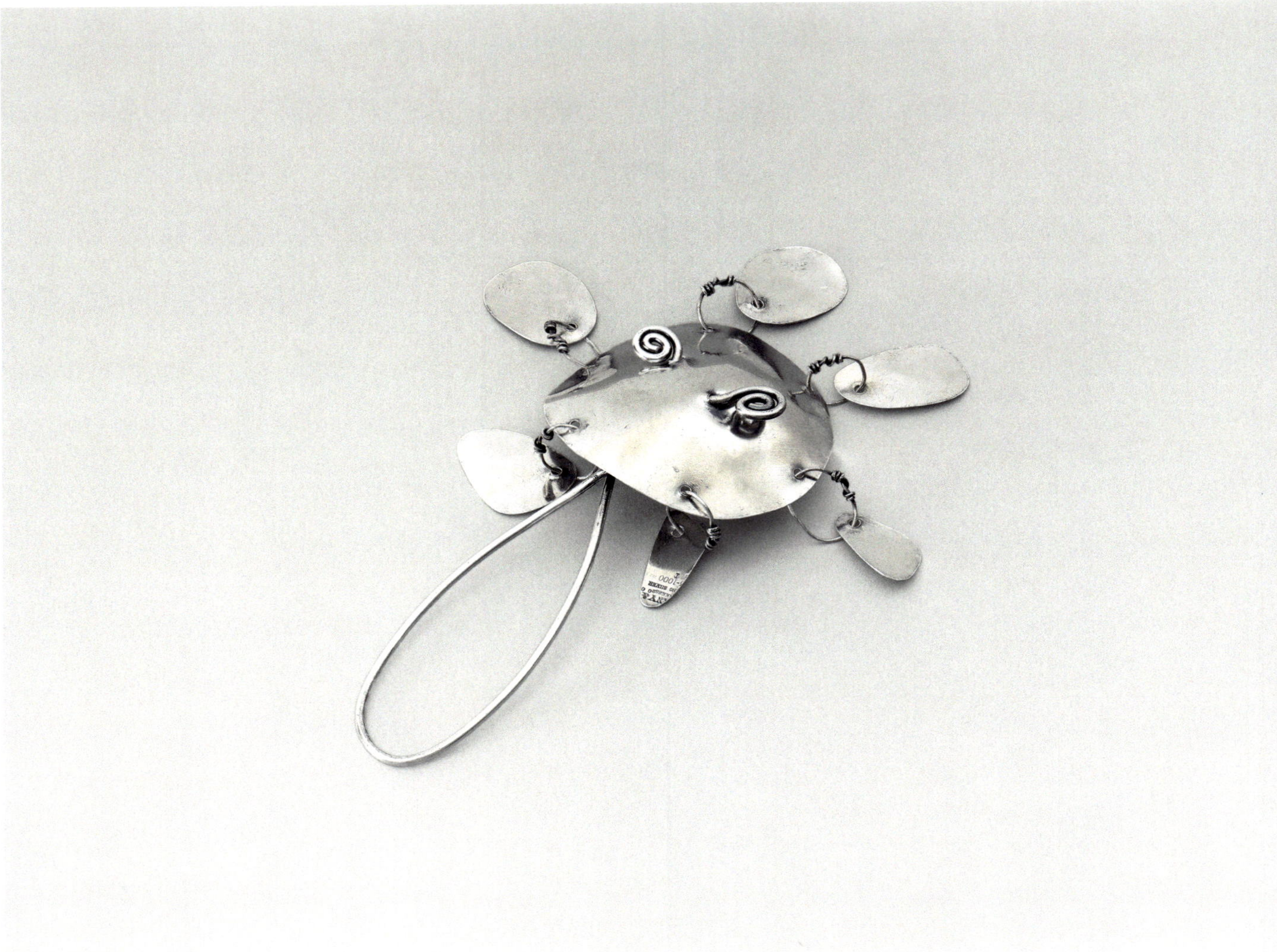

Above:
Baby rattle, c. 1935
Silver sheet metal and wire
10 × 7 ½ × 1 ¼ in. (25.4 × 19.1 × 3.3 cm)

Right:
Dinner bell, c. 1942
Glass and wire
6 ⅝ × 4 ¼ × 3 ¾ in. (16.8 × 10.8 × 9.5 cm)

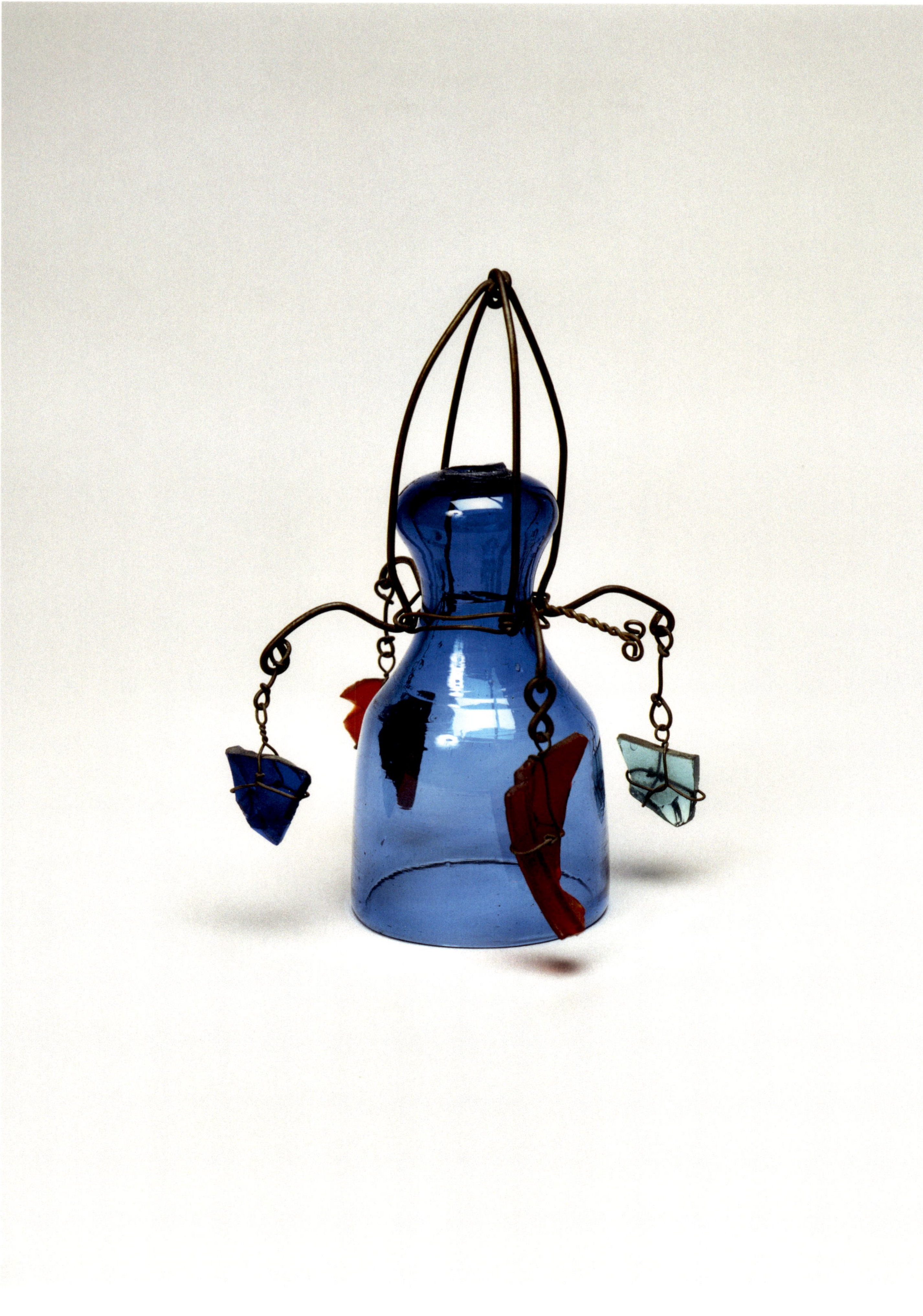

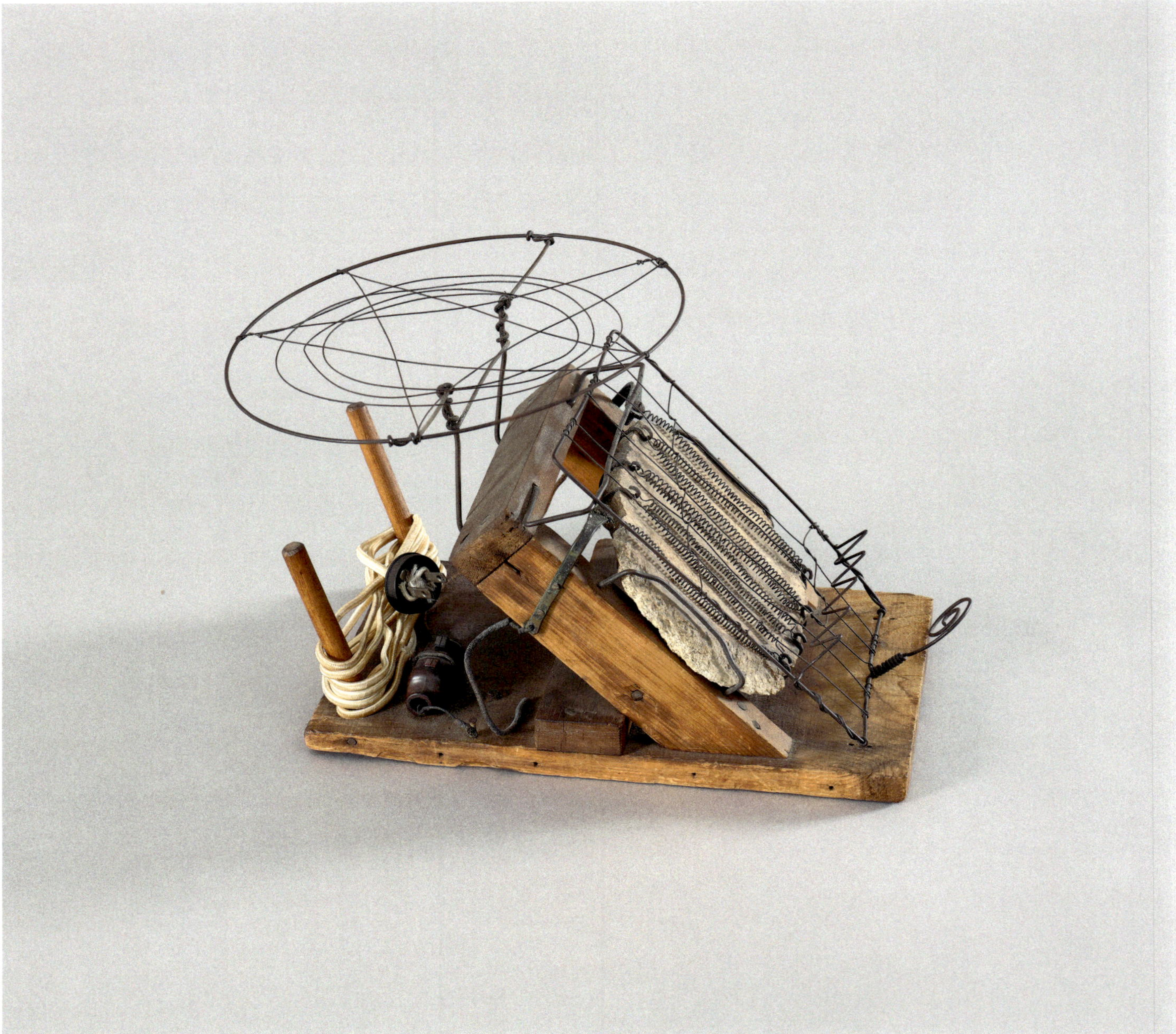

Toaster, c. 1942
Wood, wire, and stone, with electrical wiring
12 × 9 × 8 ¼ in. (30.5 × 22.9 × 21 cm)

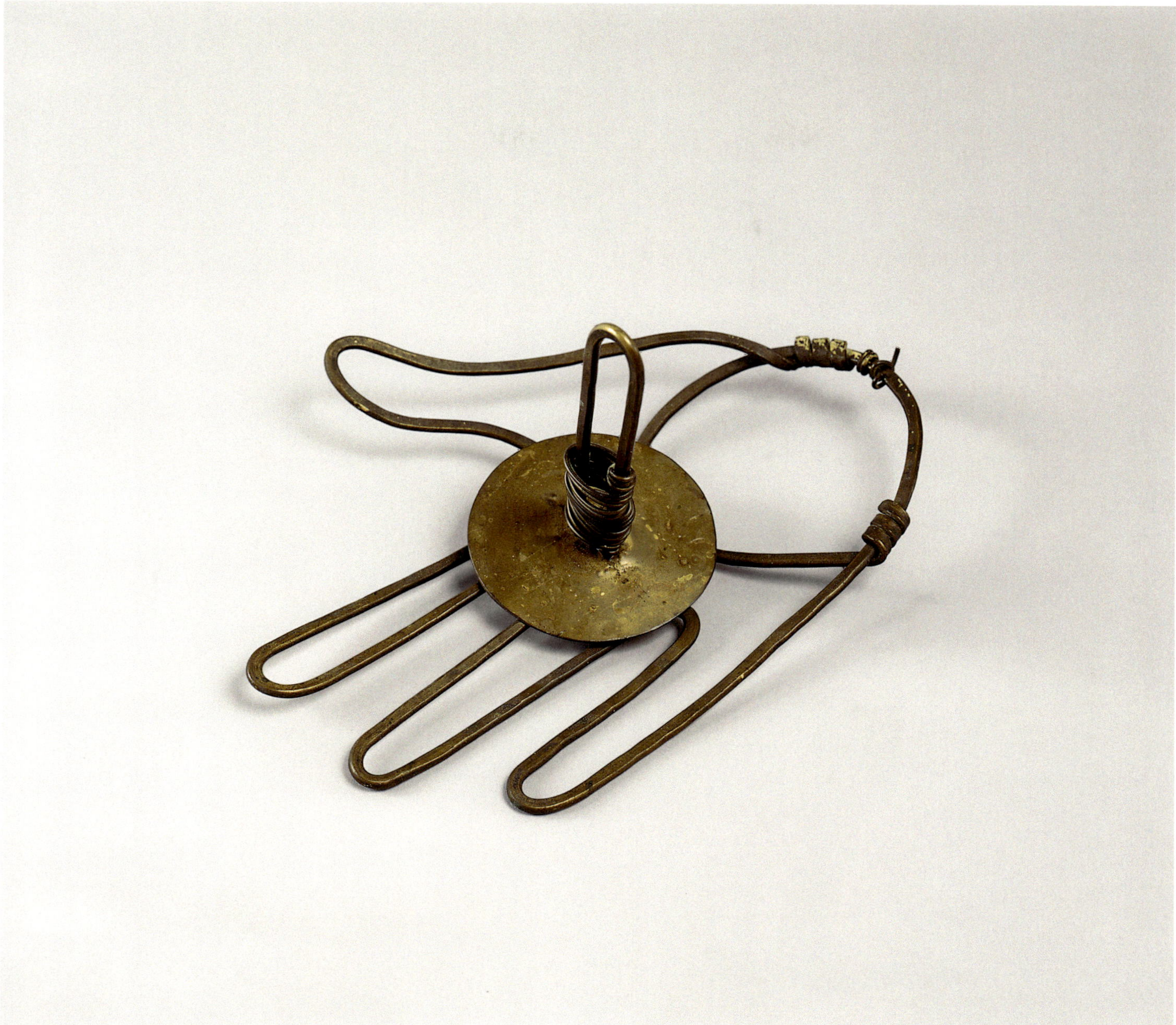

Toilet paper holder, 1949
Brass wire and sheet metal
11 ⅞ × 9 × 6 ¾ in. (30.2 × 22.8 × 17.1 cm)

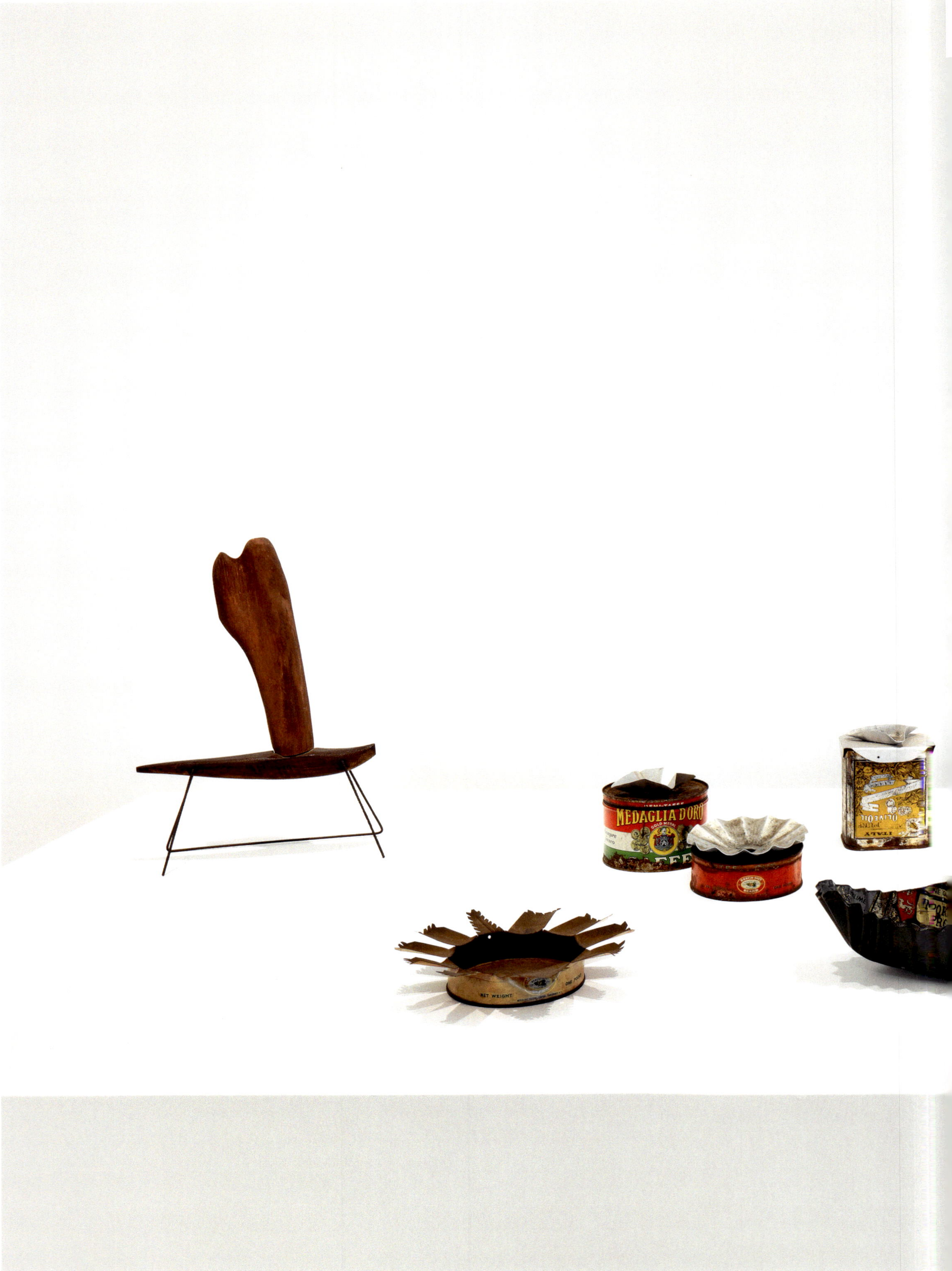
MEDAGLIA D'ORO

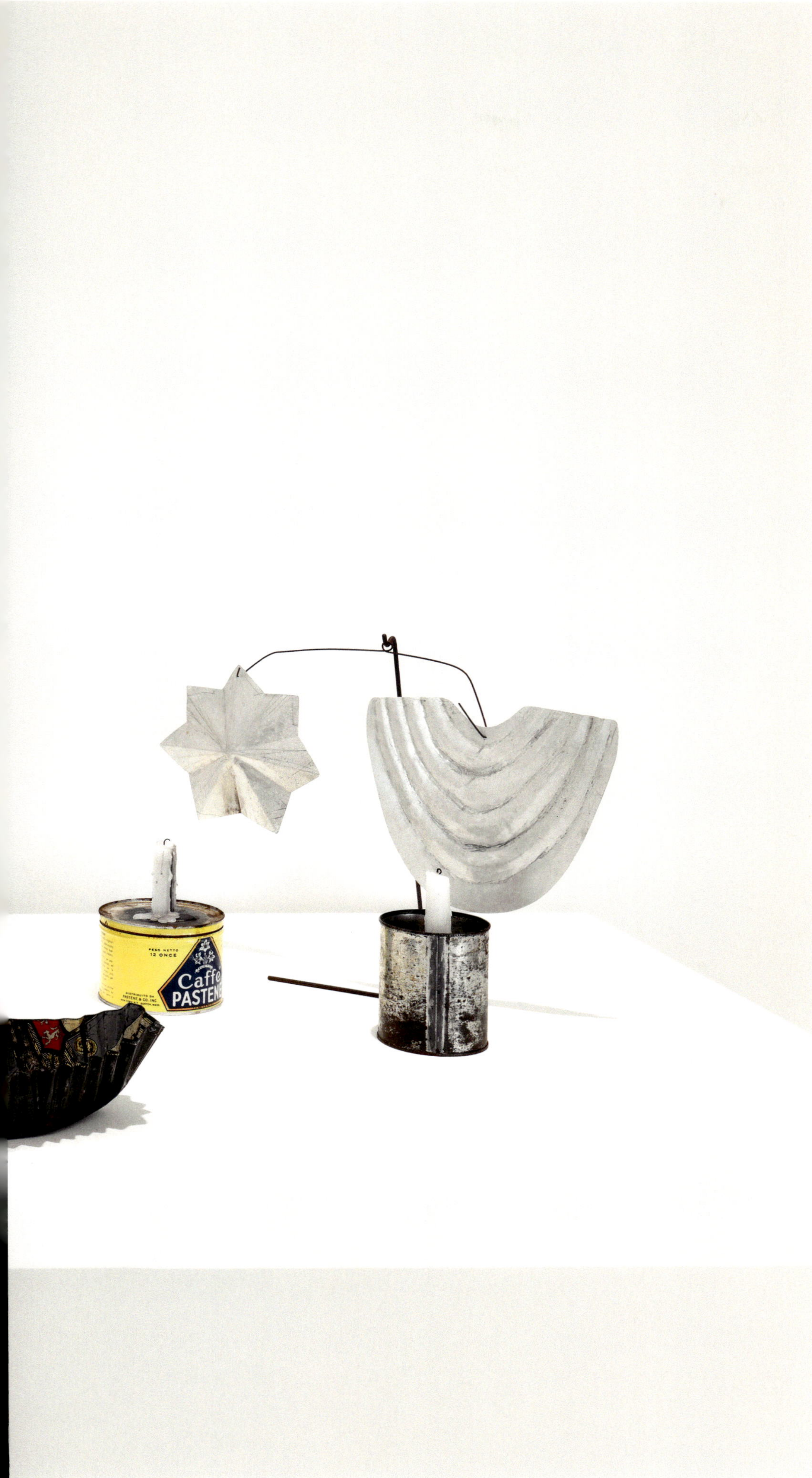

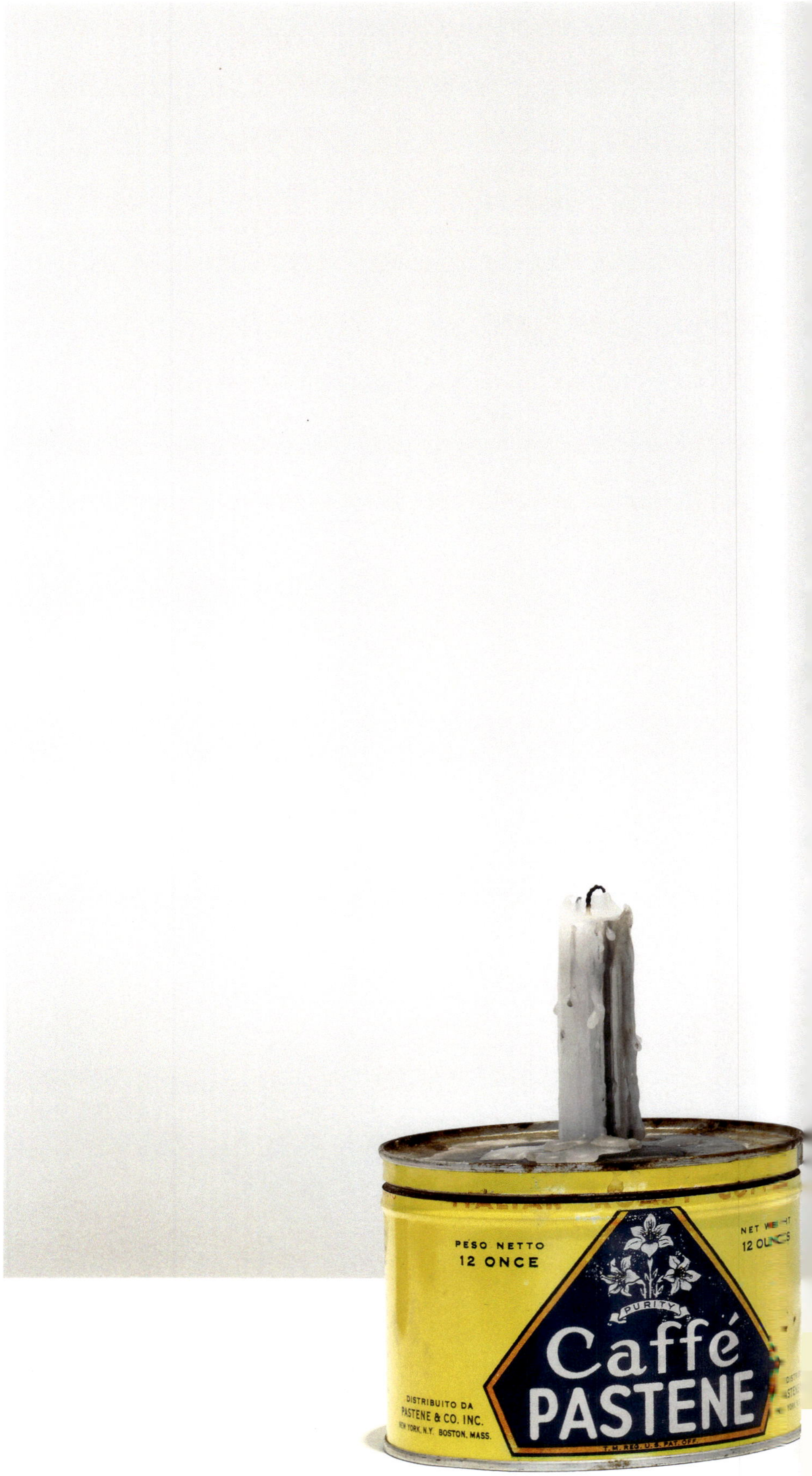
PESO NETTO
12 ONCE
PURITY
Caffé
PASTENE
DISTRIBUITO DA
PASTENE & CO. INC.

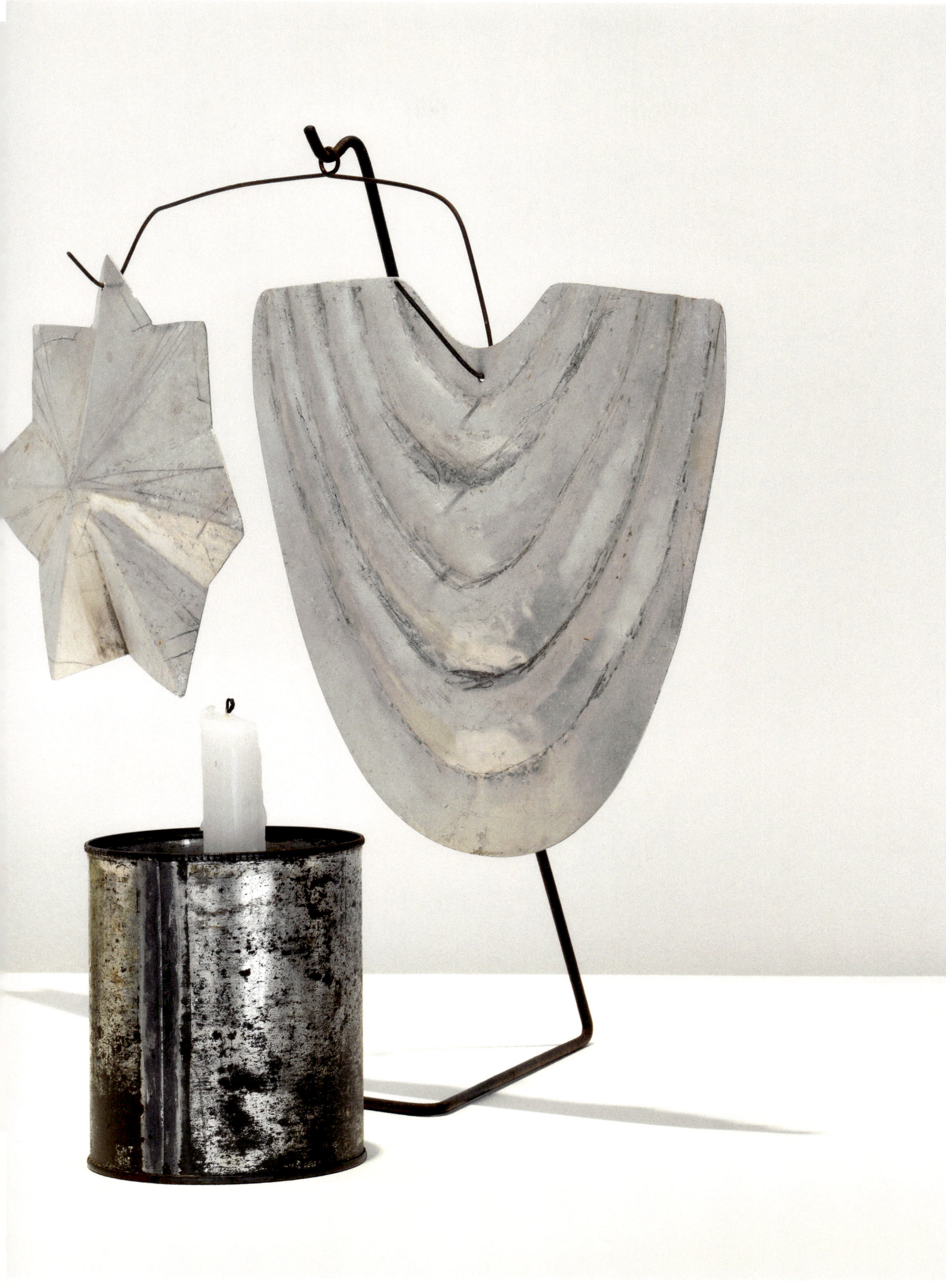

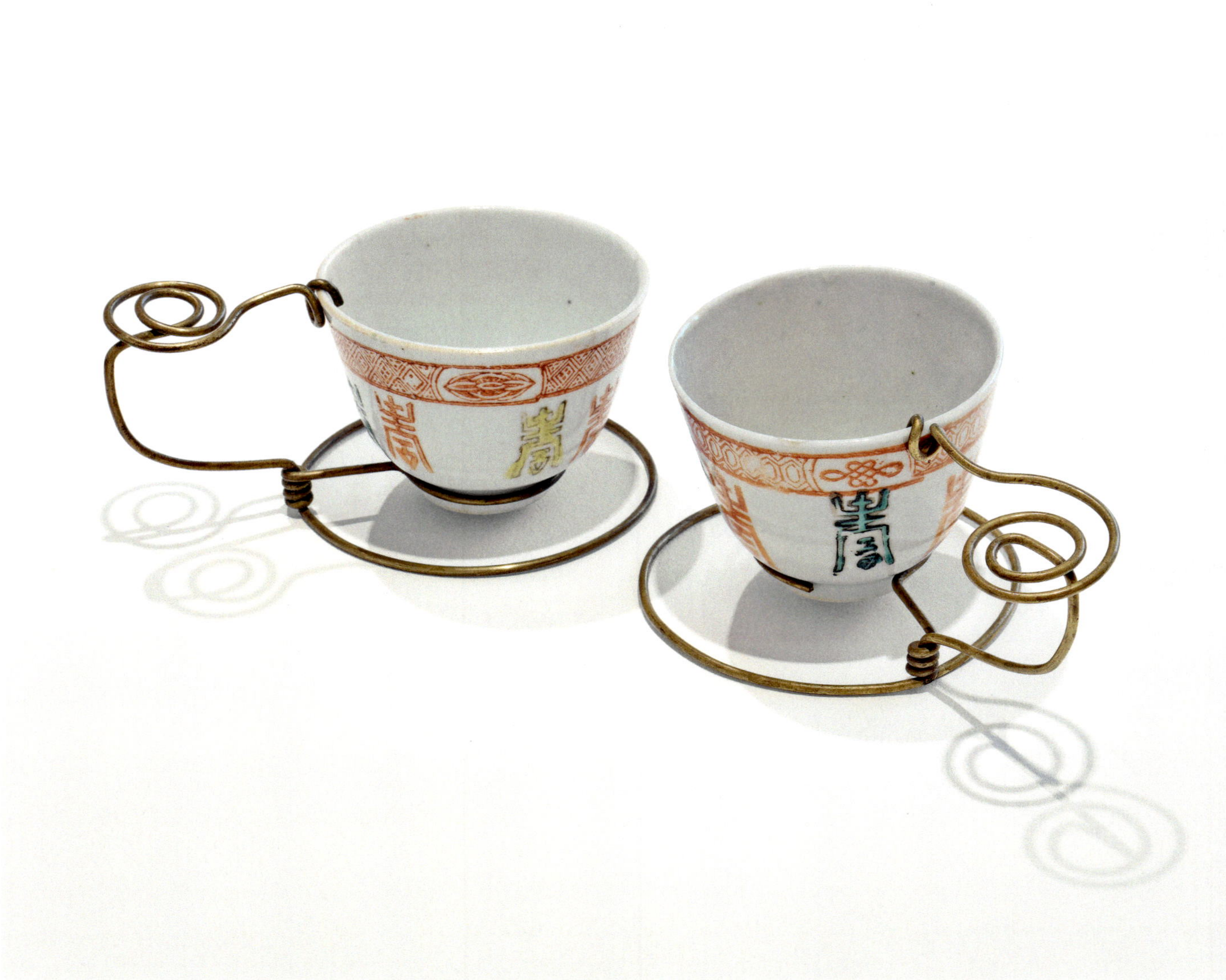

Above:
Zarfs, c. 1940
Brass wire
5 ⅛ × 2 ⅛ × 3 ½ in. (13 × 5.4 × 8.9 cm) (left)
4 ⅝ × 2 ¼ × 2 ¾ in. (11.4 × 5.7 × 7 cm) (right)

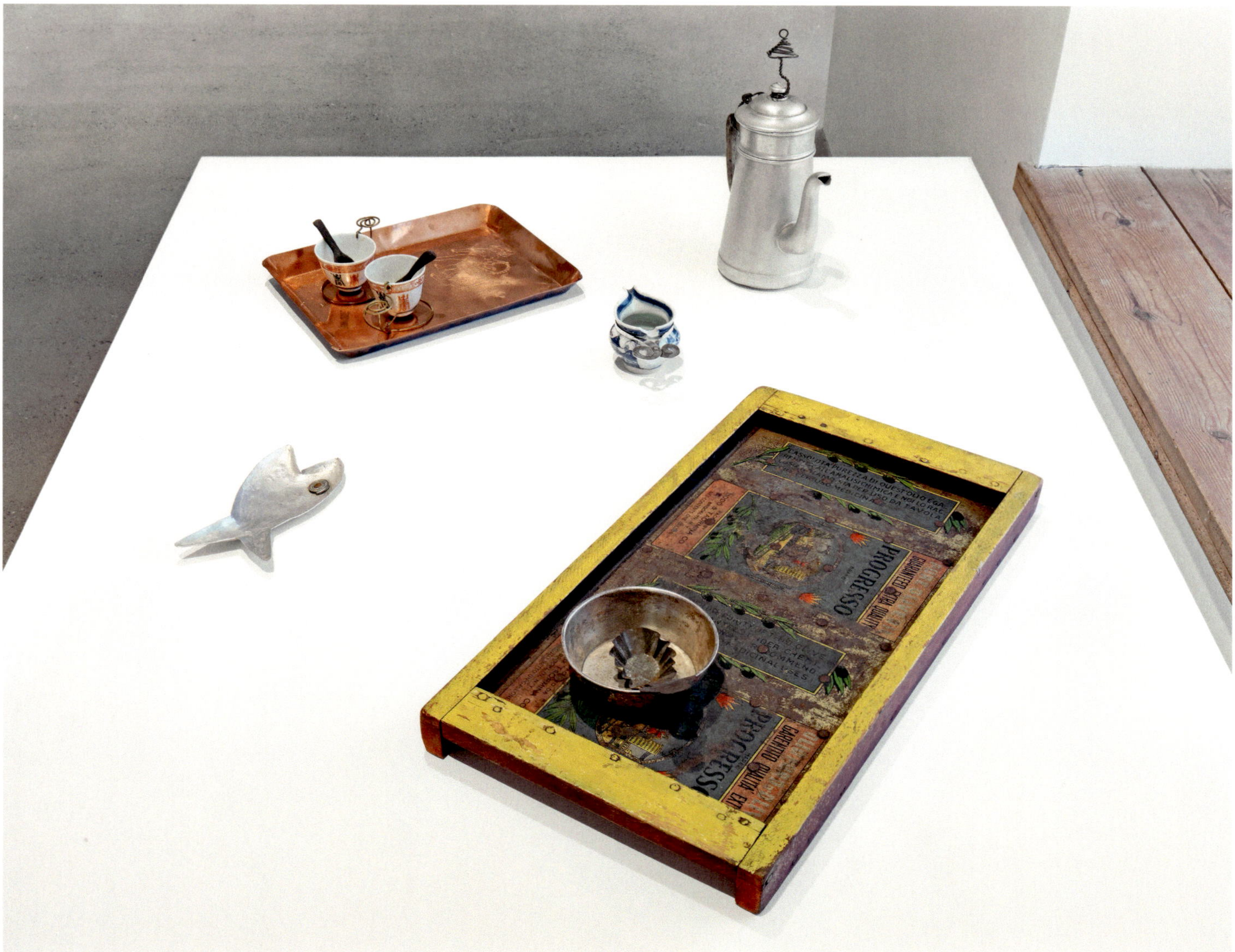
PROGRESSO
PROGRESSO

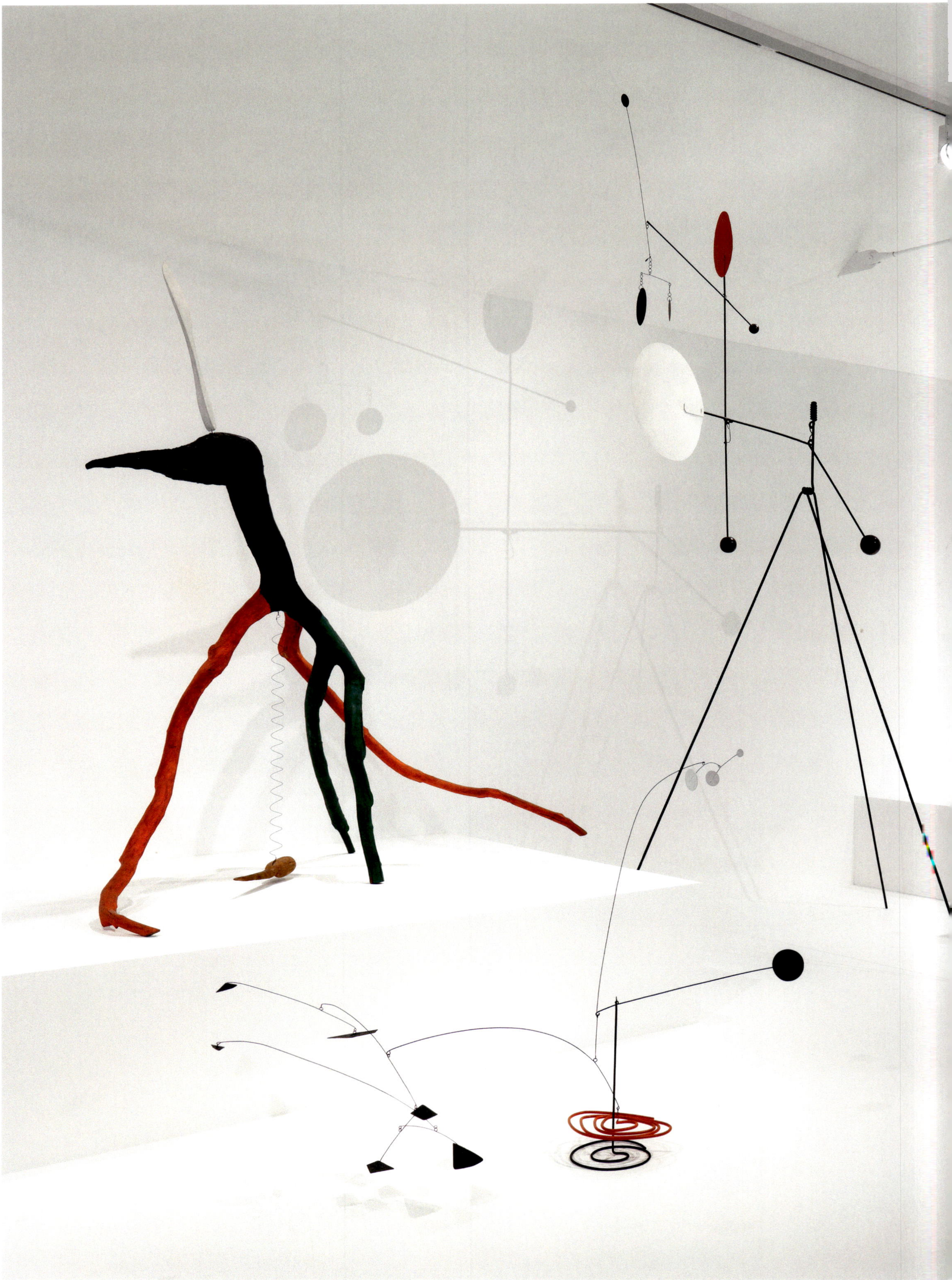

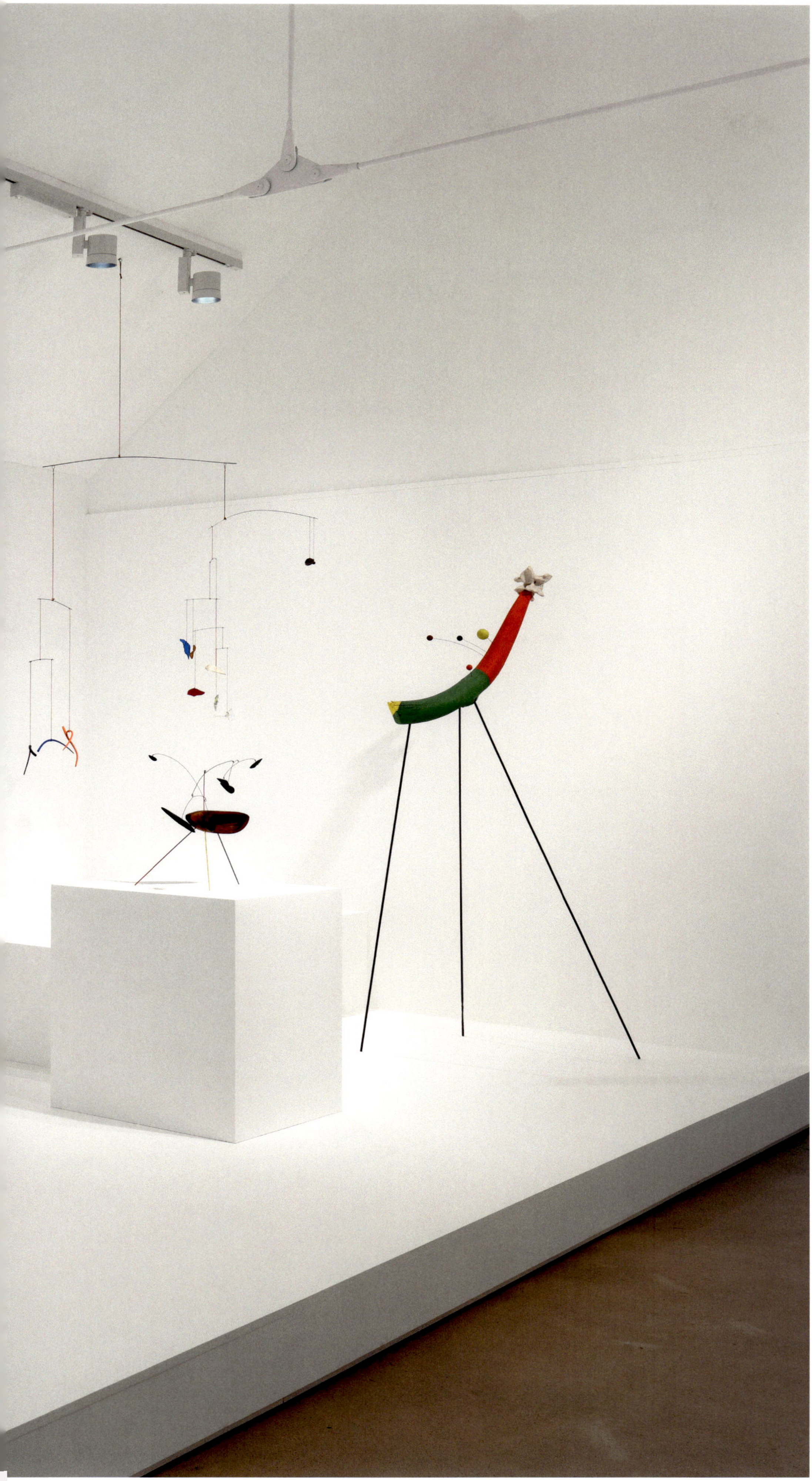

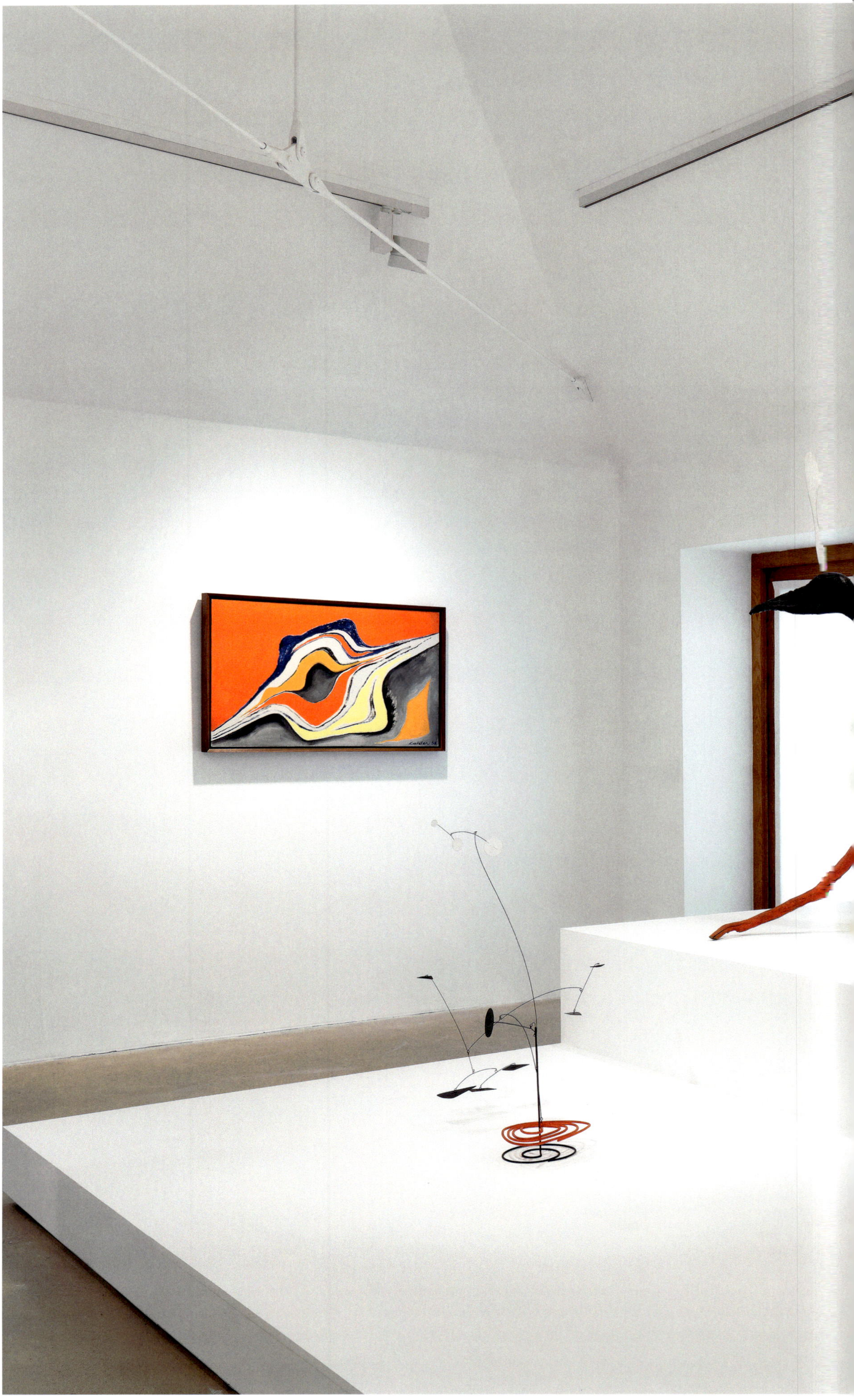

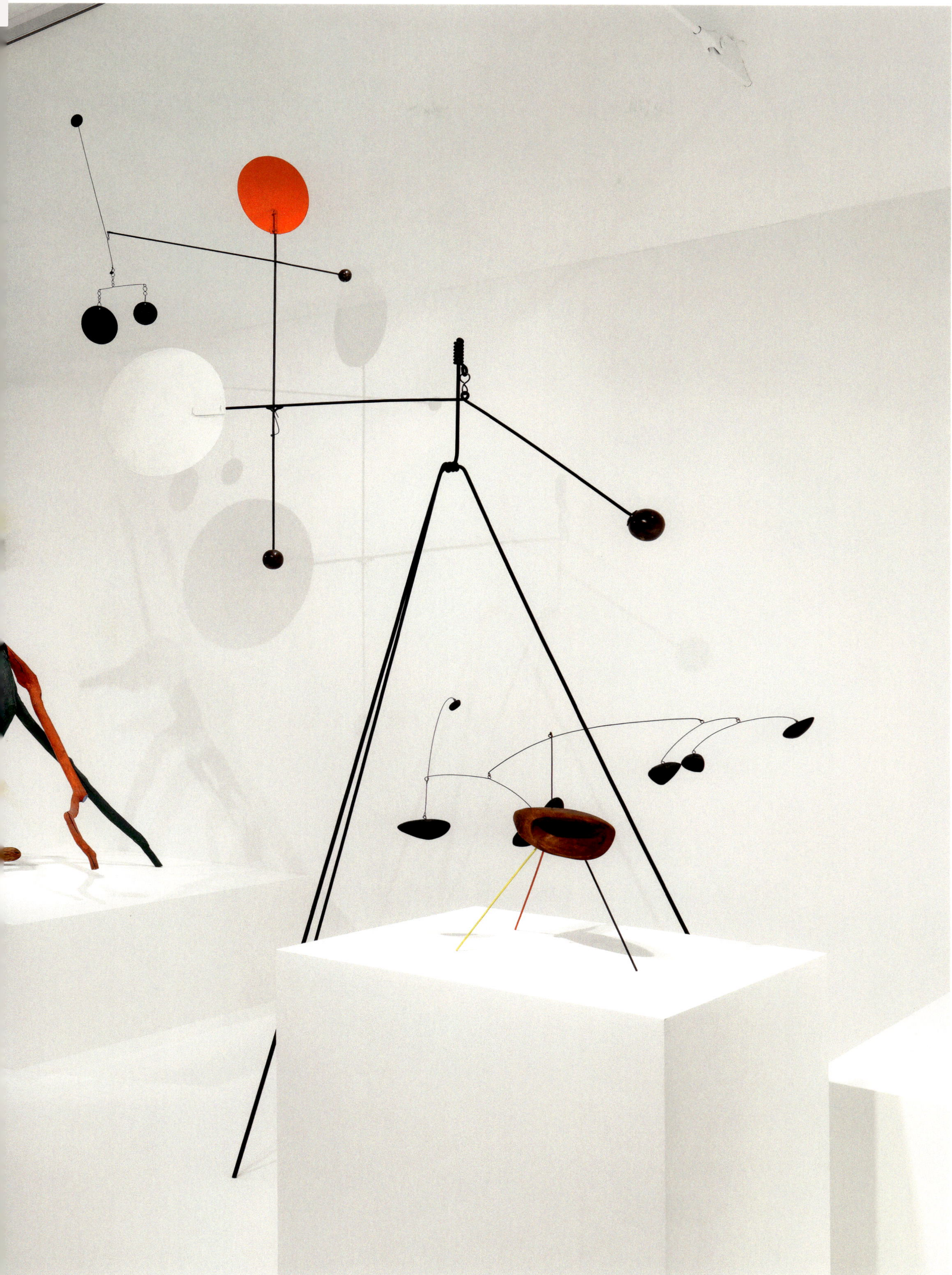

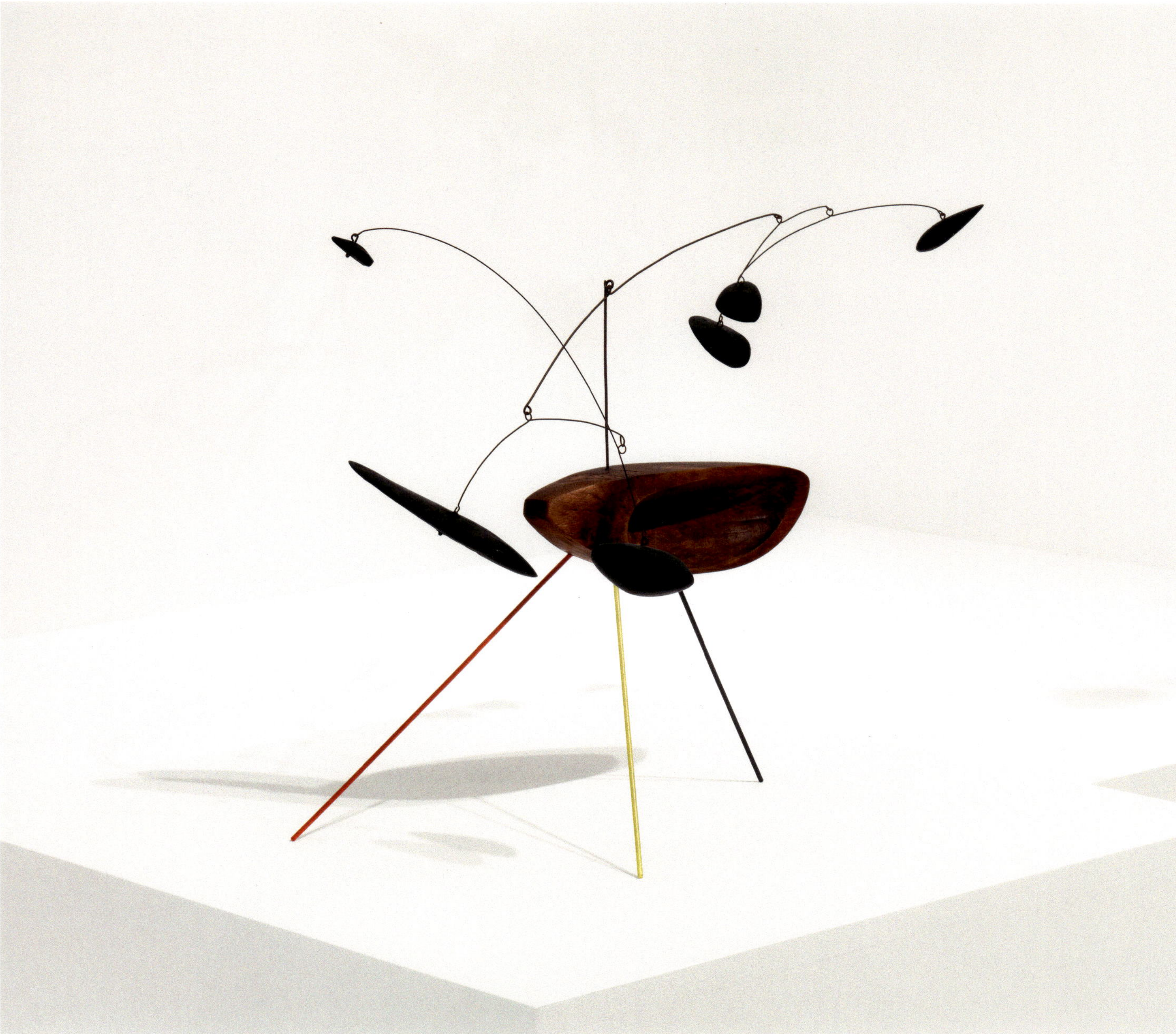

Untitled, 1945
Wood, rod, wire, and paint
15 ¼ × 21 ¼ × 12 in. (38.7 × 53.9 × 30.4 cm)

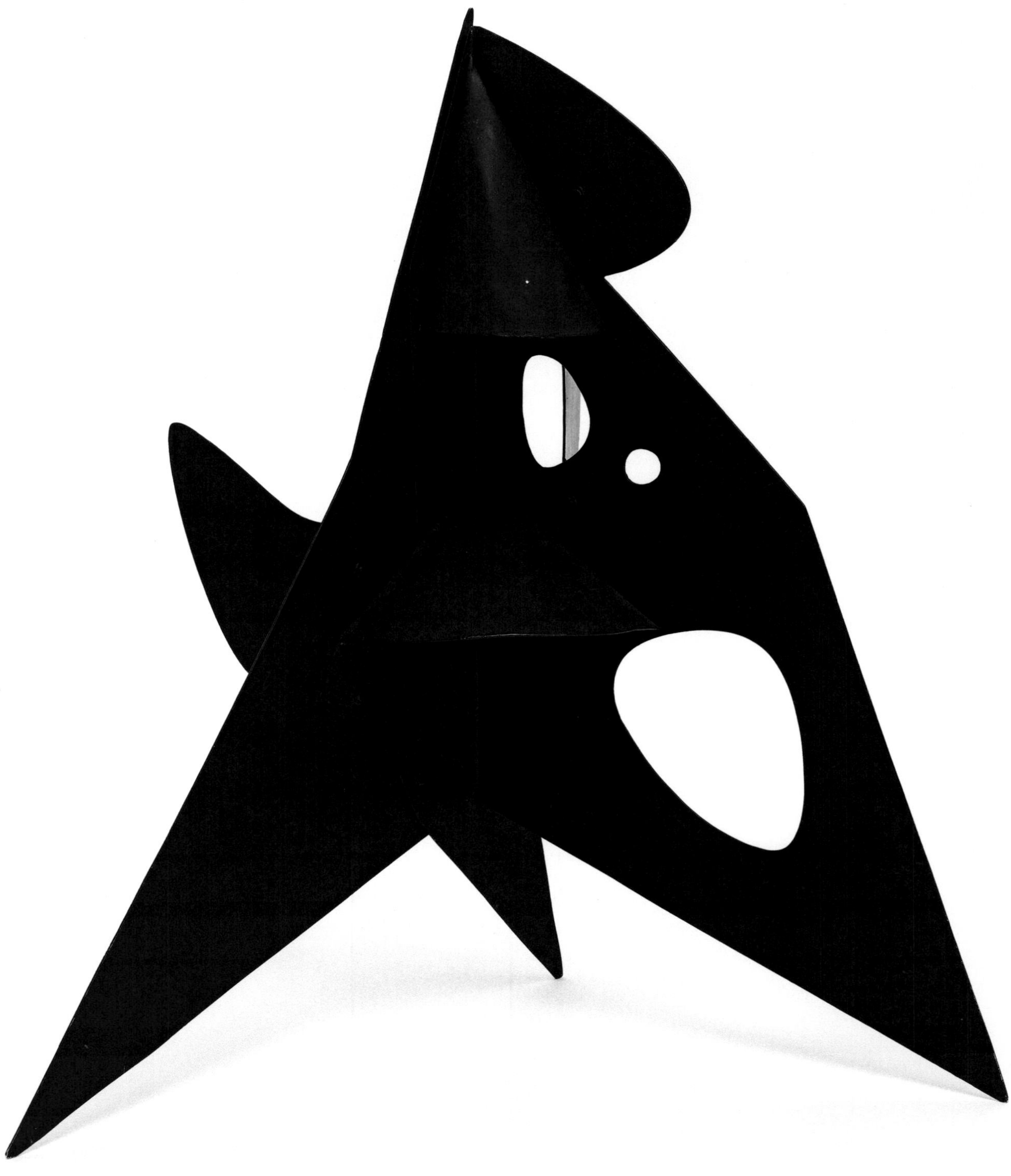

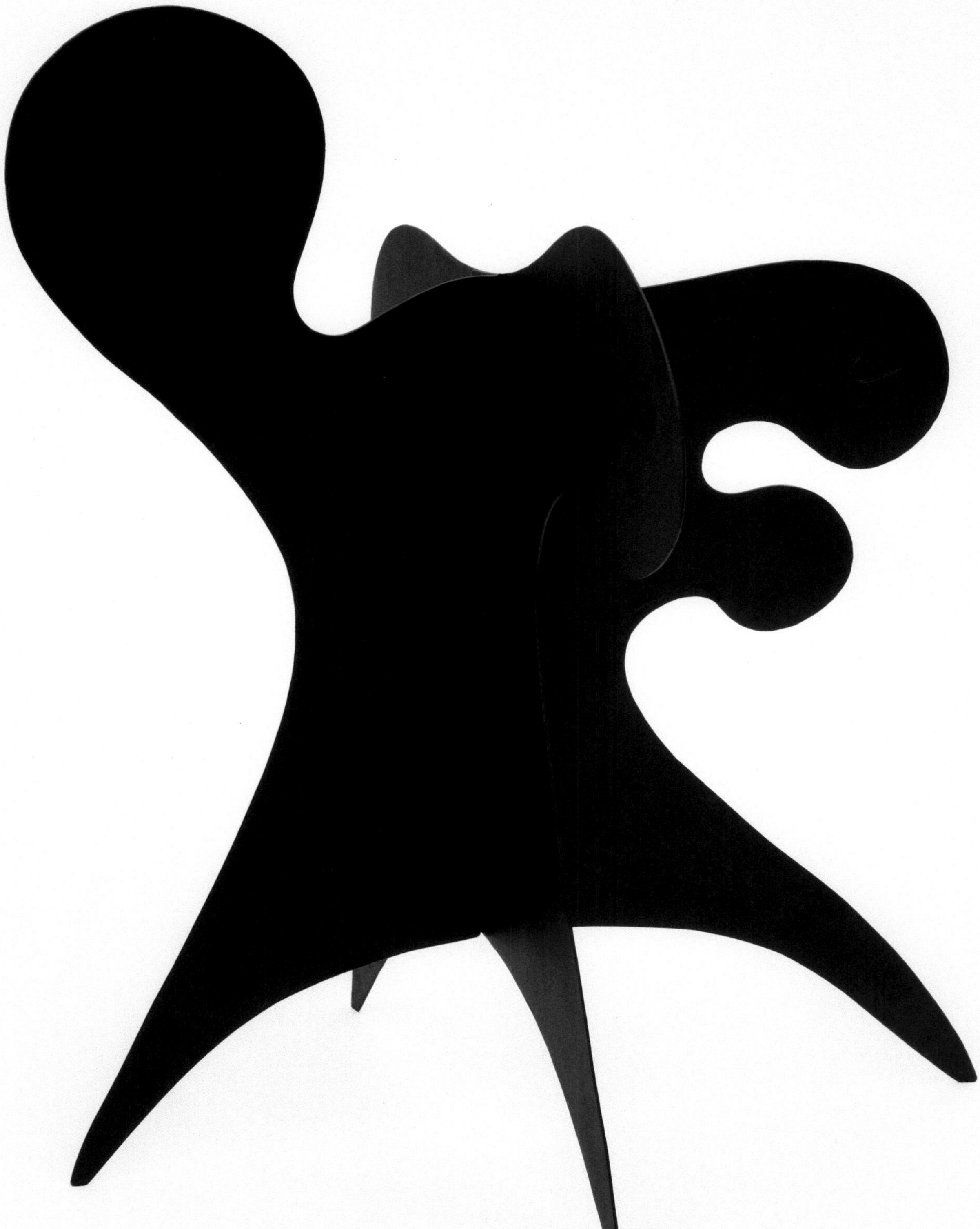

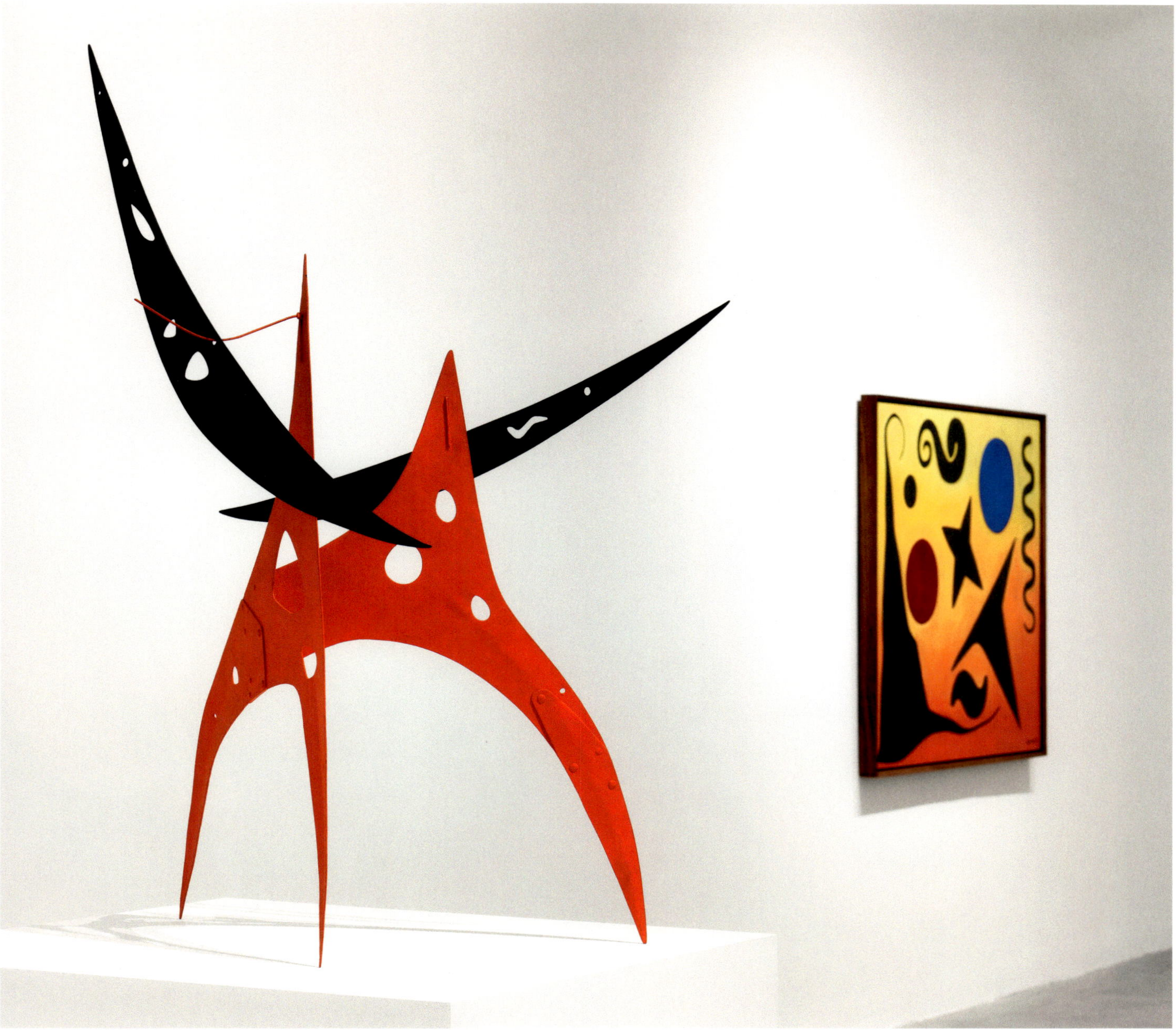

Sword Plant, 1947
Sheet metal, wire, and paint
38 ½ × 31 × 28 ½ in. (97.8 × 78.7 × 72.4 cm)

Seven Black, Red and Blue, 1947
Oil on canvas
48 ⅛ × 60 ¼ in. (122.3 × 153 cm)

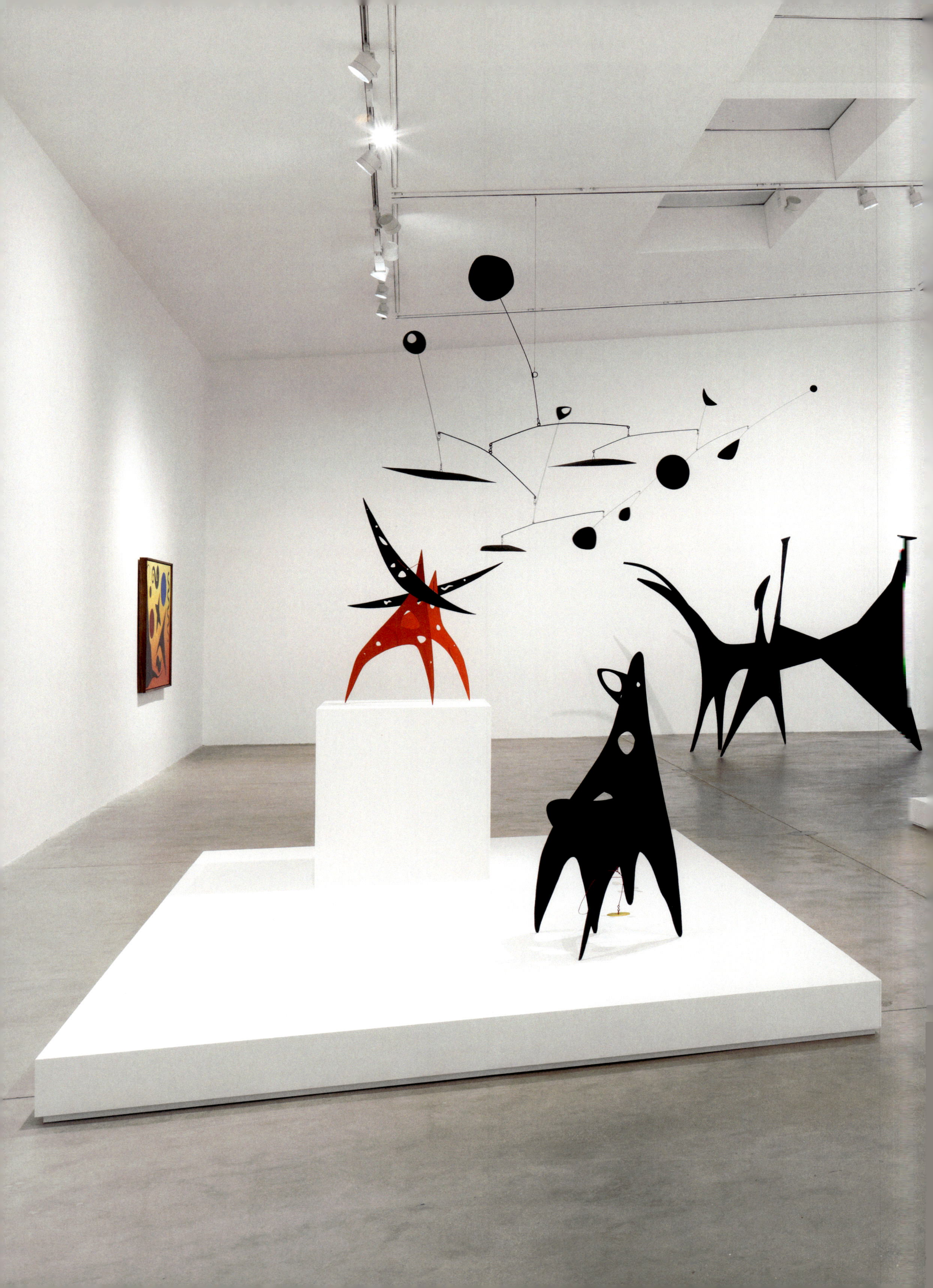

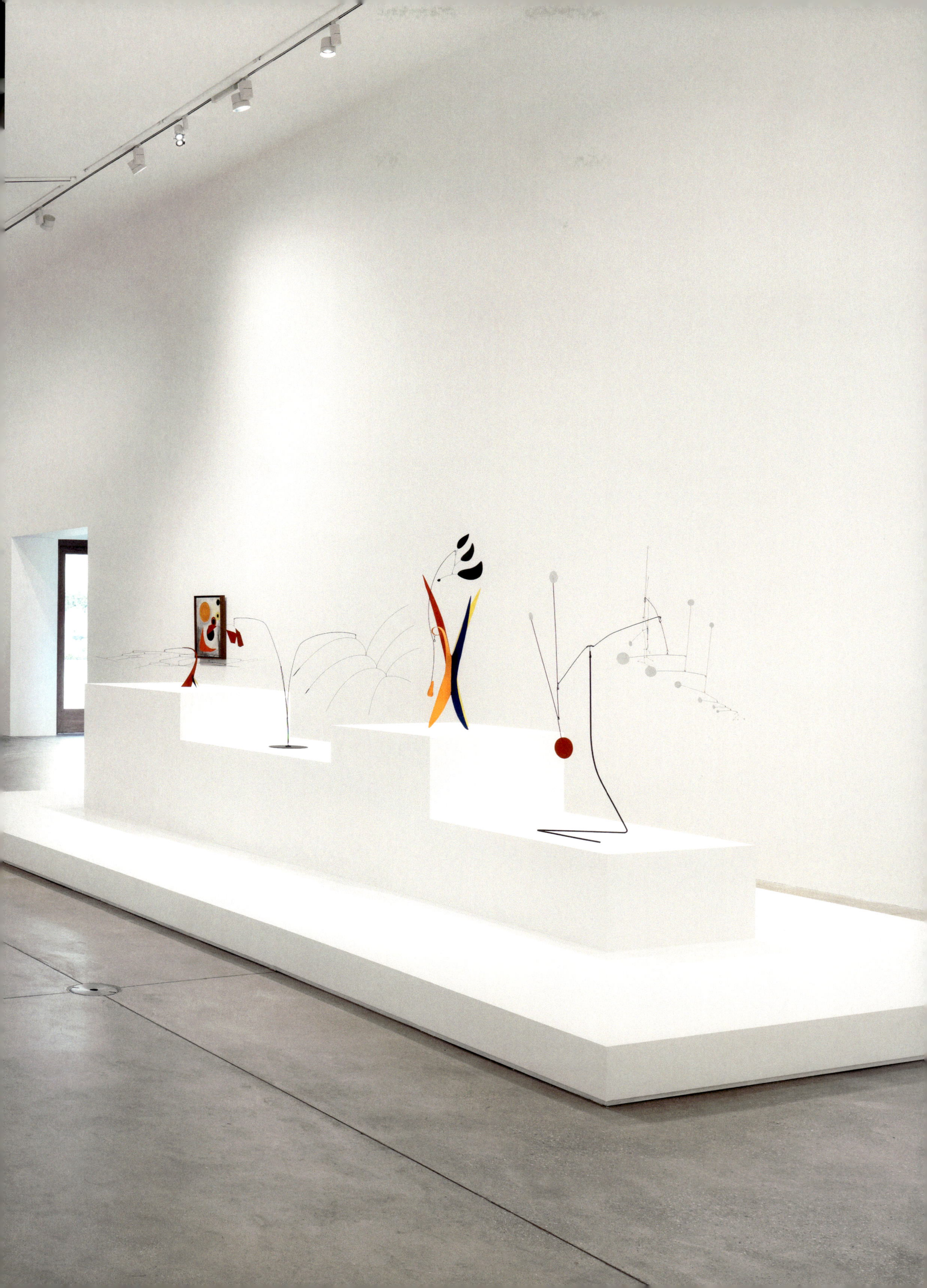

Root, 1947
Sheet metal, wire, and paint
48 × 26 × 33 in. (121.9 × 66 × 83.8 cm)

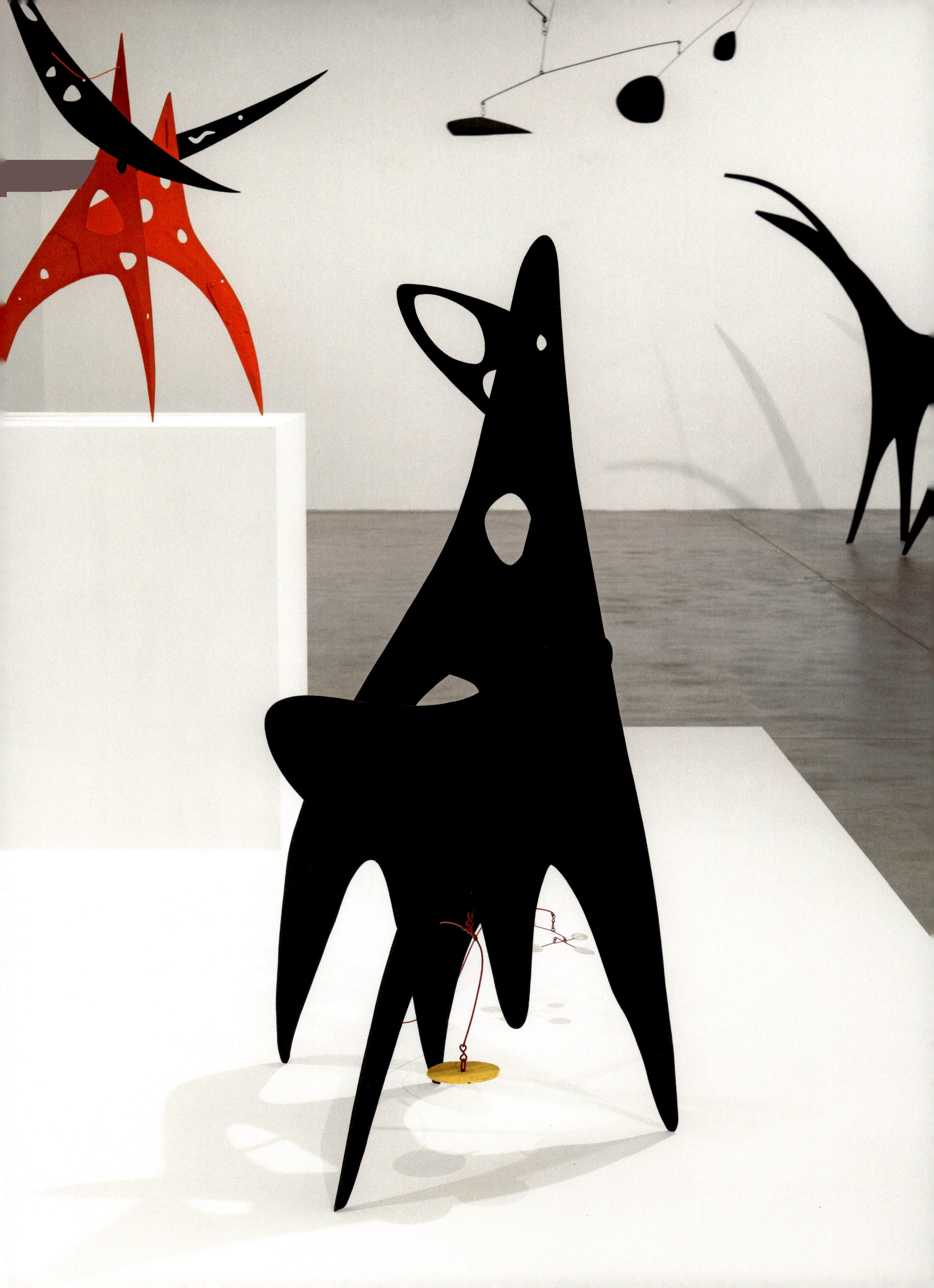

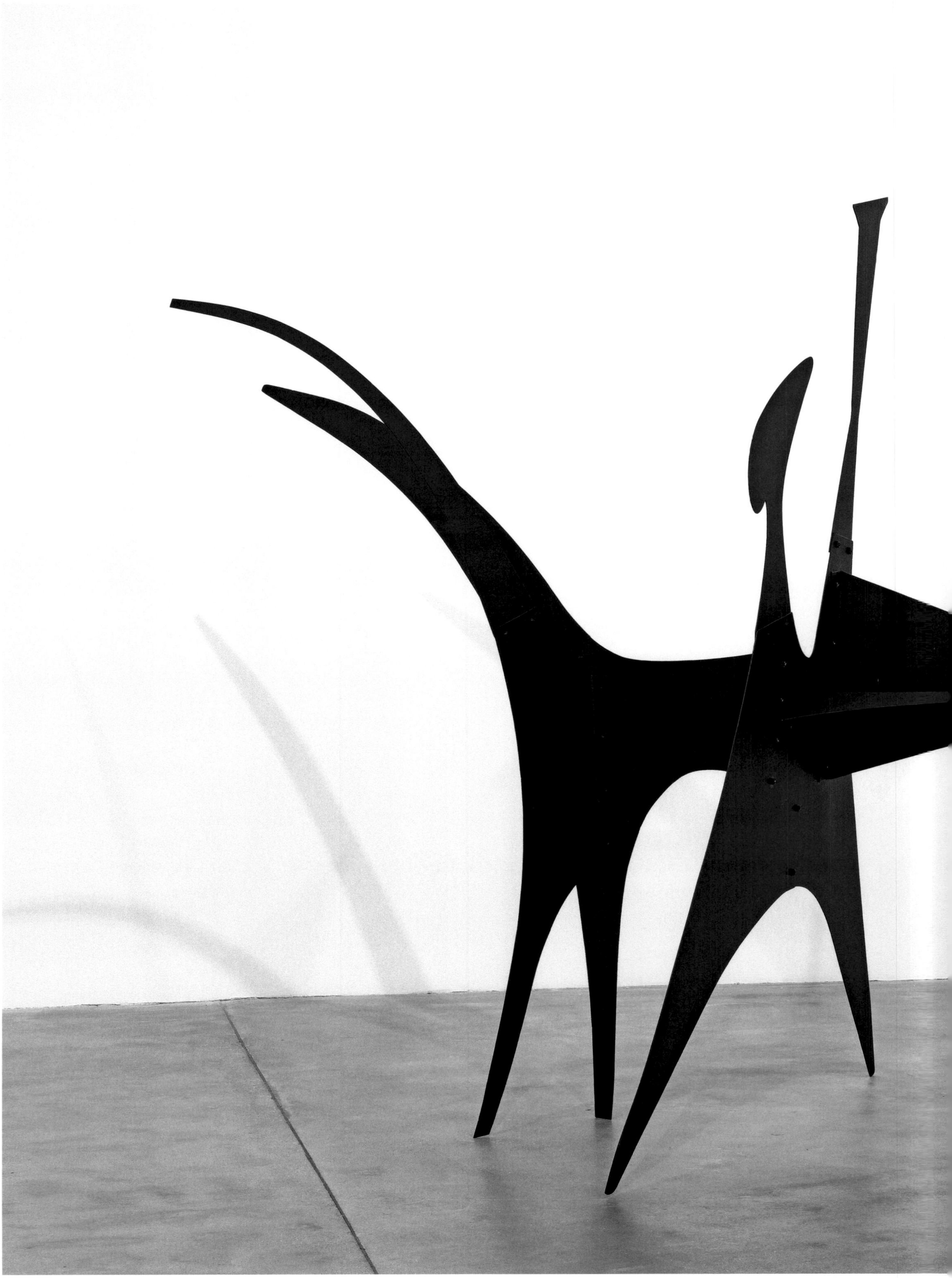

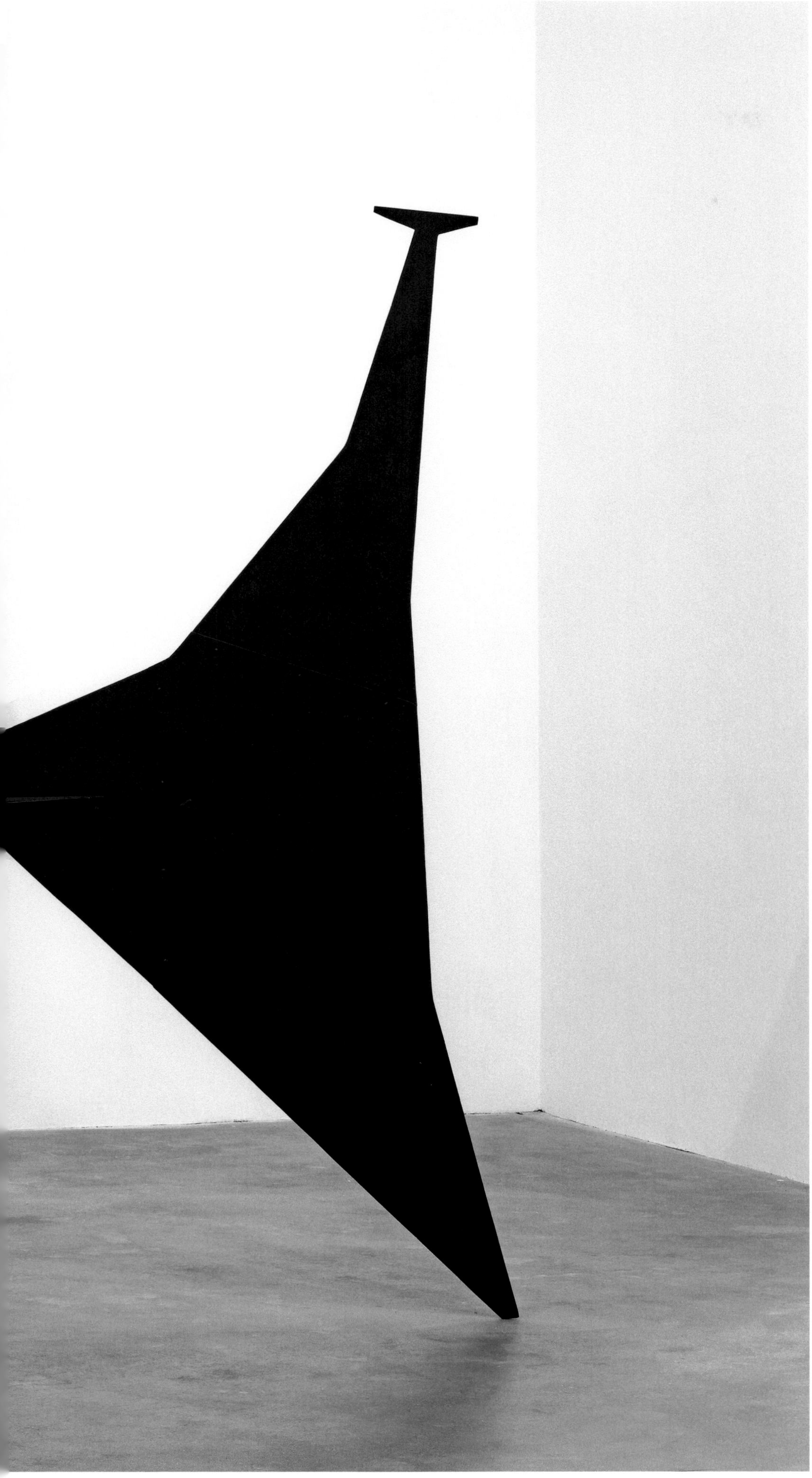

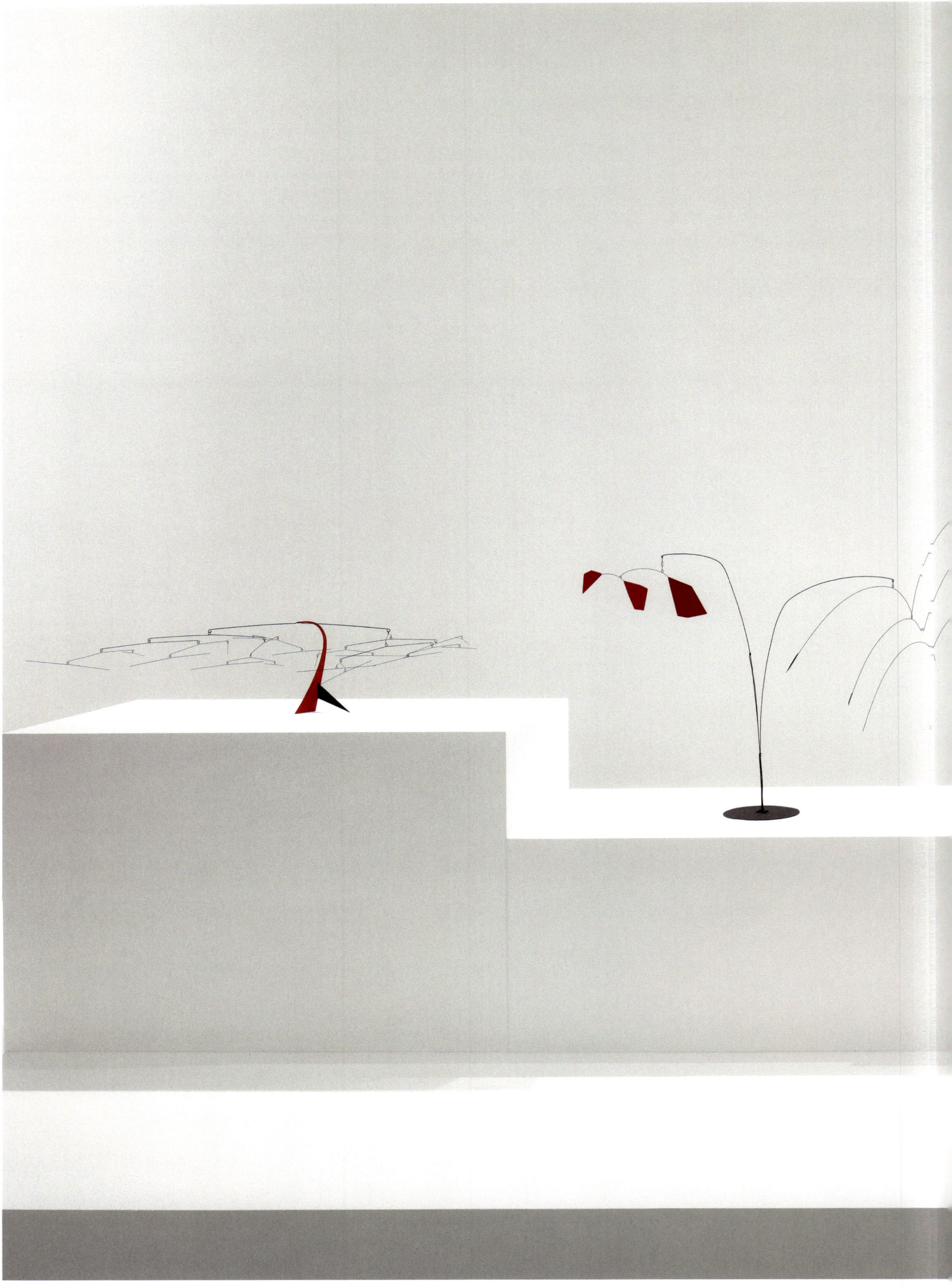

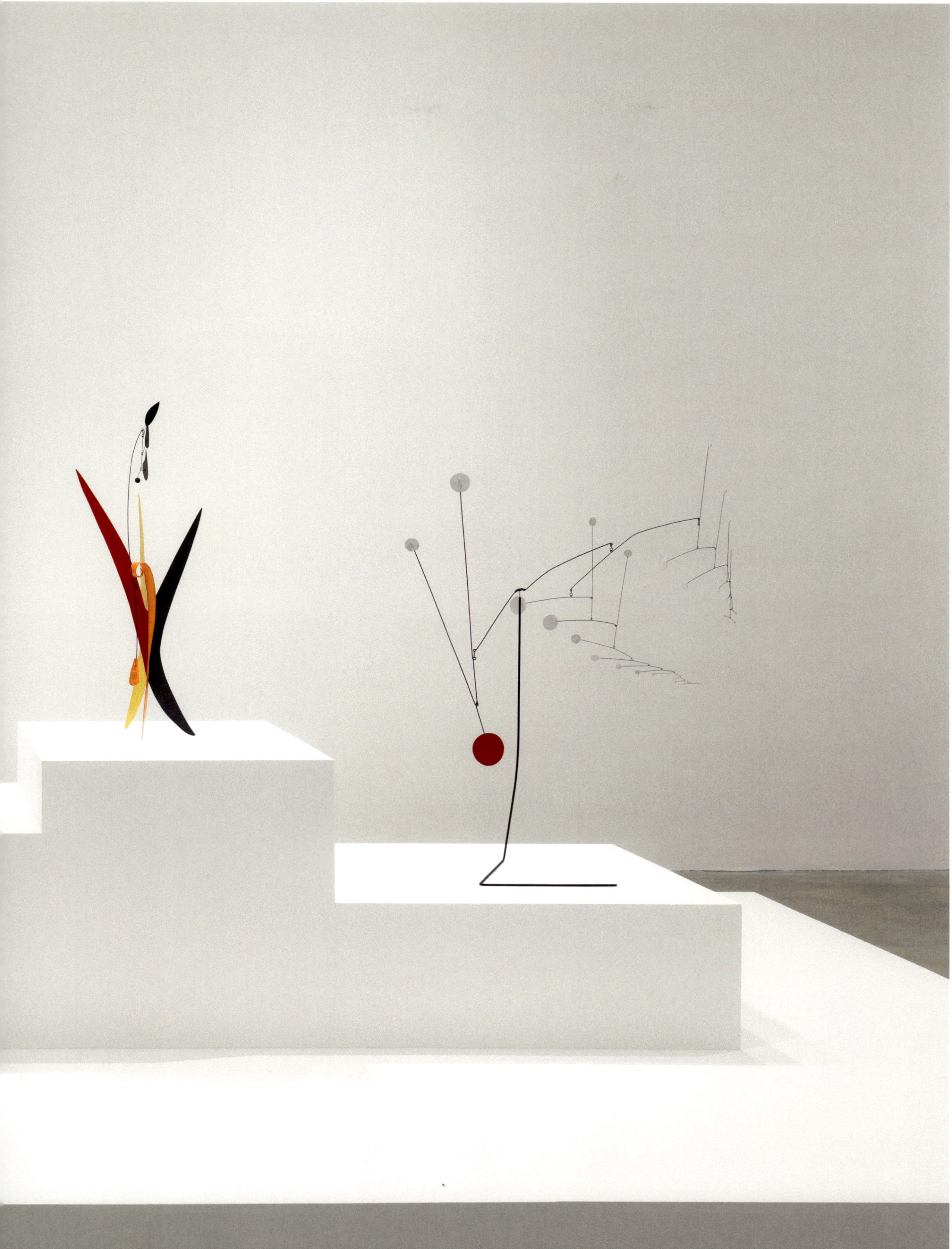

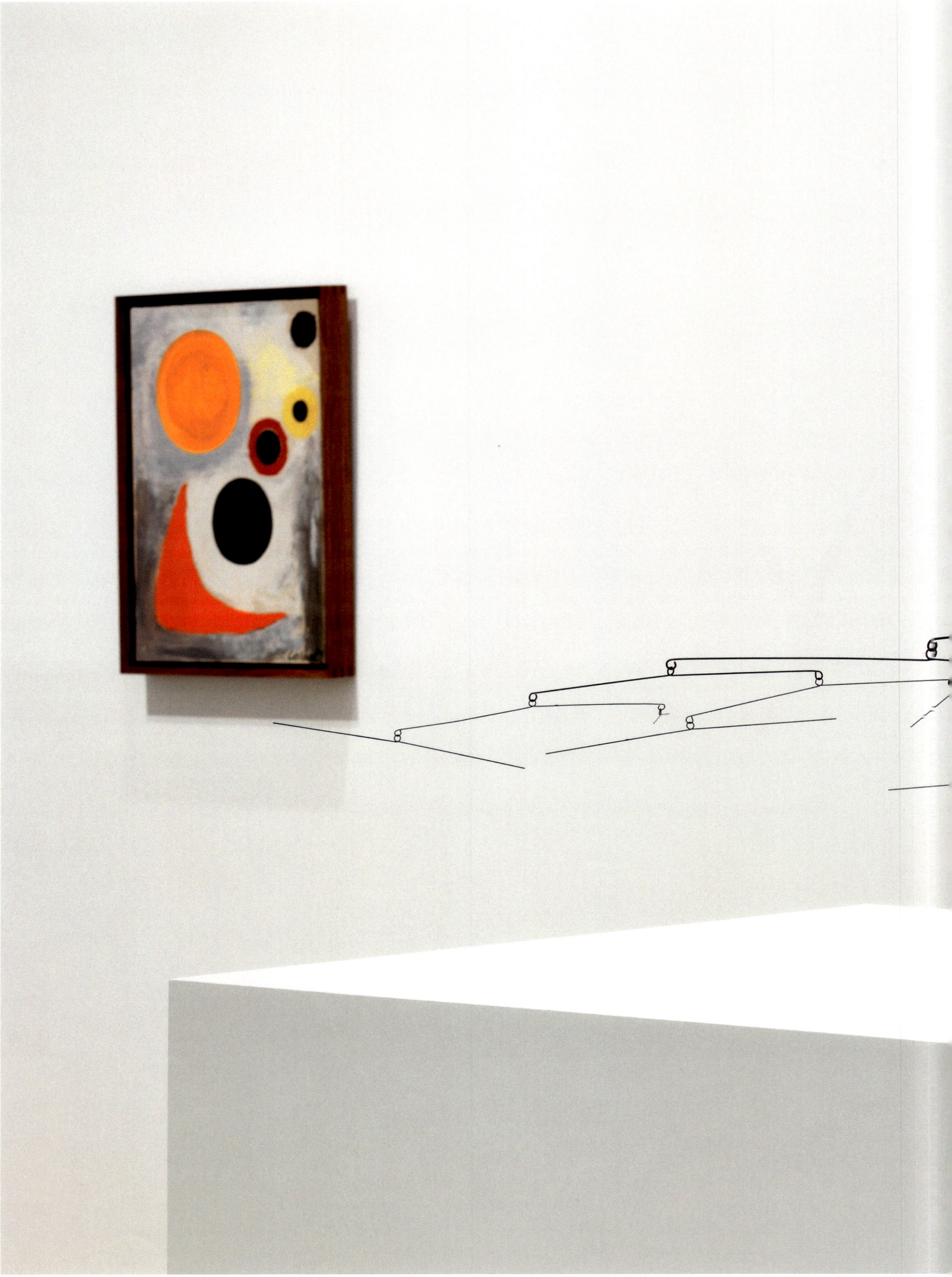

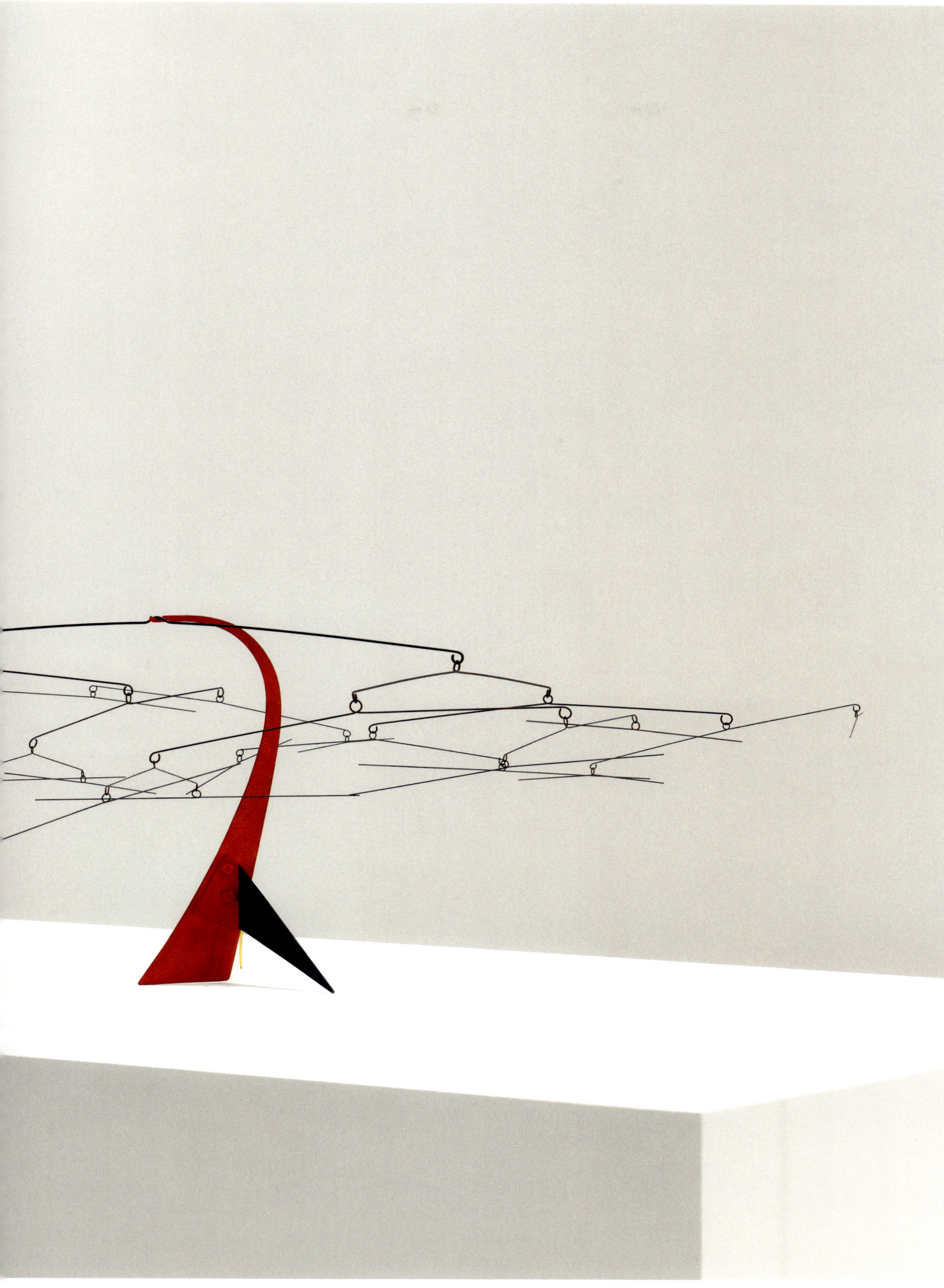

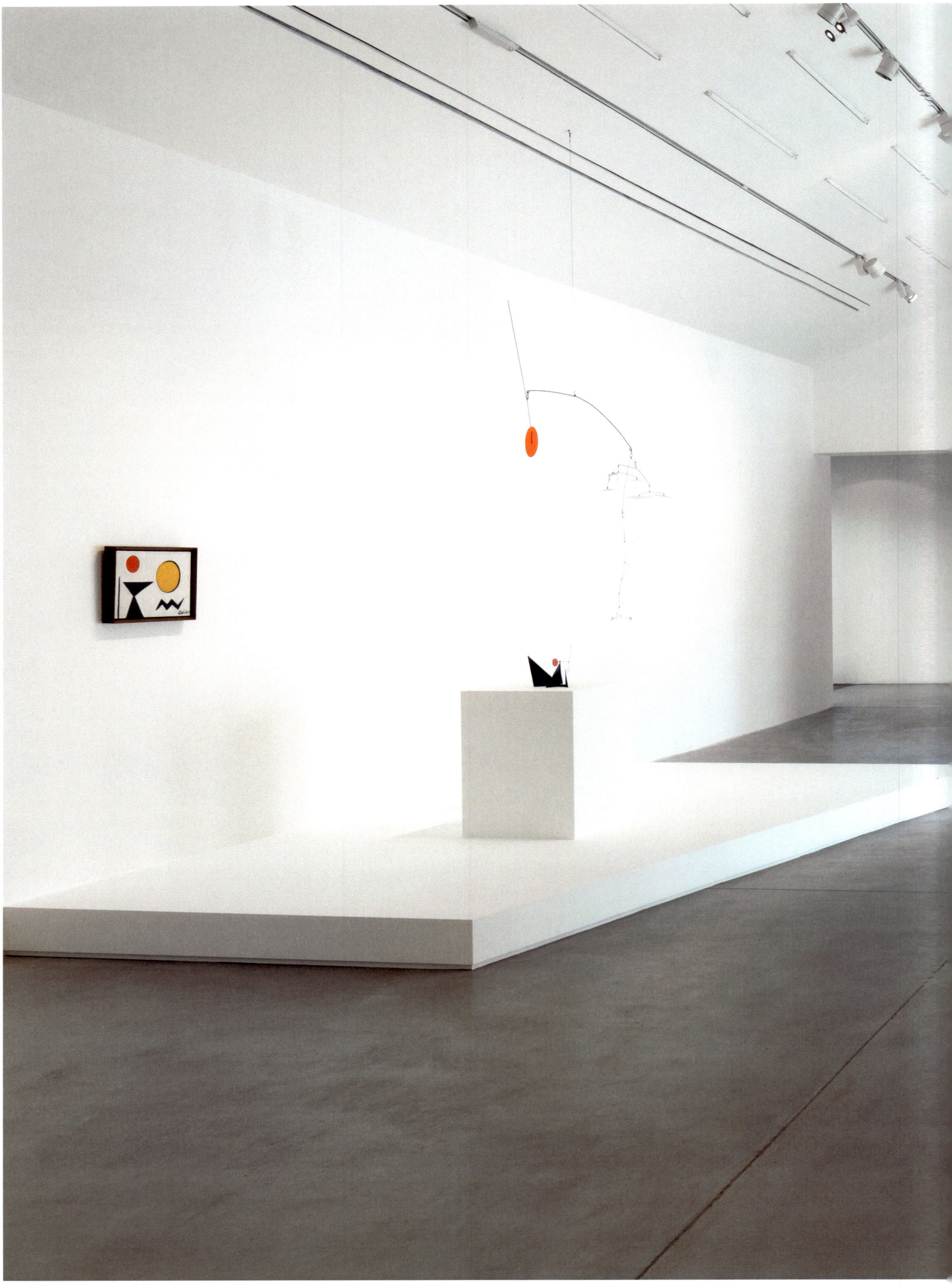

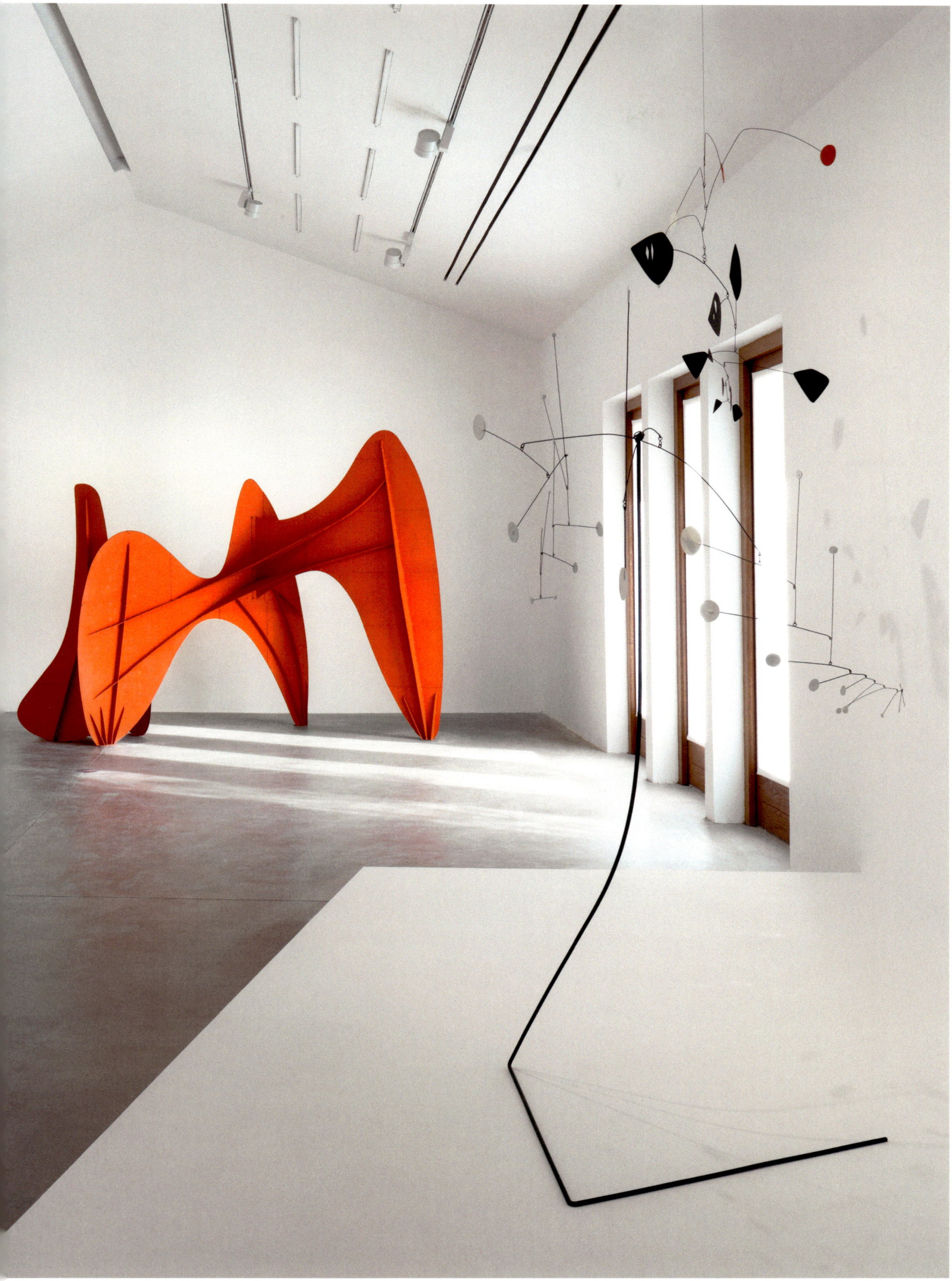

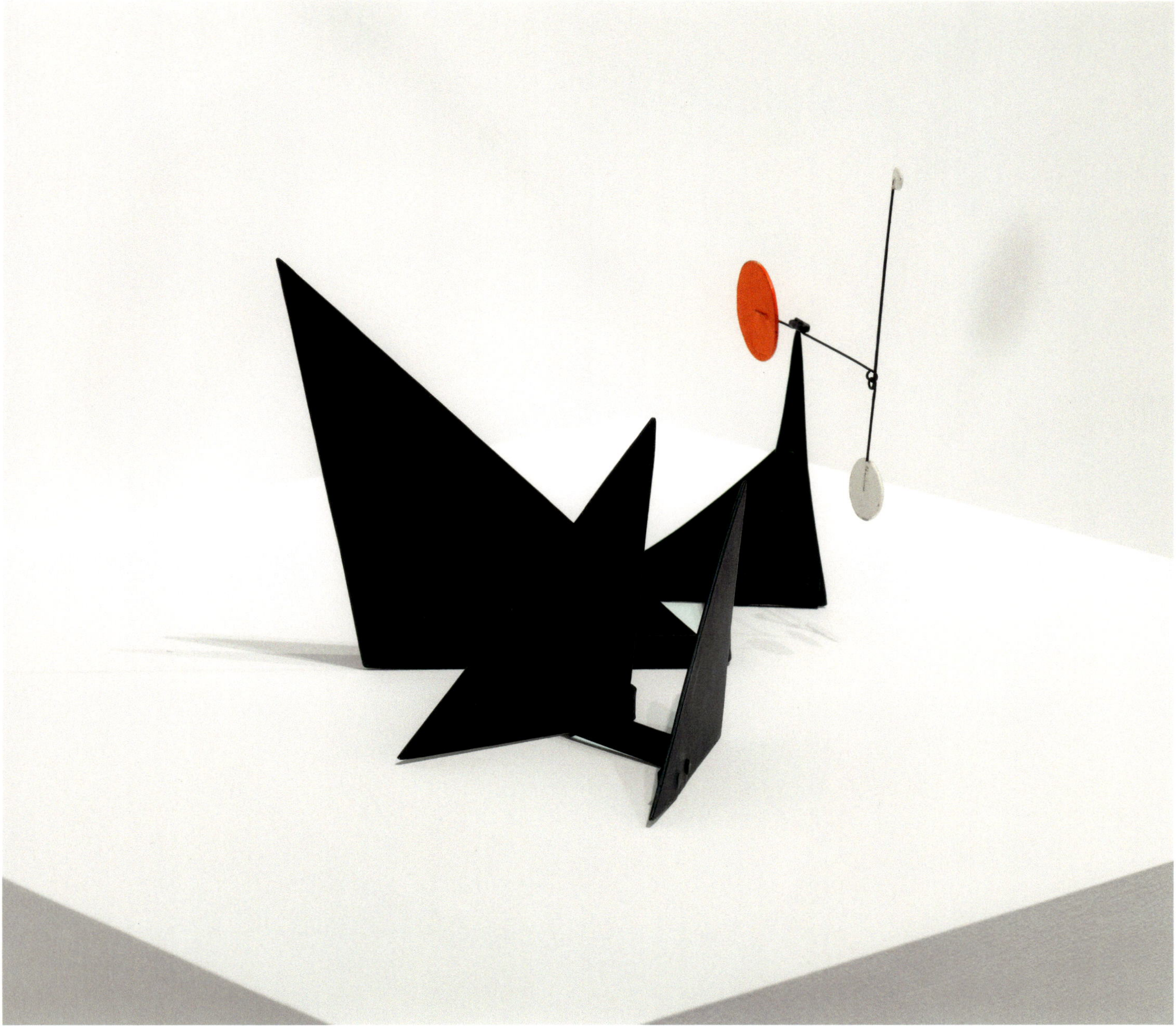

Small City, 1964
Sheet metal, wire, and paint
8 × 14 ½ × 7 in. (20.3 × 36.8 × 17.8 cm)

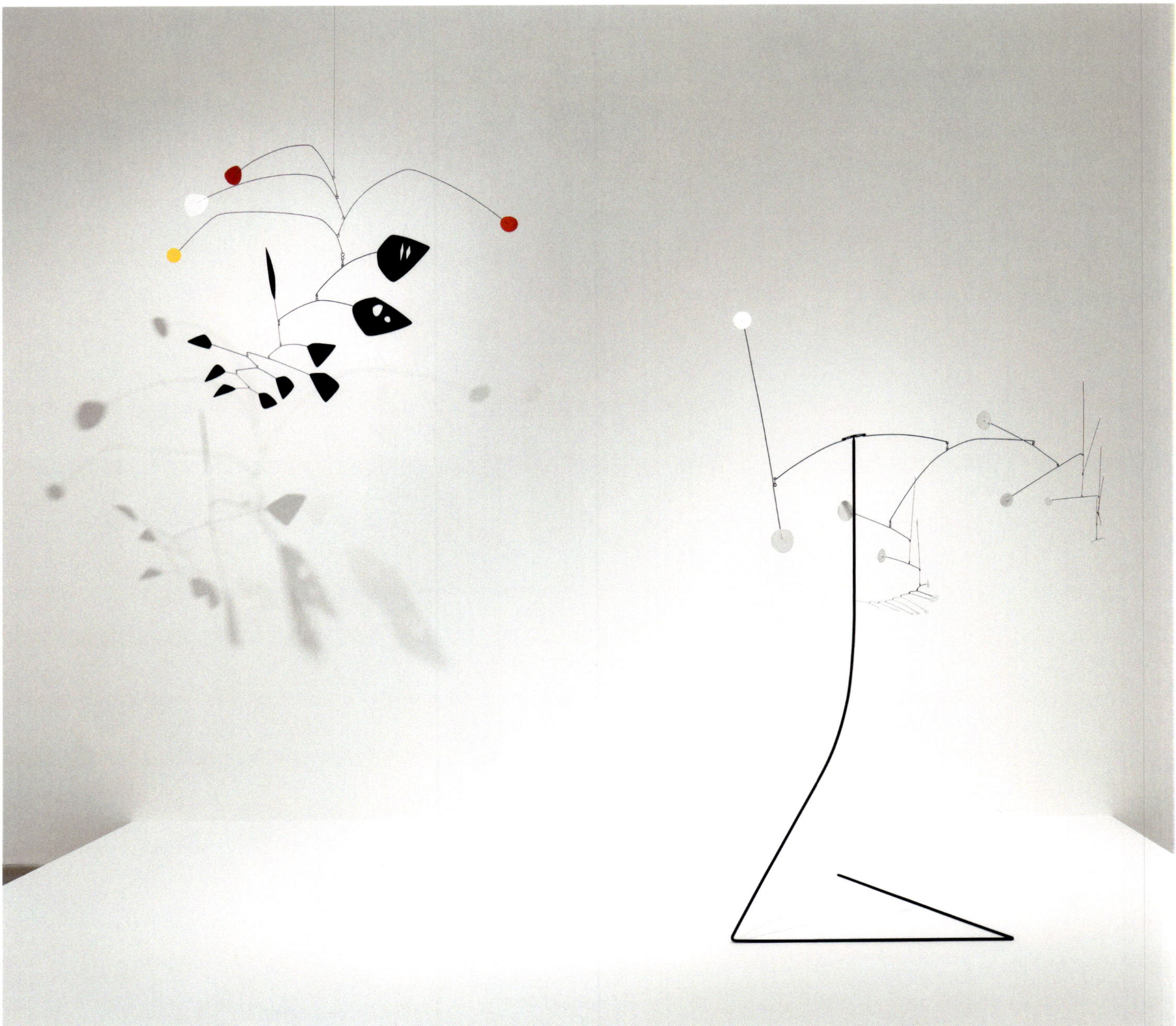

Untitled, c. 1955 (left)
Sheet metal, wire, and paint
43 × 59 in. (109.2 × 149.9 cm)

Franji Pani, 1955 (right)
Sheet metal, rod, wire, and paint
81 × 53 ½ × 30 ¾ in. (205.7 × 135.9 × 78.1 cm)

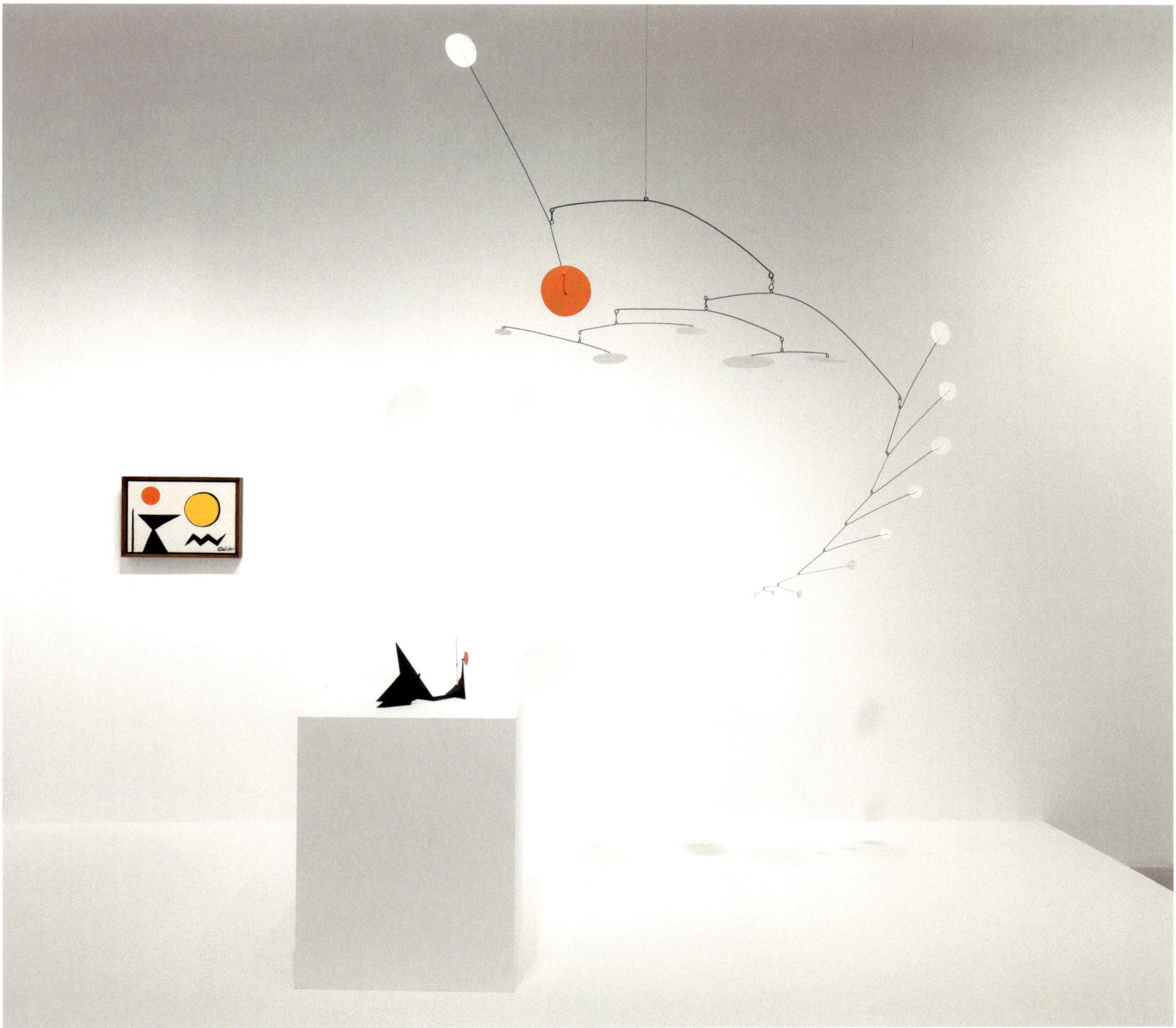

The Anvil, 1950 (left)
Oil on canvas
12 × 18 in. (30.5 × 45.7 cm)

Small City, 1964 (middle)
Sheet metal, wire, and paint
8 × 14 ½ × 7 in. (20.3 × 36.8 × 17.8 cm)

Untitled, 1969 (right)
Sheet metal, wire, and paint
79 × 61 in. (200.7 × 154.9 cm)

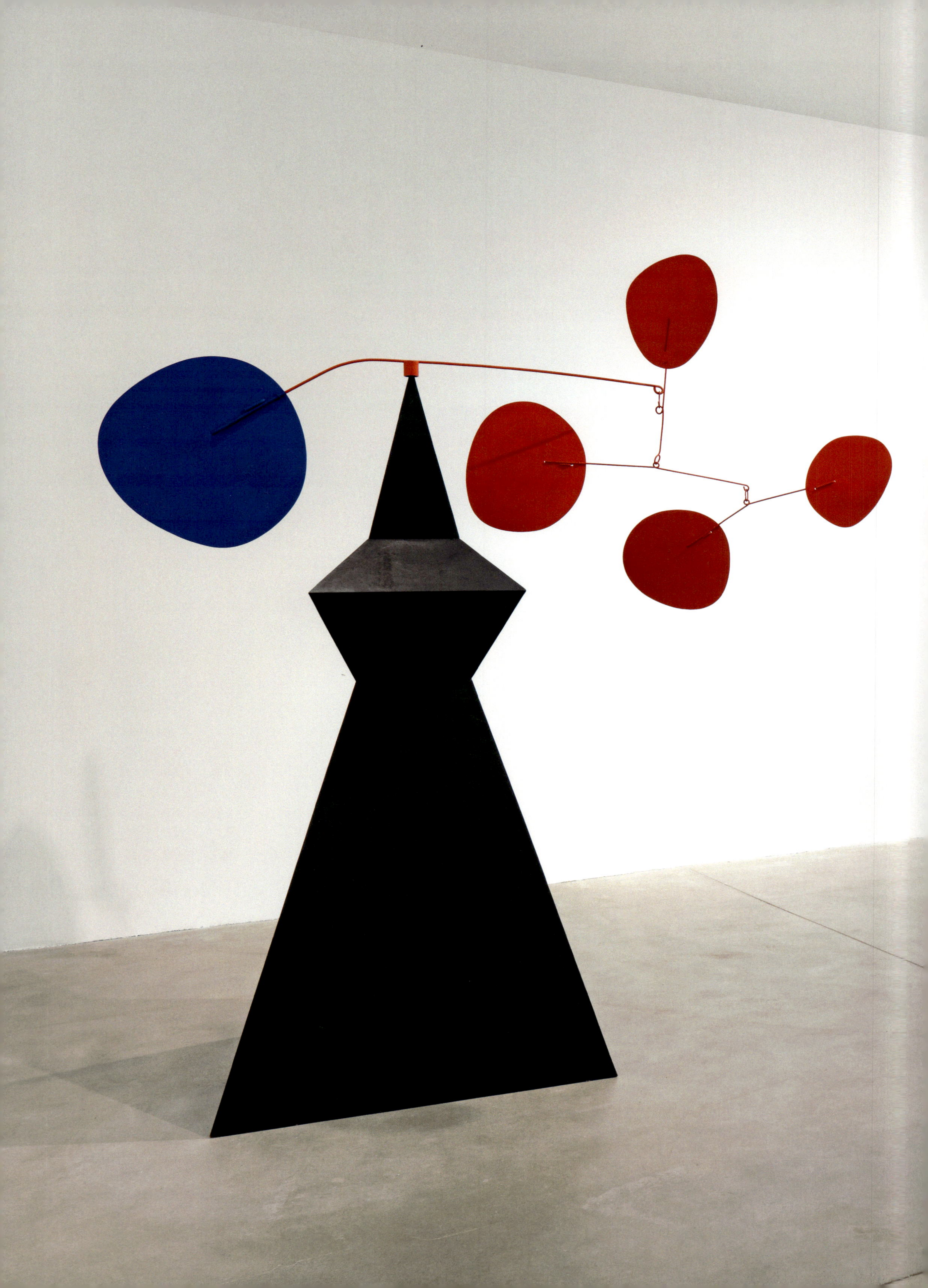

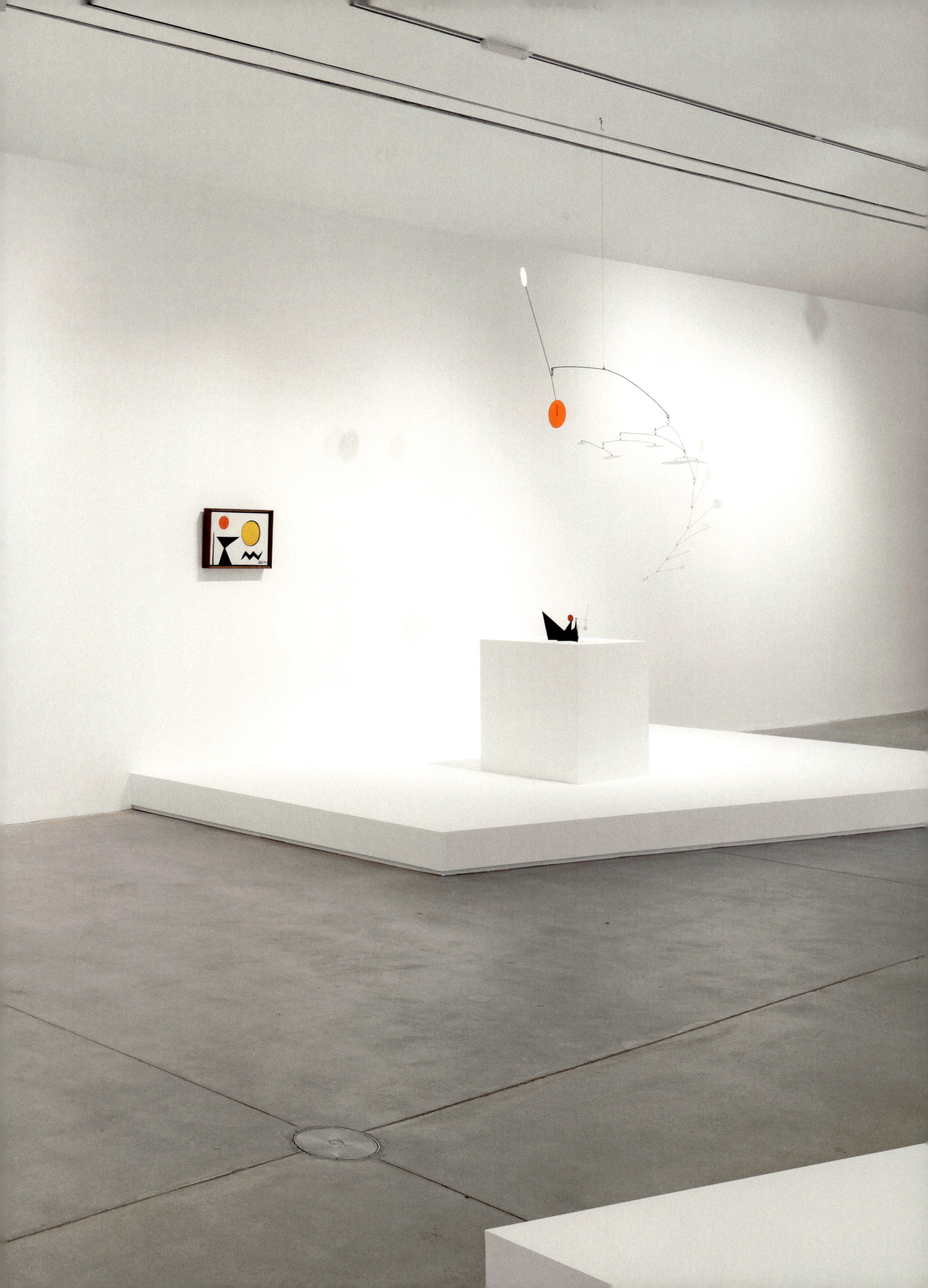

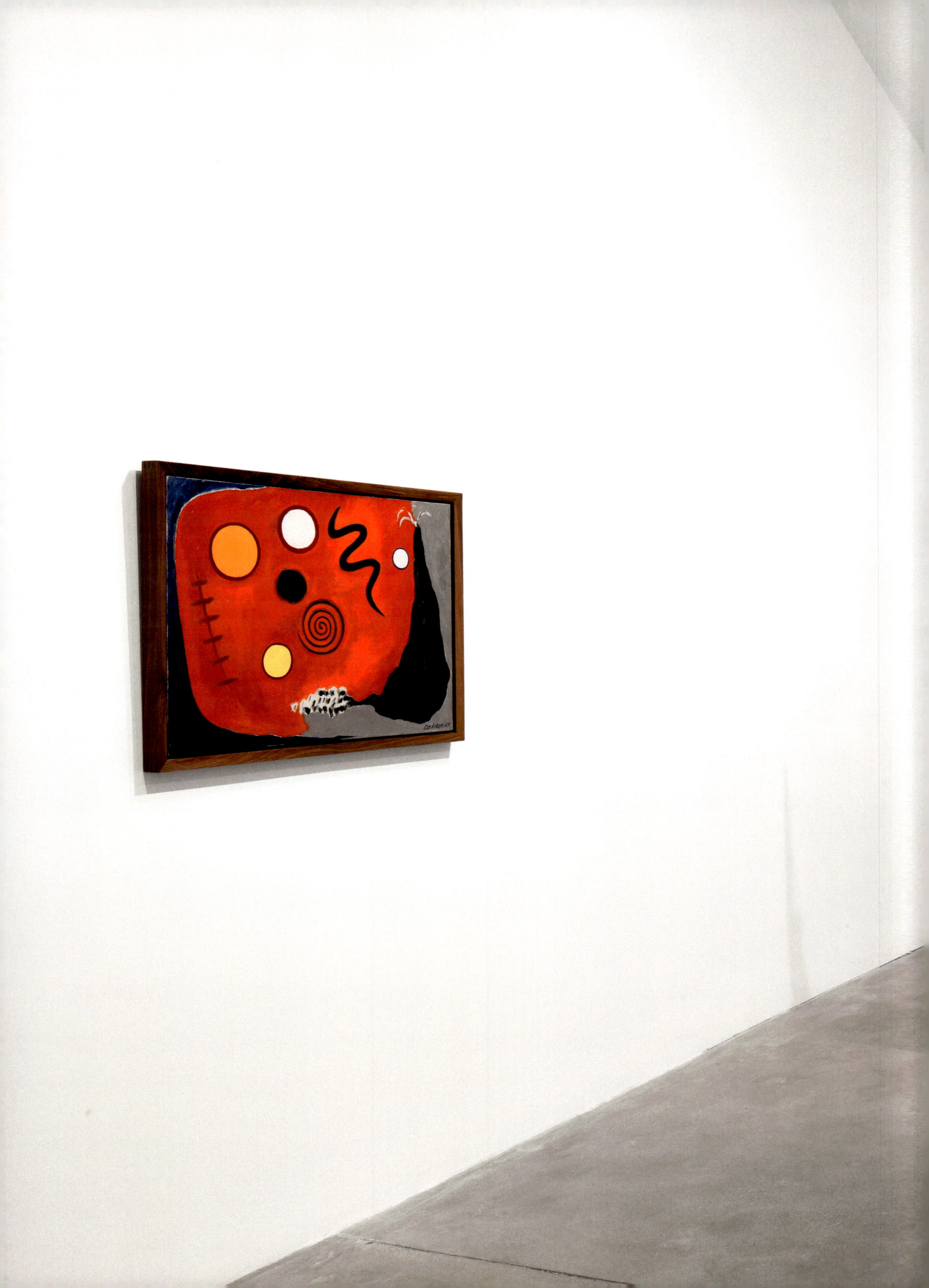

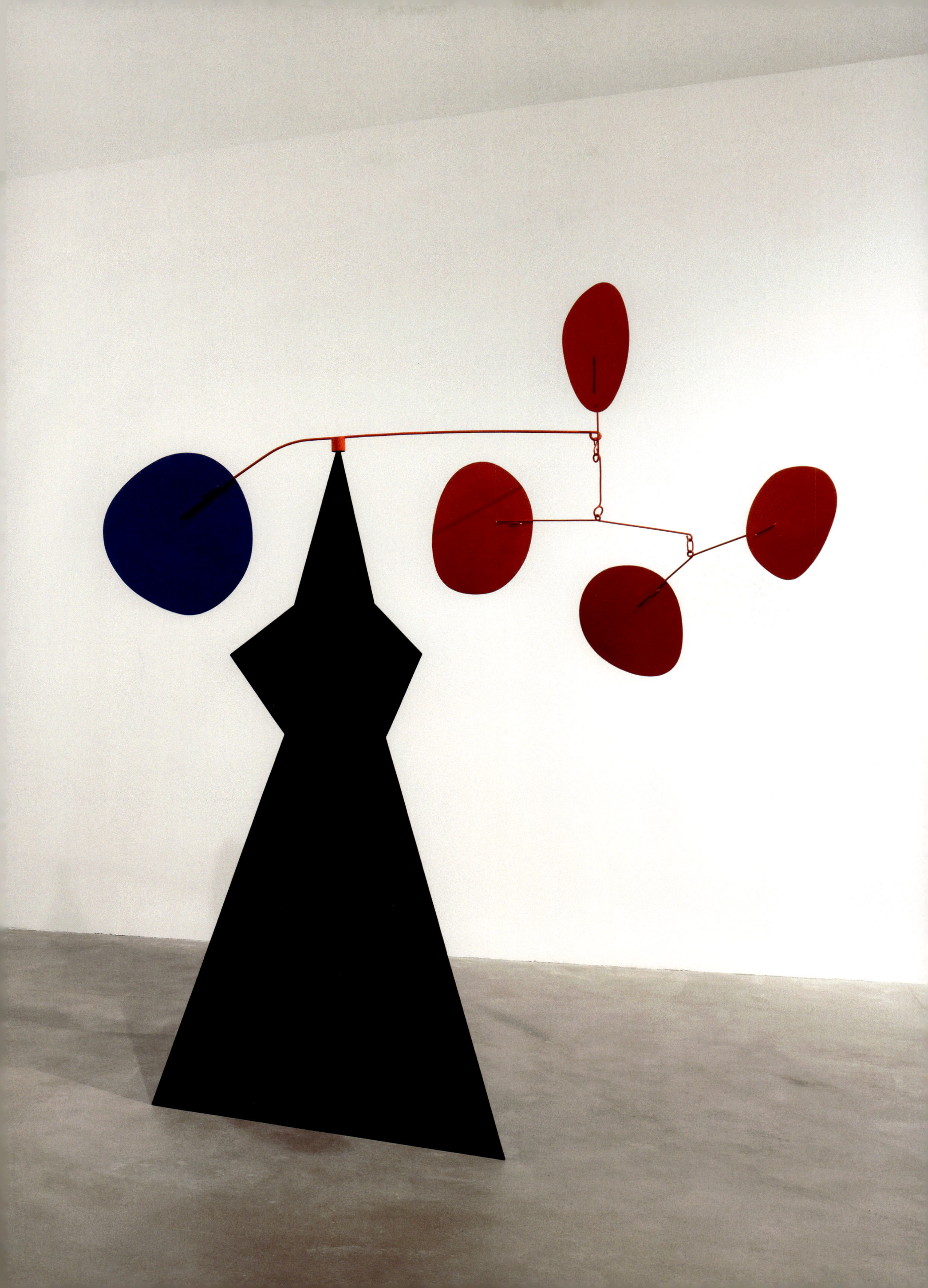

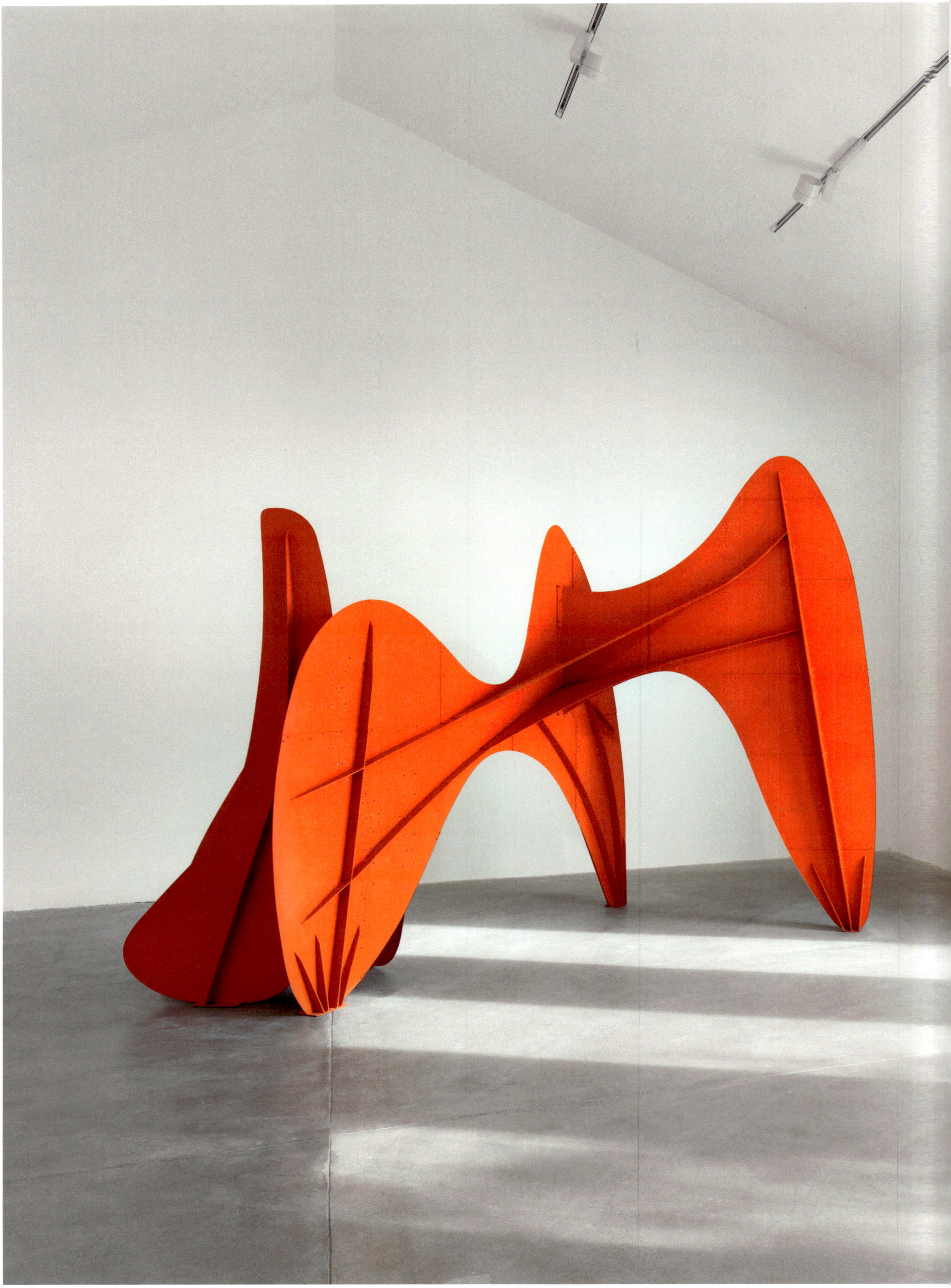

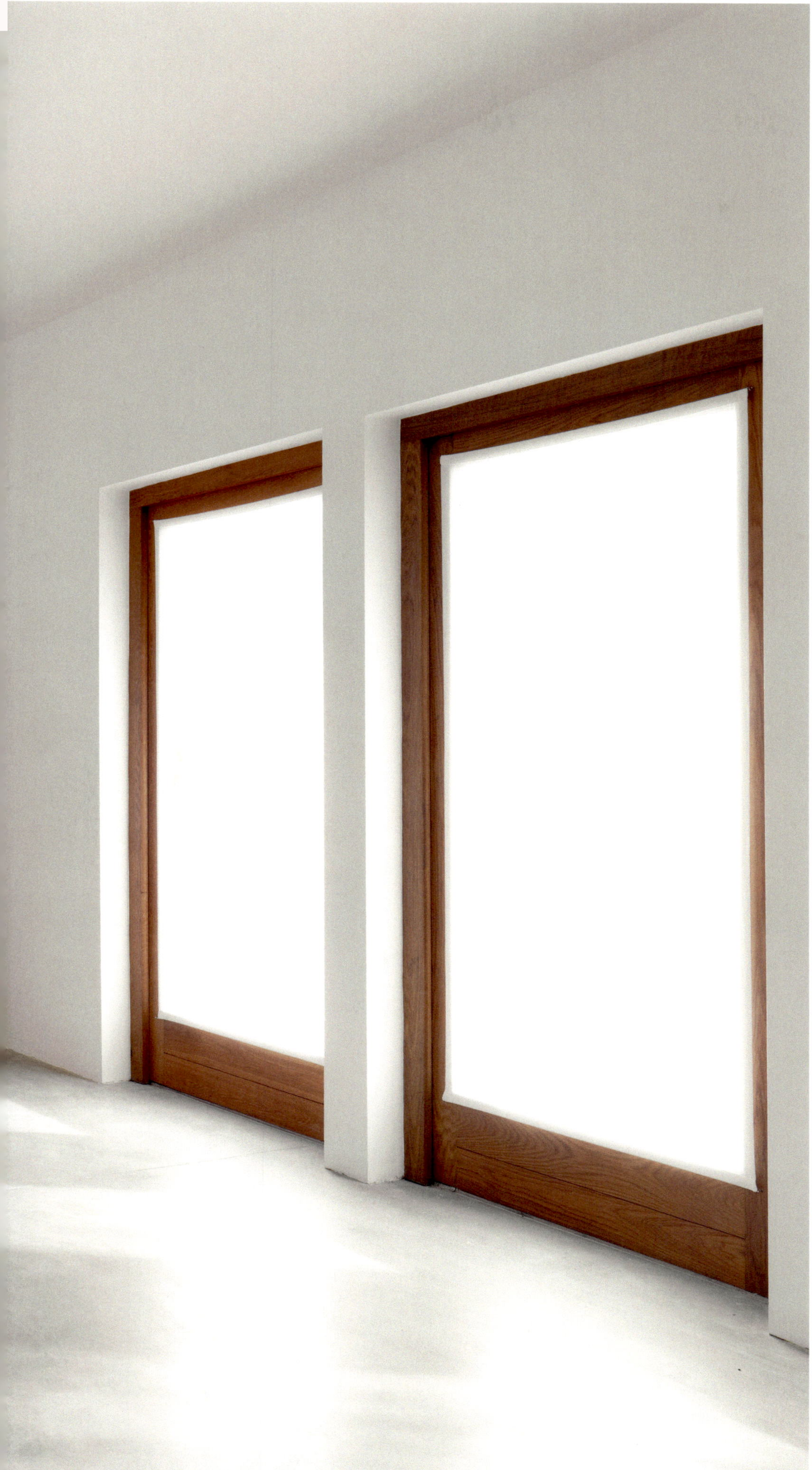

LIST OF WORKS

OUTDOOR WORKS

pp. 42–55

Sabot, 1963 (pp. 42, 43)
Sheet metal, bolts, and paint
146 × 132 ½ × 77 ½ in.
(370.8 × 336.6 × 196.9 cm)
Calder Foundation, New York

Funghi Neri, 1957 (p. 44)
Sheet metal, bolts, and paint
112 × 91 × 72 in.
(284.5 × 231.1 × 182.9 cm)

Gui, 1976 (pp. 46, 48)
Sheet metal, bolts, and paint
117 ⅛ × 104 7⁄16 × 74 in.
(297.5 × 265.3 × 188 cm)

Knobs, 1976 (p. 47)
Sheet metal, bolts, and paint
141 × 65 ¾ × 97 ½ in.
(358.1 × 167 × 247.7 cm)

Polygons on Triangles, 1963
(pp. 51, 52)
Sheet metal, bolts, and paint
114 × 73 ¼ × 96 in.
(289.6 × 186.1 × 243.8 cm)

Slender Legs, 1959 (pp. 53, 54, 55)
Sheet metal, rod, bolts, and paint
139 ½ × 154 × 75 in.
(345.4 × 391.1 × 190.5 cm)
Private Collection

THRESHING BARN

pp. 56–59

The Yellow Disc, 1958 (p. 56)
Oil on canvas
35 × 48 in. (88.9 × 121.9 cm)

Guava, 1955 (p. 57)
Sheet metal, rod, wire, and paint
71 ¼ × 146 ½ × 46 ½ in.
(181 × 372.1 × 118 cm)
Private Collection

Red Maze I, 1954 (pp. 57, 58)
Sheet metal, wire, and paint
51 ½ × 43 in. (130.8 × 109.2 cm)

Morning Cobweb (intermediate
maquette), 1967 (p. 57)
Sheet metal, bolts, and paint
64 × 40 ¼ × 40 in. (162.6 × 102.2 × 101.6 cm)

Onion Running Away, c. 1950 (p. 57)
Oil on canvas
36 × 32 ¼ in. (91.5 × 82 cm)

WORKSHOP GALLERY

pp. 60–67

Untitled, 1949 (far wall, p. 61)
Oil on canvas
20 × 16 in. (50.8 × 40.6 cm)

Necklace, c. 1942 (pp. 63, 67)
Silver wire
17 × 12 in. (43.2 × 30.5 cm)

WORKSHOP GALLERY

Vitrine on p. 62

*Works listed anti-clockwise
as shown in the vitrine*

Brooch, c. 1938 (top right)
Brass wire, glass, and steel wire
6 ¾ × 7 in. (17.1 × 17.8 cm)

Hair comb, c. 1940 (top middle)
Brass wire
10 ⅜ × 4 ⅝ in. (26.3 × 11.7 cm)

Figa hair comb, c. 1948
(top left and p. 65)
Silver wire
7 ½ × 3 ⅛ in. (19.1 × 7.9 cm)

Hair comb, c. 1940
(middle left and p. 64)
Brass wire
9 ¾ × 7 ¼ × 2 ¼ in. (24.8 × 18.4 × 5.7 cm)

Necklace, c. 1938 (middle)
Silver wire
8 ⅝ × 8 ¼ × ¼ in. (22 × 21 × 0.5 cm)
Loop: 20 in. (50.8 cm)
Each element: 1 ¾ in. (4.4 cm)

Bracelet, c. 1940 (bottom left)
Brass wire
2 ½ × 3 ⅛ × 2 ⅝ in. (6.4 × 7.9 × 6.7 cm)

Bracelet, c. 1938 (bottom center)
Brass wire
1 ¾ × 2 ¾ × 2 in. (4.4 × 7 × 5.1 cm)

Jewelry Box, c. 1940 (bottom right)
Leather
4 ½ × 6 ¼ × 3 in. (11.4 × 15.8 × 7.6 cm)

WORKSHOP GALLERY

Vitrine on pp. 68–69

*Works listed anti-clockwise
as shown in the vitrine*

Untitled, 1957
(bottom right on p. 69)
Wool and canvas
42 × 36 in. (106.7 × 91.4 cm)
Calder Foundation, New York.
Promised Gift of Alexander S. C. Rower

Andirons, c. 1935
(middle right on p. 69)
Brass rod and steel bar
26 × 15 ¾ × 9 ¾ in. (66 × 40 × 24.8 cm)

Hand of Fatima, c. 1948
(top right on p. 69)
Sheet metal and wire
Hand: 14 ½ × 9 ⅝ in. (36.8 × 24.4 cm)
Height with wire: 25 ½ in.
(64.8 cm)

Bird ornament, c. 1945
(top, second from right on p. 69)
Brass wire
9 × 10 ⅜ in. (22.9 × 26.2 cm)

Grill, c. 1940
(middle left on p. 69)
Rod and wire
25 × 11 ½ × 2 ¾ in. (63.5 × 29.2 × 7 cm)

Chair, c. 1935 (p. 69)
Wood
36 ¾ × 20 ⅜ × 27 in. (93.3 × 51.8 × 68.6 cm)

Caged Stone and Fourteen Dots,
c. 1948 (p. 68)
Sheet metal, wire, stone, rod, and paint
36 ½ × 34 × 10 in. (92.7 × 86.4 × 25.4 cm)

Coffee table, c. 1935 (p. 68)
Sheet metal, rod, and tubing
18 ¾ × 30 × 30 in. (47.6 × 76.2 × 76.2 cm)

Fetishes, 1944 (p. 68)
Oil on canvas
28 × 24 in. (71.1 × 61 cm)

Chair, c. 1935 (p. 68)
Wood
38 × 18 ⅝ × 29 ¼ in. (96.5 × 47.3 × 74.3 cm)

Lamp, c. 1935 (p. 68)
Wood, sheet metal, wire, and paint,
with electrical wiring
67 ½ × 24 ½ × 26 ½ in.
(171.5 × 62.2 × 67.3 cm)

Chess set, c. 1944 (p. 68)
Wood and paint
18 × 18 in. (45.7 × 45.7 cm)
Calder Foundation, New York.
Mary Calder Rower Bequest, 2011

Ashtray, c. 1940 (p. 68)
Sheet metal
1 ¼ × 3 ½ × 4 ¾ in. (3.2 × 8.9 × 12.1 cm)

Clogs, c. 1935 (p. 69)
Leather, wood, and paint
4 ½ × 11 × 4 ¾ in. (11.4 × 27.9 × 12.1 cm)

WORKSHOP GALLERY

Vitrine on pp. 70–71

*Works listed anti-clockwise
as shown in the vitrine*

Toilet paper holder, 1949
(bottom right on p. 71 and p. 77)
Brass wire and sheet metal
11 ⅞ × 9 × 6 ¾ in. (30.2 × 22.8 × 17.1 cm)

Hand mirror, 1949
(top right on p. 71)
Brass wire and sheet metal,
with mirror
13 ½ × 4 ⅞ × ⅝ in. (34.3 × 12.4 × 1.6 cm)

Toaster, c. 1942
(top left on p. 71 and p. 76)
Wood, wire, and stone, with electrical
wiring
12 × 9 × 8 ¼ in. (30.5 × 22.9 × 21 cm)

Pepper mill, c. 1945
(far right on p. 70)
Pepper mill repaired with brass wire
3 ⅝ × 2 ⅛ × 2 ⅛ in. (9.2 × 5.4 × 5.4 cm)

Dinner bell, c. 1942
(top right on p. 70 and p. 75)
Glass and wire
6 ⅝ × 4 ¼ × 3 ¾ in. (16.8 × 10.8 × 9.5 cm)

Measuring spoon, c. 1940
(top left on p. 70 and p. 72)
Sheet metal
17 × 3 ⅜ × 3 ½ in. (43.2 × 8.5 × 8.9 cm)

Measuring spoon, c. 1940
(top left on p. 70 and p. 72)
Sheet metal
16 ½ × 3 ⅝ × 3 ½ in. (41.9 × 9.2 × 8.9 cm)

Measuring spoon, c. 1940
(top left on p. 70 and p. 72)
Sheet metal
16 × 3 × 3 ½ in. (40.6 × 7.6 × 8.9 cm)

Milk skimmer, c. 1940
(left on p. 70 and p. 73)
Silver wire
10 ⅜ × 5 ⅝ in. (26.4 × 14.3 cm)

Figa fork, c. 1948
(bottom middle on p. 70)
Silver wire
12 ¼ × 2 ¾ × ½ in. (31 × 7 × 1.3 cm)

Spoon, c. 1935
(bottom right on p. 70)
Wood
⅝ × 8 × 1 ½ in. (1.6 × 20.3 × 3.8 cm)

Scissor guard, c. 1940 (left on p. 71)
Brass wire
7 ⅜ × 1 ⅝ in. (18.7 × 4.1 cm)
Calder Foundation, New York.
Gift of Sandra Calder Davidson, 2010

Baby rattle, c. 1935
(middle on p. 71 and p. 74)
Silver sheet metal and wire
10 × 7 ½ × 1 ¼ in. (25.4 × 19.1 × 3.3 cm)

WORKSHOP GALLERY

Vitrine on pp. 78–79

Works listed anti-clockwise as shown in the vitrine

Untitled, c. 1947 (pp. 79, 81)
Sheet metal, rod, wire, tin cans, and candles
15 ⅜ × 20 × 12 in. (39 × 50.8 × 30.5 cm)

Ashtray, c. 1935 (right on p. 78)
Tin can and sheet metal
6 ½ × 4 ½ × 3 ¾ in. (16.5 × 11.4 × 9.5 cm)

Ashtray, c. 1935
(second from right on p. 78)
Tin can and sheet metal
5 ⅝ × 5 ½ × 2 ¾ in. (14.2 × 13.9 × 6.9 cm)

Ashtray, c. 1935
(third from right on p. 78)
Tin can and sheet metal
5 ½ × 5 ⅛ × 4 ½ in. (13.9 × 13 × 11.4 cm)

Untitled, 1935 (p. 78)
Wood and wire
15 ⅞ × 11 ¼ × 4 ½ in. (40.4 × 28.6 × 11.5 cm)

Animal astray, c. 1943
(bottom middle on p. 78)
Tin can
2 × 9 × 9 in. (5 × 22.8 × 22.8 cm)

Unspillable ashtray, c. 1940
(pp. 78–79)
Sheet metal
14 ¼ × 6 ½ × 3 ¼ in. (36.2 × 16.5 × 8.3 cm)

WORKSHOP GALLERY

Vitrine on p. 83

Works listed anti-clockwise as shown in the vitrine

Tray, c. 1935 (bottom right)
Wood, sheet metal, and paint
21 ½ × 11 ½ × 2 in.
(54.6 × 29.2 × 5.1 cm)

Sugar scoop, c. 1935
(bottom right in bowl on tray)
Sheet metal
4 ¼ × 2 × 2 ¾ in. (10.8 × 5.1 × 7 cm)

Creamer, c. 1940
(second from top right)
Creamed repaired with silver wire
2 ¾ × 5 × 3 ½ in. (7 × 12.7 × 8.9 cm)

Moka pot, c. 1928 (top right)
Moka pot modified with wire
11 ½ × 8 ½ × 4 ½ in. (29.2 × 21.6 × 11.4 cm)

Coffee serving tray, 1948 (top left)
Sheet metal
12 ¼ × 9 ¼ × 1 in.
(31.1 × 23.5 × 2.5 cm)

Zarf, c. 1940
(second from left on tray and p. 82)
Brass wire
5 ⅛ × 2 ⅛ × 3 ½ in. (13 × 5.4 × 8.9 cm)

Coffee spoon, c. 1935
(second from left on tray in cup)
Wood
3 ⅛ × ¾ × ½ in. (7.9 × 1.9 × 1.3 cm)

Zarf, c. 1940 (left on tray and p. 82)
Brass wire
4 ⅝ × 2 ¼ × 2 ¾ in. (11.4 × 5.7 × 7 cm)

Coffee spoon, c. 1935
(left on tray in cup)
Wood
3 ⅜ × ⅞ × ⅜ in. (8.6 × 2.2 × 1 cm)

Fish ashtray, c. 1935 (middle left)
Sheet metal and wire
7 × 3 ⅜ × ¾ in. (17.8 × 8.6 × 1.9 cm)

PIGSTY GALLERY

pp. 84–87

Apple Monster, 1938 (pp. 84, 86, 87)
Wood, wire, and paint
66 × 55 ½ × 32 ½ in. (167.6 × 141 × 82.6 cm)
Calder Foundation, New York.
Gift of Alexander S. C. Rower in memory of Mary Calder Rower, 2015

Untitled, c. 1946 (pp. 84, 86)
Sheet metal, wire, and paint
35 × 43 × 21 in. (88.9 × 109.2 × 53.3 cm)

Red, White, Black and Brass, 1934
(pp. 84, 87)
Sheet metal, rod, wire, brass, and paint
113 × 68 × 53 in. (287 × 172.7 × 134.6 cm)
Calder Foundation, New York.
Promised Gift of Alexander S. C. Rower

Untitled, 1938 (p. 85)
Wood, bone, rod, wire, and paint
70 ¼ × 37 × 23 ½ in. (178.4 × 94 × 59.7 cm)
Calder Foundation, New York.
Gift of Holton Rower in memory of Howard Rower, 2014

Untitled, 1945 (pp. 85, 87, 89)
Wood, rod, wire, and paint
15 ¼ × 21 ¼ × 12 in. (38.7 × 53.9 × 30.4 cm)

Tines, 1943 (p. 85)
Pitchfork tines, glass, wire, shell, string, and paint
50 × 58 × 3 ½ in. (127 × 147.3 × 8.9 cm)
Calder Foundation, New York.
Promised Gift of Holton Rower

The Giant Mollusc, 1958 (p. 86)
Oil on canvas
24 × 36 in. (61 × 91.4 cm)

Conical Gussets, 1956 (p. 90)
Sheet metal and paint
15 ½ × 13 ½ × 8 ½ in. (39.4 × 34.3 × 21.6 cm)

Ex-Octopus (maquette), 1936 (p. 91)
Sheet metal and paint
17 ⅛ × 17 × 10 ½ in. (43.5 × 43.2 × 26.7 cm)

Bleu, jaune, rouge sur base courbe, 1969 (not illustrated)
Sheet metal, wire, and paint
12 ½ × 14 × 14 in. (31.8 × 35.6 × 35.6 cm)

RHOADES GALLERY

pp. 93–103

Sword Plant, 1947 (pp. 93, 94, 97)
Sheet metal, wire, and paint
38 ½ × 31 × 28 ½ in. (97.8 × 78.7 × 72.4 cm)

Seven Black, Red and Blue, 1947 (pp. 93, 94, 97)
Oil on canvas
48 ⅛ × 60 ¼ in. (122.3 × 153 cm)

Root, 1947 (pp. 94, 97)
Sheet metal, wire, and paint
48 × 26 × 33 in. (121.9 × 66 × 83.8 cm)

Untitled, 1954 (p. 94)
Sheet metal, rod, wire, and paint
96 × 138 × 72 in. (243.8 × 350.5 × 182.8 cm)
Private Collection

Black Beast, 1940 (pp. 94, 98, 99)
Sheet metal, bolts, and paint
103 × 163 × 78 ½ in. (261.6 × 414 × 199.4 cm)
Calder Foundation, New York

Orange Disc, Red Boomerang, 1955 (pp. 95, 102)
Oil on canvas
24 × 18 in. (61 × 45.7 cm)

Untitled (Mobile with N Degrees of Freedom), 1946 (pp. 100, 102, 103)
Sheet metal, wire, and paint
11 ¼ × 49 × 37 in. (28.6 × 124.5 × 94 cm)
Calder Foundation, New York.
Purchase, 2009

Untitled, 1941 (pp. 95, 100)
Sheet metal, wire, and paint
33 ½ × 56 × 9 in. (85.1 × 142.2 × 22.9 cm)

Yucca, 1941 (pp. 95, 101)
Sheet metal, wire, and paint
40 ¾ × 15 × 11 in. (103.5 × 38.1 × 27.9 cm)

Puntos Blancos, 1955 (pp. 95, 101)
Sheet metal, rod, wire, and paint
51 × 46 × 25 in. (129.5 × 116.8 × 63.5 cm)

Arctic Landscape, 1958 (not illustrated)
Oil on canvas
20 × 28 in. (50.8 × 71.1 cm)

BOURGEOIS GALLERY

pp. 104–115

The Anvil, 1950 (pp. 104, 109, 111)
Oil on canvas
12 × 18 in. (30.5 × 45.7 cm)

Small City, 1964 (pp. 104, 107, 109, 111)
Sheet metal, wire, and paint
8 × 14 ½ × 7 in. (20.3 × 36.8 × 17.8 cm)

Untitled, 1969 (pp. 104, 109, 111)
Sheet metal, wire, and paint
79 × 61 in. (200.7 × 154.9 cm)

La Grande vitesse (1:5 intermediate maquette), 1969 (pp. 105, 114)
Sheet metal, bolts, and paint
102 × 135 × 93 in.
(259.1 × 342.9 × 236.2 cm)

Untitled, c. 1955 (pp. 110, 113)
Sheet metal, wire, and paint
43 × 59 in. (109.2 × 149.9 cm)

Franji Pani, 1955 (pp. 105, 108)
Sheet metal, rod, wire, and paint
81 × 53 ½ × 30 ¾ in.
(205.7 × 135.9 × 78.1 cm)

Untitled, 1967 (pp. 105, 108)
Sheet metal, rod, wire, and paint
92 ¾ × 85 ¼ × 33 in.
(235.6 × 216.5 × 83.8 cm)

Fuse, 1947 (p. 112)
Oil on canvas
24 × 32 ⅞ in. (61 × 83.6 cm)

London (maquette), 1962 (not illustrated)
Sheet metal, wire, and paint
35 × 45 × 10 in. (88.9 × 114.3 × 25.4 cm)

Published on the occasion
of the exhibition

Alexander Calder
From the Stony River to the Sky

Hauser & Wirth, Somerset
26 May – 9 September 2018

Texts
Susan Braeuer Dam
and Jessica Holmes

Book design and typography
Atelier Dyakova

Copy editing and proofreading
Emma Capps

Pre-press by
prints professional, Berlin

Printed by
DZA Druckerei zu Altenburg GmbH,
Altenburg

Photo Credits

All archival photographs courtesy Calder Foundation, New York / Art Resource, New York

Unless indicated below, all archival images: © 2018 Calder Foundation, New York
Page 20 (fig. 10): © Centre Pompidou, MNAM-CCI Bibliothèque Kandinsky, Dist. RMN-Grand Palais / Fonds Marc Vaux; pages 30–31, 34: © 2018 Estate of André Kertész / Higher Pictures; page 33 (fig. 5): Jerry L. Thomson © 2018 Calder Foundation, New York; page 37: © Estate of Evelyn Hofer; page 40: © Ugo Mulas Heirs. Photographs by Herbert Matter: pages 16 (figs. 7, 8), 18 (fig. 6), 20 (fig. 9), 22–23 (fig. 11), 29 (fig. 4), 36 (figs. 6, 7, 8) © 2018 Calder Foundation, New York. Photograph by James Thrall Soby page 17 (fig. 5) © 2018 Calder Foundation, New York. All rights reserved.

Unless indicated below, all installation views by Ken Adlard
Pages 75–77: Calder Foundation, New York / Art Resource, New York; page 90: Tom Powel Imaging © 2018 Calder Foundation, New York; page 91: Bonnie Morrison © 2018 Calder Foundation, New York.

Every effort has been made to trace copyright ownership and to obtain reproduction permissions. Corrections brought to the publisher's attention will be incorporated in future reprints or editions of this book.

Cataloguing-in-Publication Data is available from the Library of Congress.

Available worldwide, outside of Europe, through
ARTBOOK | D.A.P.
75 Broad Street, Suite 630
New York, NY 10004
Tel 212 627 1999 | Fax 212 627 9484

ISBN: 978-3-906915-25-8

Printed and bound in Germany